Two week

loan

Please return on or before the
date stamped below.
Charges are made for

Ethnic Resurgence in Modern Democratic States

Pergamon Policy Studies on Ethnic Issues

Hall *Ethnic Autonomy — Comparative Dynamics*

Related Titles

PERGAMON
POLICY
STUDIES

ON ETHNIC ISSUES

Ethnic Resurgence in Modern Democratic States
A Multidisciplinary Approach to Human Resources and Conflict

Edited by
Uri Ra'anan
with the participation of
John P. Roche
and other contributions

Pergamon Press

NEW YORK • OXFORD • TORONTO • SYDNEY • FRANKFURT • PARIS

Pergamon Press Offices:

U.S.A   Pergamon Press Inc., Maxwell House, Fairview Park, Elmsford, New York 10523, U.S.A.

U.K.   Pergamon Press Ltd., Headington Hill Hall, Oxford OX3 0BW, England

CANADA   Pergamon of Canada Ltd., 150 Consumers Road, Willowdale, Ontario M2J 1P9, Canada

AUSTRALIA   Pergamon Press (Aust) Pty. Ltd., P.O. Box 544, Potts Point, NSW 2011, Australia

FRANCE   Pergamon Press SARL, 24 rue des Ecoles, 75240 Paris, Cedex 05, France

FEDERAL REPUBLIC OF GERMANY   Pergamon Press GmbH, 6242 Kronberg/Taunus, Pferdstrasse 1, Federal Republic of Germany

Library of Congress Cataloging in Publication Data

Main entry under title:

Ethnic resurgence in modern, democratic states.

(Pergamon policy studies)
Bibliography: p.
Includes index.
1. Minorities—Addresses, essays, lectures.
2. Ethnicity—Addresses, essays, lectures.   I. Ra'anan, Uri, 1926-   II. Roche, John Pearson, 1923-
JC311.E86 1979   301.5'92   79-15551
ISBN 0-08-024647-8

Publisher's note: The type employed in this book made utilization of diacritical marks unfeasible. Consequently, the German umlaut has been rendered as "ae," "oe," or "ue," respectively, in accordance with traditional practice, while French accents have been omitted, and so have diacritical marks in the case of Turkish, Czech, and other names.

To Estelle, Gavy, and Micha

Contents

Preface and Acknowledgments

For almost three decades, a mere handful of isolated analysts, including the editor of this volume, demonstrated reluctance to accept as gospel the facile assumption that modernization somehow would cause ethnic self-assertion and conflict to fade away. Despite the temptation to succumb to the fashionable belief that state sovereignty was about to dissolve into regional, transnational, and supranational institutions and associations of various kinds, the lonely skeptics pointed out that, if anything, indications pointed in the opposite direction – i.e. toward the emergence of substate actors capable of breaking down existing political units into smaller entities. In the view of this minority, such actors would be motivated by aspirations of a primarily ethnic nature, and the more developed regions, particularly the West, would prove especially susceptible to this trend. Today the beliefs articulated by such voices – few and sometimes unpopular – have become well-nigh axiomatic in the light of irrefutable evidence concerning ethnic resurgence in Europe and North America, that appears on the pages of almost every current newspaper. With a selective forgetfulness that is typical of the profession, however, not many care to remember how recent their own conversion has been to this point of view. (Incidentally, no normative implications should be read into the points noted in this paragraph. The few who anticipated the developments of the present era of ethnicity may or may not have welcomed them.)

Since 1967, the editor of this volume has devoted a considerable segment of his teaching to an attempt to bring some conceptual and semantic order into existing chaos, particularly in the English language, with regard to the problematic area of ethnic and nationality issues. (The Fletcher School of Law and Diplomacy has encouraged such efforts, since its leadership comprehends fully that a plethora of factors must be analyzed and taught if a modern graduate curriculum in international affairs is to be viable.) In 1973 the editor of this book was able to devote a sabbatic leave, with the generous assistance of the

Battelle Seattle Research Center, to systematizing in writing his thoughts on this topic. Since 1975 the generous support of the Rockefeller Foundation has enabled him to embark upon the essential field research trips for an in-depth investigation of such phenomena as nationalism in Scotland, the problems of migrant labor (from the Mediterranean littoral) in Northwestern Europe (particularly Germany), linguistic conflict in Belgium, and the nexus between the Cyprus question and Aegean tension. The Foundation, moreover, made it possible for him to interact with experts on these topics from various governments, political parties, and research and academic institutions. Some of the colleagues in question assisted in a consultative capacity and/or as contributors to this volume. The talents of Fletcher's excellent young graduates have been utilized with the aid of the Rockefeller Foundation and they are well represented as authors of several chapters. Moreover, thanks to the Rockefeller project, The Fletcher School's International Security Studies Program, chaired by the editor of this work, was able to hold two major conferences. The first, on Scarce Resources and International Conflict, took place in May 1977, and specific material contained in Chapters 1 and 3 was presented and discussed on that occasion (which also presented an opportunity for exchanges of views on nationalism with Professor Eli Kedourie, on migrant labor with Dr. Ursula Mehrlaender, and on disputes in the Aegean with Professors Leo Gross and Richard Baxter). The second conference, dealing with Development and Security, was held in April 1978, and provided more general inputs. Although the issues discussed in Chapters 4 and 5 (Scotland and Belgium) have been tested further at the polls since this work was completed, the analyses presented remain valid.

The editor wishes to express his appreciation particularly to Dr. John J. Stremlau, Dr. Elmore Jackson and Dr. Mason Willrich of the Rockefeller Foundation, and to Dr. Raymond Gastil of the Battelle Seattle Research Center, for their support, and to his collaborators on this book, for their excellent contributions. Among his colleagues, Professor Rosemarie S. Rogers was most helpful in a consultative capacity with regard to migrant labor problems. The editor wishes also to thank his research assistants, Mrs. Amy Redlick, Mr. Marios Evriviades, and Mr. Richard H. Feen.

The editor received assistance beyond the call of duty during his field research trips from the following: Mr. Alfred Vigderman (Department of State, Ret.), Ambassador William R. Crawford (United States Embassy, Nicosia), his DCM, Mr. Fred Brown, and his Political Officer, Mr. Richard Erdman; the two most remarkable personalities of the two Cypriot communities, Mr. Glavkos J. Clerides and Mr. Rauf Denktash (Mr. Clerides particularly has earned deep appreciation and respect), as well as Mr. Christophides of the Cyprus Broadcasting Corporation, Mr. Constantinou and Mr. Kalimas (in charge of rehabilitation of refugees), and Mr. Evriviades (of the Larnaca Security Forces). Others helpful in Cyprus were Mr. Andreas Azinas, Mr. Dimitriades (mayor of Nicosia), and Mr. Katsambas.

In Athens, the editor met with special kindness and help from Dr. and Mrs. Pan Vandoros, Mr. Monteagle Stearns (DCM of the United States Embassy), Mr. Mavros (former Greek Foreign Minister), Mr. John Tsounis (Director General of the Greek Foreign Ministry), Mr. Gunaris (Greek Foreign Ministry-Cyprus Affairs), Mr. Philoptopoulos (Ministry of Information), Madame Vlachou (distinguished Editor-in-Chief of <u>Kathimerini</u>), Mr. Angelos Vlachos (former Greek Ambassador to Moscow), Professor Dimitras, General M. Alexandrakis (former Greek representative to NATO), and many others.

In Istanbul, special mention should be given to the assistance provided by Mr. Howard Mace (United States Consul General) and his Cultural Affairs Officers, Mr. Langham and Mr. Ritchotte, as well as Professors Ergin, Tuna, Dereli, Giritli, and Ari, and also the distinguished journalist, Mr. Balci. In Ankara, similar help was given by Ambassador Macomber, his DCM, Mr. Donald Bergus, and his Political Officer, Mr. George A. MacFarland, Jr., as well as by Mr. Guvandiren (Turkish Foreign Ministry-Cyprus Affairs). Mr. Dimitras, at Harvard and Mr. Zannetos, at Sloan, have also been very helpful.

In London, special assistance was rendered by Dr. Michael J. Dobbs (British Conservative Party, Research Office), and Brigadier Kenneth Hunt (International Institute of Strategic Studies). In Edinburgh, Professors John Erickson and Henry Drucker went out of their way to be helpful, and so did Mr. William Wolfe, Titular Head of the Scottish National Party, and its theoretician, Mr. Stephen Maxwell.

In Brussels, special gratitude is owed to Major and Mrs. Roy Stafford (United States Mission to NATO), to Ambassador Strausz-Hupe, and to Mr. Andre J. Navez (United States Embassy).

In Bonn, Counselor and Mrs. W.R. Smyser of the United States Embassy devoted an extraordinary amount of time and effort to make the trip a success, with the help of Mr. and Mrs. John R. Mapother, old friends, and Mr. Simeon Moats. Particular assistance was given by Dr. Ursula Mehrlaender of the Friedrich Ebert Institute, Dr. Herbert Becher and Mrs. Erpenbeck of the Catholic Bureau in Bonn, Dr. Dieter Oberndoerfer of the Konrad Adenauer Institute, Dr. Wolfgang Bodenbender of the Federal Ministry for Labor and Social Structure, and Mr. Makris of the Greek Embassy.

To all these personalities, to Mrs. Gayle Praeger for her excellent work in organizing the 1977 and 1978 conferences, to his secretary, Mrs. Helene M. Nelson, for her unfailing patience and sunny temperament, and to his family for all their help and devotion, the editor owes gratitude.

Uri Ra'anan
Lexington, Mass.

Introduction — The Resurgence of Ethnic Self-Assertion in the West: Causes and Effects

Uri Ra'anan

CAUSES

The last two decades have witnessed population mobility in the West on a scale equaled only by the massive dislocations of World War II and its immediate aftermath. However, in the latter case, population transfers, voluntarily (by flight) or under duress (expulsions), produced greater ethnic homogeneity (ethnic Germans leaving Eastern Europe for the FRG; Hindus leaving Pakistan for India and Moslems moving in the opposite direction; Palestinian Arabs moving from Israel to Arab countries, and Jews from Arab and Moslem countries migrating to Israel). More recent population movements, on the other hand, in most instances have increased ethnic and cultural heterogeneity.

The causes for this phenomenon are twofold:

1. Increasing aversion to manual (particularly menial) work in "postindustrial societies" (absorbing a constantly increasing proportion of their labor force in service and other white collar occupations). Consequently, semiskilled workers have been "imported" by such societies, particularly in Northwestern Europe, from somewhat less developed, Mediterranean regions.

2. The debris of empire. Metropolitan European states (former centers of overseas empires in the process of "decolonization") have given former supporters and collaborators in the ex-colonial areas the option of coming to the mother country once its military "umbrella" was being withdrawn. In some cases, this has not led to changes in the cultural pattern (e.g., Portuguese settlers from Africa returning to Portugal or British settlers from Kenya coming back to the British Isles). In other instances, however, the ethnic kaleidoscope has become more varied — e.g., the migration of Moluccans to

The Netherlands (with adverse results of late), the flight of Indians and Pakistanis from East Africa to the United Kingdom (providing political ammunition for neoracists of the extreme right), and the mass movement of Algerians to France after independence. (Some of the Algerians have come to seek work; the majority, however, fled, and this includes Moslems who had fought in the French security forces, Jews who had obtained French citizenship, and nearly one million "French colons" many of whom, in fact, are of Spanish and Italian rather than French descent.) To some extent, perhaps, the exodus of Vietnamese "boat people" and their attempt to enter pro-Western states, particularly the United States, belongs to the same general category. In this, as in some of the other cases, there have been regrettable instances of a "nativist" backlash, accompanied by unpleasant phenomena.

Geographical mobility across international frontiers is aided, with regard to the absorption of surplus labor, by the development of such supranational entities as the European Economic Community (EEC), and, in the context of movement between portions of former empires, by such institutions as Commonwealth Passport regulations.

This phenomenon must be viewed together with the escalation of intrastate migration in postindustrial societies. In the United States, in 1970, no less than 35 million persons lived in a county or state other than the one in which they have been residing a mere five years previously, and the cumulative total over a 70-year life span well may be in the neighborhood of 50 percent of the population. (In a period of only two years, 1975 to 77, the bureau of the census reports that no less than 27.5 percent of the United States population moved, with well over one-half of this total being involved in movement over major distances.) Such fluidity in residential data is enhanced by the large degree of social mobility so typical of the current stage of development in the West, involving, as it does, not merely the conversion of the labor force from rural to urban occupations, but from manual to service or "white collar" occupations. While the former trend geographically involves in-migration into the metropolitan conglomerations, the latter leads to movement from inner cities to suburbia. "Smokeless" industries, such as electronics, frequently are found along suburban belts, such as Route 128.

In countries that were composed to start with of more than one major ethnic and cultural element, but where the separate nationalities had lived in large, compact, and fairly homogeneous hinterlands (e.g., Flemings in predominantly agrarian Flanders and Walloons in the mining and industrial centers of southern Belgium; Quebecois in agrarian belts along the lower St. Lawrence and "Anglophones" further west in Canada), the confluence of geographical and social movements has caused confrontation, competition, and conflict in focal areas in which two or more ethnic groups have been "thrown together" (e.g., Brussels or Montreal).

Which of the following two phenomena is more conflict prone is not established:

The movement of migrant workers into Northwestern Europe essentially creates two societies within relatively narrow geographical confines – an "indigenous" white collar stratum, functioning in close proximity to a "foreign" manual labor element. In the immediate future, this development is less "problematic," paradoxical as this may seem, since there is relatively little direct competition (or contact) between these strata at the initial stages. Moreover, it takes time before there is wide recognition that one is not dealing with a transitory phenomenon and that the countries affected de facto have become immigration societies. In the longer run, as this perception spreads and as the "culture shock" becomes more pronounced, particularly with the appearance of a second generation of migrant families (or the children of "mixed" marriages), rivalry and conflict are likely to become more endemic and pronounced.

The in-migration of two or more "indigenous" ethnic groups into central urban (and adjacent suburban) areas to compete for prestigious posts in service occupations, including the government bureaucracy, has a greater chance of leading to serious friction (with a high degree of "visibility" in the media), even during the initial stage. On the other hand, in such instances, it is less likely that the cultural chasm will coincide for prolonged periods with a social gap since the groups in question are moving, more or less simultaneously, into white collar occupations.

In either one of the two categories discussed, however, the conflict element is pronounced, whether it is immediately visible or smoldering beneath the surface.

In a very fundamental sense, these are expressions of a "resource" problem relating to the utilization of the most precious of "natural" resources, the human factor. Moreover, friction in some of the instances mentioned revolves around the "resource" of most immediate concern to human beings, namely job opportunities (the obvious channel whereby most men and women obtain access to other "resources"). That is not to say, of course, that there is a dearth of meaningful linkages between ethnic conflict and other "resource" problems (in the usually accepted meaning of the word). In fact, there is a "spillover" effect in both directions:

1. According to some analysts, it is the odor of North Sea oil and the revenues accruing from this development that have provided a much-needed credibility factor for the Scottish nationalist movement which was considered politically less respectable prior to the appearance of this element.

2. In the case of Cyprus, Greece, and Turkey, on the other hand, the escalation of a major ethnic struggle on the disputed island has exacerbated to a serious extent a previously marginal dispute over Aegean oil. (Its presence in significant quantities, however, was and continues to be putative at best.) The result has been to raise a host of other "Aegean problems" relating to jurisdiction, navigation, demilitarization, and so forth.

EFFECTS

Alienation

One of the more apparent concomitants of the phenomena discussed here has been "alienation," both in the broader social and psychological aspects of the term. This factor, of course, was noted as a by-product of mobility (and of geographical and social uprooting) at an earlier stage of development of Western society, i.e. the industrial revolution. At that stage too there was massive migration, primarily overseas, but also from rural to urban regions within individual countries. However, social mobility, of the dimensions associated with the current massive growth of the service sector of the population, was far less evident then. Moreover, it may be assumed that the contemporary migration pattern has not yet reached its peak, but may be intensified considerably, given the fact that both natural and human resources are distributed most unevenly and that geographic concentrations of either rarely coincide. It seems probable that population will continue to move in the direction of (relatively) resource-rich areas, but at a much more spectacular rate in view of the global resource shortage that our planet, for the first time, is beginning to experience. (This particular aspect was lacking, on the whole, in the earlier period of industrial revolution.)

"Alienation" was duly noted by contemporary analysts of nineteenth century industrialization, but some of its effects were mitigated by the appearance of a partial substitute for lost traditional values in the form of a new, working class subculture, with its distinct loyalties, affinities, mores, and even ideologies. The current, broad service stratum of society, on the other hand, lacks the cohesive elements provided, in terms of locale and economic solidarity, by the factory or the coal mine. Both geographically and socially, this highly visible service sector of the population in postindustrial societies tends to be diffuse; it lacks the essential ingredients of a class or subculture.

In view of all of these considerations, the atomization occurring within contemporary Western societies is likely to be more intense than the phenomena noted earlier, and the need (and search) for substitute values is bound to be all the more urgent. It is one of the lessons of history, however, that for such values to be meaningful, they cannot be artificially created or contrived, but will have appeal only to the extent that they evoke deeply rooted sentiments and associations (even if these remain well hidden under the surface). To some extent, of course, elements of this type are to be found within the nuclear family. However, in societies that employ gainfully the vast majority of the population, both male and female, a large proportion of waking hours is spent away from the protective environment of home life, necessitating the invocation of sentiments and loyalties that go beyond the immediate framework of the nuclear family.

Judging by the political and sociopolitical data that can be gathered from most highly developed contemporary states, the affinities that can be evoked and that come to the surface most readily, beyond the parameters of the nuclear family, are essentially cultural and can be identified most simply with the factor subsumed generally under the title of "ethnic." To use an analogy from the American scene (which can be applied, with appropriate changes, to other contemporary cultures), a "three generational" phenomenon is becoming apparent.

The "first generation" moved to the United States during the period of industrialization, retaining most of its linguistic, religious, and other "ethnic" characteristics. Since these factors made that generation stand out as "different," within a generally WASP environment, it tended to keep to itself within its own social and philanthropic associations. The "second generation" tended to feel generally ashamed of these "peculiarities," and did its best therefore to "pass," including deliberate severing of cultural, linguistic, and other "ethnic" roots. The "third generation," maturing in the era in which postindustrial phenomena, including "alienation," are becoming very apparent, has been searching for some of these very roots, being unable, however, to find them with the aid of the previous generation which had gone out of its way to slough them off. Consequently, the current generation has had to go back, as it were, to the "grandparents" to help resuscitate an ethnic framework which provides both a source of identity and renewed pride. Of course, like all analogies this portrayal contains oversimplifications, but it does appear to reflect reality to a meaningful extent. This can be seen even by examining some of the cruder and more simple visual data. Hollywood, between the 1920s and 1950s, portrayed heroes who, almost without exception, had impeccably "American" (i.e. descended from the British Isles) names and characteristics (although many of the actors, in fact, were descended from a very different environment). Where a different ethnic origin of a folk hero could not be disguised (e.g. the German parentage of Lou Gehrig), it was portrayed usually as a lovable eccentricity, to be regarded as light comic relief.

Five minutes of glancing through any recent television guide, on the other hand, will reveal a totally different scene. The heroes and heroines of situation comedies and of thrillers alike not only are unmistakably "ethnic," but their affinities and pride in their ethnicity are emphasized. (Thus five of the most successful detective shows of the last few years have featured one proudly Greek, one equally proudly Polish, and three no less proudly Italian heroes.) It may be argued, of course, that Hollywood and its lineal descendants in television are not necessarily the best mirrors of real life. However, there is little doubt that they like to accommodate the Zeitgeist (or at least what they perceive to be the fashion of the day).

The reappearance of the ethnic factor as a significant element both socially and politically is common currency in the developed portion of the globe, as borne out by the national movements of the Quebecois, the Bretons, the Corsicans, the Occitanians, the Basques, the Catalans, the Walloons, the Flemings, the Scots, the Welsh, the Jurassiens – to mention only a few.

Emergence of Substate Actors

As evidenced by newspaper headlines during the last decade or two, this phenomenon is conflict prone. Not in all instances does this imply resort to physical violence, although in many cases force has been employed (whether of the "low-level violence" type – terrorism, kidnapping, hijacking, indiscriminate explosions, etc. – or of a more endemic kind).

In almost all circumstances, however, the result has been conflict in the political arena, with considerable impact upon the party system as a whole (particularly in Britain, Belgium, Spain, and Canada). To take only one example, the vicissitudes experienced by the Scottish National Party (SNP) have been important not only for the future of Scotland, but for parliamentary options in Westminster, particularly with regard to the electoral chances of the British Labor Party as a contender for power over the United Kingdom.

Indeed, the consequences have been felt even on the supranational level, i.e., they have affected the international system as a whole – at least within Europe. To mention one aspect: The emerging substate actors, particularly Scotland and Wales, have been striving for separate representation within the Council of Europe (a potentially significant first step toward recognition as a member of the global system).

Thus, at the very time when so many observers have been under the impression that large supranational, "regional," conglomerations (such as the Organization of African Unity or the Organization of American States) are beginning to replace individual states as primary actors on the international scene, the centrifugal phenomenon described here has led to the increasing self-assertion of subnational entities (with aspirations, in some instances, to fully fledged statehood).

In that context, it is neither helpful nor particularly illuminating to resort to pejoratives such as "Balkanization," or "tribalism." This development constitutes a distinct factor in international relations, and the task of the observer is to analyze and to comprehend it rather than to confuse himself and others with terminology of a normative type.

This is not to deny that the twofold proliferation of international actors (i.e., the tripling of the number of sovereign states resulting from decolonization, plus the introduction of a growing number of increasingly significant substate elements) complicates the structure of international relations and, by multiplying options to the point of a geometric progression, probably destabilizes the system as a whole.

That is not to say that the only substate actors appearing in recent years have represented ethnic groups. Quite obviously, some of the most active organizations, particularly in the arena of terrorism, have been of a rather inchoate type (in terms of aspirations, although certainly not of operations), reflecting neither ethnic nor perhaps even clearly ideological or social aims.

However, those elements that do possess a clearly ethnic base are the more significant because, in most instances, they also have reasonable, well-defined territorial parameters. The seizure of power, in modern as in classical times, is linked intimately with control over territory. Clearly, therefore, these are the substate actors most likely to attain fully fledged statehood, the highest rank of membership in the international system. Their very existence complicates – and may endanger – existing structures, particularly alliance systems such as NATO, which are founded upon the concept (and consist) of sovereign states that have been a familiar feature on the scene for a long time. The recent growth of centrifugal movements that weaken (if they do not actually break up) individual member states poses serious problems for the alliance as a whole (which has its hands full, as it is, trying to tackle such issues as standardization of weapons and centralization of command and control among governments pursuing divergent "national interests" and speaking different languages). Within this context, relations are complicated still further by ethnic conflicts that cause such dissention between member states (e.g., Cyprus vis-a-vis Greece and Turkey) as to bring about the alienation of one or more from the alliance as a whole (particularly since the disputing parties expect other allies to support them, and interpret neutrality as lack of friendship). Moreover, such conflicts have other forms of fallout as well. Ethnic strife along linguistic lines, for instance (e.g., Canada and Belgium), is likely to complicate even more the problems posed by language of command within a multinational alliance, particularly given the split second decisions made essential by contemporary technology. The recent controversy concerning the language to be employed by air control tower personnel within the province of Quebec is a typical example.

CENTRIFUGAL PHENOMENA AND THE
REVOLUTION IN WEAPONS TECHNOLOGY

The developments analyzed in this study assume particular significance in view of their coincidence in time with the revolution in weapons technology – the emergence of ultrahigh precision hardware and software, and the beginning of postnuclear technologies.

At least during the current period (of deployment and use of the first generation of the new Precision Guided Munitions), the character of these weapons, perhaps temporarily, offers peculiar advantages to small and dispersed groups operating against static and relatively large targets such as airports or massed concentrations of regular forces. The reasons for this rather startling reversal are quite simple. The new technologies, while highly complex, provide weapons that are fairly simple to operate, as well as being frequently small and light to carry (e.g., the launchers for infantry operated antitank and antiair missiles of the "Sagger" and "Strela" type). Many can be operated by one or at most two individuals and are relatively recoilless, so that they can be deployed and used almost anywhere. In view of their unprecedented accuracy, these weapons may have a 99 percent or higher probability of destroying the target as soon as it is "acquired" (i.e., sighted visually or through electronic means). Consequently, dispersal and concealment provide a partial answer to the new technology. Preventing a target from being "acquired" may be the simplest way to preserve it from destruction. As a result, it is precisely the small and dispersed groups which, while being quite adequate for the purpose of operating these weapons, may also be best suited for avoiding serious casualties at the hands of opposing forces using the same technology.

A few individuals operating heat-seeking antiair projectiles from a hotel room window may be able to hold to ransom or obliterate the air traffic or major utilities of a major city. The same type of weapons may not be very effective against such individuals, particularly if they disperse among the civilian population. Massed regular forces, including armor and aircraft, on the other hand offer tempting and highly vulnerable targets for Precision Guided Munitions.

It is obvious that these technological developments offer a positive inducement for centrifugal elements in the body politic to take on the modern state and its forces. This may be one of the reasons why even ethnic movements that have successfully established themselves as a viable competitor in the party political structure of a country (e.g., the separatist P.Q. in Quebec and the autonomist P.N.V. in the Basque Provinces) have not been able to eliminate permanently more violent and overtly conflict oriented splinters (such as the terrorist F.L.Q. in Quebec and the E.T.A. in the Basque Provinces).

To some extent, these developments tend to blur the more traditional distinctions between low level violence and warfare. From the point of view of the political leverage that the threat of either provides, the differences are not unbridgeable. Of course, there are other arenas in which ethnic and national conflict can be conducted – "by other means." (The domain of sports provides just one such example – from the full scale "soccer war" between Honduras and El Salvador to the Innsbruck Winter Olympics, during which the Tyrolese authorities and spectators found the most ingenious ways of demonstrating their political support for their South Tyrolese kinsmen across the Italian frontier who had to participate at the games as "Italians.")

SPECIAL STUDIES

The considerations presented here reflect preliminary conclusions of the author's investigations within the parameters of the Rockefeller Foundation project, as well as additional special studies supported by that project and contained within this book. These include a conceptual and analytical approach to the problem of multiethnic states, including a discussion of models of conflict resolution (by the author); an analysis of national and ethnic conflict in an immigration society – the United States (by Professor John P. Roche); a survey of problems and remedial measures, social, economic, educational, and legal, relating to the migrant labor phenomenon in Northwestern Europe (conducted by the Friedrich-Ebert Foundation in the German Federal Republic under Dr. Ursula Mehrlaender); a review of the political "fallout" as well as the roots of an ethnic/regional movement – the new Scottish Nationalism (conducted by Dr. H. Drucker at the University of Edinburgh); and three country studies of "indigenous" ethnic problems in Northwestern Europe (Belgium), the Mediterranean (Cyprus-Greece-Turkey), and the Far East (Japan) by three Fletcher graduates (J.E. Kane, G.D. Ra'anan, and G.F. Rhode).

These studies have been supplemented by the author's own research trips to Scotland, Belgium, the German Federal Republic, Cyprus, Greece, Turkey, and Canada.

It is by design that the various chapters of this volume represent contributions by practitioners from different disciplines, including contemporary political history, United States constitutional history, the social sciences (particularly sociology), political party analysis, conflict studies, and anthropology. It was the purpose of this work to acquaint the reader not merely with the particular cultural style that ethnic resurgence has assumed in selected modern democratic states, but also to present the public with representative samples of the way in which different disciples view this significant phenomenon. The editor hopes that this variegated approach may prove more useful to students of this topic than an artificial attempt to force the individual portions of the book into a single monolithic mold.

1 Ethnic Conflict: Toward a New Typology *
Uri Ra'anan

It has been one of the fallacies of contemporary political thought, particularly in the West, to assume that the international arena of the twentieth century is occupied largely, if not almost exclusively, by "nation-states" and — some sophisticated minds would add — "nation-states-to-be." (This term is either tautological or, if it is to be lucid and coherent, presumably a "nation-state" would have to refer to a polity, the territorial and juridical frontiers of which coincide with the ethnic boundaries of the national entity with which that state is identified, frequently by its very name.) Indeed, the generally accepted adjective "international," in place of the more accurate terms "interstate" or "intergovernmental," itself reflects the fallacious assumption that "nation-state" may be regarded more or less as a synonym for "independent state."(1)

Publisher's note: The type employed in this book made utilization of diacritical marks unfeasible. Consequently, the German umlaut has been rendered as "ae," "oe," or "ue," respectively, in accordance with traditional practice, while French accents have been omitted, and so have diacritical marks in the case of Turkish, Czech, and other names.

*This chapter contains concepts developed by the author in the 1950s and early 1960s, systematized in his teaching at the Fletcher School of Law and Diplomacy from 1967 onward, reflected and applied during the 1970s in case studies by some of his students (and eventually by others), distilled in definitive written form in 1973 during sabbatic leave assisted generously by the Battelle Seattle Research Center, and finalized, as well as updated, as part of the wider project generously supported by the Rockefeller Foundation.

To be sure, protagonists of this currently fashionable view will admit usually that one portion of the globe — consisting of the so-called developing areas — does not quite fit their conceptual framework. However, then they will assert that in this region a process is under way, subsumed under the facile heading of "nation building," which will result almost inevitably in the area's "normalization," its Gleichschaltung with the rest of the world. They will dismiss with the scornful expletive "tribalism" any rejoinders pointing out that this region already does contain many genuine national entities, frequently numbering millions of members and possessing a well-developed culture, language, and historical consciousness, such as the Yoruba, Ibo, Ewe, and others, but that the arbitrary boundaries of the postcolonial states usually cut across or ignore these natural ethnic units. Consequently, the attempt to "build nations" on the basis of the current, artificial frontiers and states actually entails undermining or destroying existing nationalities. Most of the advocates of the prevailing trend in political thought will regard such arguments at best as anachronistic and likely to hamper their beautifully streamlined models of "modernization" and economic and functional "efficiency" to be implemented by highly centralized states and their bureaucracies.

The most informed among such followers of contemporary political science fashions perhaps will allow that, in addition to the "developing areas," their terminology also does not provide an entirely appropriate description of conditions within the successor states of the three former great multinational conglomerates of Southern, Eastern, and Central Europe — the Ottoman, Romanov, and Habsburg Empires. However, generally they will be inclined to downplay these discrepancies by categorizing the current nationality conflicts of that part of the world as mere "minority problems."

As for the rest of the globe (approximately the region known as the West), apparently it is regarded in contemporary thought as the very birthplace of the modern "nation-state" and its primary showcase.

In fact, however, instances on the political map of the world in which the territorial frontiers of the state and the ethnic boundaries of the constituent nation coincide amount to a negligible minority (Iceland, metropolitan Portugal, Norway, and a few others) of the approximately 150 more or less sovereign countries existing today. In very many cases, the state is larger than the "nation," i.e., the juridical limits of the state extend well beyond the area settled by its "Staatsvolk" (that is to say, the ethnic group which created the state, is largely identified with it, constitutes the bulk of its elite, and is the source of the predominant culture).

For instance, Great Russians make up only just over one-half the population of the U.S.S.R., and even if, by a very wide stretch of the political imagination, one were to accept as "co-Staatsvoelker" of the U.S.S.R. the 14 other national groups after which the various constituent Soviet Republics are named, the boundaries of the Soviet Union would still embrace some 26 million additional citizens (almost one-ninth of the total population), belonging to "other" or "minority" ethnic entities and occupying considerable portions of the country. Similarly, in the Yugoslav case, the original Staatsvolk, the Serbs, number little more than 40 percent of the inhabitants. Even if Croats, Slovenes, Macedonians, and Montenegrins, whose names the other Yugoslav Republics bear, were to be regarded in the same light as the Serbs, this would still leave Yugoslavia with "other" or "minority" nationalities amounting to nearly one-fifth of her total citizenry and inhabiting sizable stretches of her territory.

Nor is the West exempt from such situations:

France, the classical "nation-state" of the political textbooks, contains, adjacent to its outer limits, German-speaking Alsatians; Italian-speaking inhabitants of the eastern Riviera and Corsica; Catalans and Basques at either end of the Pyrenees; Celtic Bretons; and Flemings southwest of the Belgian frontier – amounting altogether to nearly one-tenth of metropolitan France's citizens (without even counting the population of French "overseas departments" or the large number of foreign laborers in the country, North Africans and others). In the Canadian case, even if one regarded as Staatsvoelker the descendants of settlers both from the British Isles and from France (Quebecois and Acadians), each in their respective sections of the country, one would still be left with a "Third Canada" including Scandinavians, Germans, Dutch, Ukrainians, Poles, Jews, Italians, Indians, Eskimos, etc., exceeding one-fourth of Canada's citizens and inhabiting considerable stretches of her territory, especially in the Prairies, the North, and the Northwest.

In the Far East, even the island state of Japan, despite its long history of relative isolation, is far from homogeneous, including not only a sizable Korean minority, but the aboriginal Ainus, persisting tenaciously in the country's northernmost reaches.

If in these, and at least 100 other instances, the state is larger in size than the area inhabited by the nation or Staatsvolk, there are conversely quite a few cases in which the boundaries of the nation exceed the territorial limits of any one state. There is a German nation, but there are several German states (the German Federal Republic, the German Democratic Republic, possibly West Berlin – if it can be regarded as a separate state – and perhaps even Austria). Switzerland, Liechtenstein, and Luxembourg, although a majority of their inhabitants speak German and/or German dialects, presumably would not be considered German states by most analysts. A Korean and a Vietnamese nation exist, but in each of these instances there were two separate, more or less sovereign, states (one of which, South Vietnam, subsequently was eliminated by conquest). Quite a few observers, in the Middle East and outside, argue that in spite of some historical, ethnic, linguistic (i.e., dialects), and religious differences, the various Arab groups constitute one single nation, whereas currently there are 19 Arab states. There is a Jewish state, but it contains less than one-fourth of the Jewish people. There is a Hungarian state, but the frontiers imposed upon it by the post-World War I and II settlements exclude nearly 3 million Magyars from the motherland (in Transylvania, southern Slovakia, and the Vojvodina), not to speak of the many hundreds of thousands in the New World who are of Magyar descent. There are two Chinese states (actually three, if one regards Singapore from the ethnic point of view), but they do not include either the Chinese inhabitants of Hong Kong or the millions of "overseas Chinese" in Southeast Asia and in the Western Hemisphere. Even in relatively homogeneous Scandinavia, the Swedish state fails to include .5 million Swedes in neighboring Finland, right across the Gulf of Bothnia, not to mention the millions of ethnic Swedes in North America. These are but a few of scores of examples in which the ethnic limits of the nation transcend the territorial frontiers of one particular state.

Thus, in the case of well over 90 percent of the independent countries existing today, the state either is considerably larger or much smaller than the area inhabited by the corresponding nation or Staatsvolk. Consequently, "nation-states," far from constituting the rule on the contemporary political map, remain a very exceptional phenomenon – certainly if a high degree of ethnic homogeneity and congruity between the geographic outlines of the state and nation are regarded as the primary criteria of the nation-state. (If they are not, then little, if any, real meaning attaches to this term.)

If this be true of the situation prevailing today, how much more was it the case during earlier decades and centuries. After all, it is one of the peculiar contributions of, roughly, the second and third quarters of the twentieth century that it has become customary to attempt "cleaning up" the ethnic map – by genocidal measures (against Jews and Gypsies under Hitler; Crimean Tatars, Volga Germans, and Chechen-Ingush under Stalin; Ibos in Nigeria; Southern Blacks in the Sudan; both Tutsi and Hutu in Rwanda and Burundi; overseas Chinese in certain parts of Southeast Asia; Kurds in Iraq, etc.). This has been done also by brutal unilateral expulsions (Asians from Uganda, Germans from most of East Central Europe, etc.) and through population exchanges, by agreement, through semivoluntary moves, as a result of fear, or in the wake of forcible measures (Hellenes from Turkey and Turks from Greece; Macedonian Bulgars from Greece and Hellenes from Bulgaria; Turks from Bulgaria and Bulgars from European Turkey – all in the 1920s; most Hindus and Sikhs from Pakistan and many Moslems from India; practically all Jews from the Arab countries and about three-fourths of the Arabs from the area which became Israel in 1948 to 1949; some of the few Ukrainians and Byelo-Russians still remaining in truncated post-World War II Poland and many ethnic Poles from former Polish territories annexed to the U.S.S.R., etc.).

Despite all of these ethnic "clean-up" measures, genuine "nation-states" have remained exceptional factors on the political landscape, as has been pointed out. Obviously, there were even fewer instances of ethnic homogeneity in the period that preceded these measures, i.e., up to 1920, not to mention the fact that, until the two Balkan Wars and World War I, there existed three great multinational states, the Ottoman, Habsburg, and Romanov Empires (only the last of these being succeeded by an equally polyglot state – the U.S.S.R.). Moreover, during the first half of the nineteenth century, there were 39 separate German and 9 Italian states. If nation-states are very much in the minority on the contemporary political scene, therefore, they have been even more exceptional in history.

Conversely, multiethnic polities have constituted the norm across the ages and still do so today. Despite this prevalence of polyglot entities – or perhaps just because of it – "nationalism" (i.e., the self-assertion of ethnic groups, ranging from primarily cultural, religious, and educational endeavors, via political organization, to the ultimate step of struggling for territorial or state power) has been a highly significant phenomenon throughout most of recorded history. Many contemporary Western political scientists, needless to say, deny this and trace back "true" nationalism, which they regard as a "modern ideology," no further than the French Revolution or, at most, to the absolutist centralized states of the seventeenth century. (Of course, anyone acquainted with the paeans to England and the English in Shakespeare, and to the concept of "Italy" in Dante, not to speak of the lyrical and epic portrayals of the struggles for cultural and religious self-expression and national survival of the Hellenes and the Hebrews in the Greek classics and in the Bible, respectively, will wonder if this view is not somewhat simplistic.)

It is not difficult really to grasp the reason for the apparent paradox that multiethnic states, rather than posing an obstacle, constitute a breeding ground for the growth of nationalistic manifestations. Awareness of national differences and a perception of incompatibility of interests is far less likely to develop in ethnically homogeneous societies, where individuals as a rule do not encounter in their daily lives problems due to the need to function (during study, work, or litigation) in a language other than their mother tongue, to adjust to unaccustomed and incomprehensible cultural traditions, or to compete economically and socially with personalities molded by an entirely different background and heritage. Conversely, the sudden impact of one ethnic group upon another, whether because of invasion, annexation, migration, or simple fluctuation in the language or cultural frontiers between two peoples, cannot but give rise to some, most, or all of these problems (which are likely to be aggravated if the nationalities concerned find themselves within the frontiers of a single state since then they are likely to seek satisfaction of their aspirations through struggle for political control of the whole country or, at least, portions thereof).

Thus, it is symptomatic that the center of French separatism in Canada is not to be found in the solidly French Quebec hinterland, but in multinational Montreal. Similarly the focus of the Belgian nationality conflict is bilingual Brussels, and not either the homogeneously Flemish farmland of the north or the overwhelmingly Walloon coal areas of the south.

One can, of course, discover instances where distinctly nationalistic tendencies have become evident even in apparently homogeneous countries, but closer investigation usually will reveal that in these cases extraneous ethnic elements actually have impinged upon the native population. For example, Iceland, an almost "pure" nation-state, recently has shown signs of somewhat strident nationalism but, in fact, these are due largely to the situation on the sea surrounding the island, where a large proportion of this nation of fishermen spends its working days and has to compete with trawlers from Britain and other countries. In a sense, therefore, Iceland is ethnically homogeneous only on land, but not on the equally important adjacent waters.

Perhaps the considerations presented so far should not be regarded as particularly revolutionary since, to a considerable extent, they relate to data with which at least historians of the period 1806 to 1939 have long been fairly well acquainted. However, for some reason, quite a few adherents of other disciplines, particularly Western economists and some political scientists concerned with development, recently seem to have discovered with surprise and sometimes with shock that even contemporary Western societies contain mutually competing, often antagonistic, culturally, religiously, and/or linguistically distinct ethnic groups which regard themselves as nationalities or even as nations-to-be and struggle for political and/or territorial power.

In fairness to the analysts and observers in question, it may be useful to review the origins and antecedents of their currently still fashionable misapprehensions. It was one of the pathetic fallacies of the period which began in the closing stages of World War II and continued after its termination to assume that the great wave of nationalism, which had swept across Europe between the Napoleonic and Hitlerian eras, had fulfilled its aspirations through the creation of a series of supposed "nation-states" and now would somehow ebb away. The futuristic literature of the period was full of patent panaceas, mostly revolving around the concept of federalism which was expected to dominate the post-World War II world and, hopefully, to fuse the remnants of nationalism into some higher, supranational amalgam, embodied in various large federations of states.

It was taken for granted, moreover, that the general direction in which national fervor supposedly had begun to fade away was eastward. After all — so most economic and political planners of the time argued — the concept of the modern nation-state was born during the sixteenth and seventeenth centuries, in the bureaucratically centralized, post-medieval societies of Western Europe — Britain, France, the Netherlands. By the nineteenth century, so they claimed, following the French revolutionary elaboration of the idea of "la nation," and in reaction to the Napoleonic expansionist drive for conquest, nationalism had reached Central Europe, leading eventually to the formation of unitary states in Germany and Italy, and then had moved eastward to the Balkans, Eastcentral, and Eastern Europe, which became known, par excellence, as the hotbeds of national strife. By the twentieth century, the wave had moved still further east to the so-called Middle East, and eventually it had reached the rest of colonial Asia and Africa.

By this time — it was taken for granted — the West (i.e. Western Europe and the Western hemisphere), where supposedly nation-states had been achieved centuries ago, already had "recovered" from, or even had proven immune to, the "infantile malady" that was now ravaging less fortunate lands. This was believed so firmly that Western states like Switzerland, France, and the United States were held up as the classical examples of societies that had "solved" the "national problem."

Needless to say, events in recent years have demonstrated that these obituary notices even of Western nationalism were, to put it mildly, premature. Belgium has become the arena of revived Flemish and Walloon separatism and the end is not in sight. France has been confronted by national movements of the Bretons and the Basques, and Spain by Basques and Catalans. The growth of French separatism in Quebec has been meteoric. The United States, after appearing for decades to move toward "homogenization," has been beset by separatism, both white and black, and, finally, has had to acknowledge that it is the "pluralistic society" rather than the "melting pot" which constitutes its realistic goal. Then there is, of course, Ulster, not to mention the rise of Welsh and Scottish nationalism in the United Kingdom. Finally, in the classical home of supposed national resolution, Switzerland, a very sharp conflict has exacerbated relations between the German Protestant majority of the Canton of Berne and the predominantly Catholic and overwhelmingly French population of the Jura, in the north of the canton (nor has the secession of the northernmost portion of the Jura from Berne resolved the problem).

One might ask why the prophets of the 1940s and 1950s have turned out to be so mistaken. The reasons, apparently, include academic prejudice and wishful thinking. All too many of the would-be prophets, as has been pointed out, seem to have been economists or adherents of certain categories of political science, especially those with a functionalist bias. Professionally they have tended to be enamored of sheer size, "efficiency," and "viability." To most of them, it has appeared axiomatic that large territorial units, with rich and variegated resources, would prove to be more competent and thus more desirable members of the global community than smaller, poorer, and more struggling states. Consequently, they are prejudiced in favor of sizeable federations and other large polities, and against national individuality and self-expression. Since, however, most of these academicians and commentators have been products of a democratic environment and, therefore, uncomfortable with open denial of self-determination, they have been compelled to pretend, to themselves and others, that existing states, (however arbitrarily their frontiers might multilate ethnic units) are in fact "nation-states" or "nation-states-to-be." Thus, they have hailed large postcolonial states, based upon entirely artificial administrative entities of the colonial period, as laboratories of a supposed process of "nation building." Conversely, they have scorned bitterly movements for national autonomy or separation of "minority" nationalities, such as Ibos, Ewe, or Kurds, as mere retrogressive moves toward "tribalism" or "Balkanization."

Most historians and anthropologists, on the other hand, have been inclined to doubt whether, even under modern (i.e., postmedieval) conditions, artificial nation building really has been successful to any degree, except perhaps temporarily in a couple of West European instances and in some immigrant societies, in as far as they were based upon the voluntary confluence of separate cultural and ethnic mainstreams (as long as geographic and ethnic lines did not coincide, as they do in Quebec and in parts of South Africa). Moreover, historians have been well aware that the Sultans in five centuries were unable to "build" an "Ottoman nation" out of Turks, Arabs, Armenians, Kurds, Greeks, etc.; the Tsars in several centuries could not "build" a single nation out of Great Russians, Ukrainians, Byelo-Russians, Poles, Finns, Georgians, etc.; nor could the Habsburg Emperor-Kings, in a similar time span, "build" one nation out of Germans, Hungarians, Czechs, Croats, etc. There is no indication, what is more, that these large, polyglot but ramshakle empires, beset by unending struggles for self-government of the subject nationalities, really were more efficient, stable, or happy societies than those of their much smaller successor states that ethnically were reasonably homogeneous, such as Esthonia, Lithuania, etc. (states that were destroyed subsequently not by internal conflict but by Soviet imperialism).

Economists, however, and even some political scientists, regrettably do not always know much history and it was they who seemed to monopolize the futuristic literature on the topic. Admittedly, for a brief period after World War II, it did appear as if the advocates of mass, size, and federation might have a point. There came into existence such entities as the E.E.C., the unions between Mali and Senegal and between Egypt and Syria (the U.A.R.). However, the latter two unions quickly broke up and, while the E.E.C. has grown in size and economic stature, Europe's political reality remains de Gaulle's "L'Europe des patries" (as the disharmonious response to recent Middle Eastern oil pressures has made painfully obvious), rather than any true European federation whose members really have merged their individual sovereignties. Moreover, centrifugal tendencies quickly became apparent and spread within existing states between Slovaks and Czechs; Croats, Macedonians, and Serbs; Ukrainians, Georgians, Lithuanians, Jews, and Great Russians; Walloons and Flemings; Basques and Castilians; Francophones and Anglophones in Canada; Kurds and Arabs in Iraq; Black Africans and Arabs in the Sudan; Ibos, Yoruba, and Hausa-Fulani in Nigeria; Bengalis and Biharis in East Pakistan (Bangladesh), etc. Thus, if anything, the trend has been toward the breakdown of existing polities into still smaller entities, rather than their merger into larger units, as suggested by futuristic literature. The survival of so-called regional organizations in Africa, the Arab World, Latin America, etc. in no way contradicts this trend, since these structures have remained mere sounding boards rather than developing in the direction of super-sovereignties, as is quite evident from the continued hostility between Ethiopia and Somalia within the OAU, between Syria and Iraq and between Algeria and Morocco within the Arab League, and between El Salvador and Honduras in the OAS. Truly, those who in the 1940s and 1950s presumed to have lipread History and to have gained foreknowledge of her ways failed, apparently, to understand her intentions and perhaps even her very language.

Conceivably, these errors might have been anticipated and pre-empted but for the well-nigh impenetrable semantic confusion, especially in the West, that has enveloped the whole topic under discussion here — a confusion which, this author believes, is due partly to the fact that there exist in the world at least three quite distinct concepts of nationality and nationalism and that these terms, therefore, have entirely different connotations in various regions of the world.

In the <u>West</u> (i.e., roughly Europe west of the Rhine and the Western Hemisphere), a primarily territorial concept of nationality (having much in common with the legal concept of jus soii) has developed during the modern era. Western Europe was the one area where classical feudalism, in the full sense of the word, really flourished. Historical myth notwithstanding, feudalism of this type did not necessarily breed anarchy but rather provided, in several cases, a congenial environment for the growth of centralization and bureaucratic statehood, as evidenced by the history of the early Norman-Angevin monarchy, from William I to Henry II, and of Norman Sicily.

On the basis of this heritage, the postmedieval, absolutist West European monarchies of the Tudors and the Valois were able to establish modern, bureaucratic, and centralized states. In these instances — and, perhaps, in these instances alone — some degree of "nation building" can be demonstrated to have occurred. In a sense, it was these new <u>states</u> that assisted the process of creating the modern French and English <u>nations</u>, rather than the other way around (although, as has already been pointed out, even in these cases this process, extended over many generations, has not been completed entirely to this very day). Allegiance to the state, therefore, residence therein, and submission to its jurisdiction, are the hallmarks of the Western idea of nationality — to the point where, in American English, one speaks of a "national" of a country when, actually, one means a "citizen." The two terms have become synonymous. It is an individual's place of residence and his passport that largely determine his nationality in the West, i.e. primarily territorial and juridical criteria (precisely as in the case of jus soli). For the same reasons, "state" and "nation" have tended to become almost synonymous in the English language, to a degree that causes many to refer to "national interests" when, in fact, they mean "state interests," while others speak simplistically of a world of nation-states. However, since, as has been demonstrated already, there are actually rather few instances in which the limits of the state and of its constituent nation (Staatsvolk) really coincide, loyalty and commitment to the state and to the nation often not only are not synonymous, but may be directly in conflict with one another. In order to unite a nation split asunder by official boundaries or to win independence for a nationality lacking sovereign territory, men sometimes feel impelled to fight the states in which they dwell and whose formal citizenship they hold. In the pre-1938 Austrian Republic, to be a "nationalist" meant supporting an Anschluss between Austria and the German Reich, i.e. attempting to obliterate the Republic and to submerge it in a Greater Germany. Thus, to be a "nationalist" and an Austrian "patriot" were antithetical terms. The interests of the "state" and the "nation" simply were incompatible. The same, of course, was true of any of the particularist German and Italian states in the first half of the nineteenth century. Similarly, to be a Jordanian or Lebanese "patriot" and a pan-Arab "nationalist," who happens to be a citizen of Jordan or Lebanon, are antithetical concepts. The creation of a pan-Arab empire, probably ruled from Cairo or Damascus, effectively would mean the end of independent Jordanian and Lebanese states (to the extent that Lebanese independence can be regarded as meaningful still under virtual Syrian occupation). In multinational states it may be possible to be a patriot and a nationalist simultaneously – provided one happens to be a member of the Staatsvolk. It is, however, hardly feasible for "minorities."

In Czechoslovakia, a Czech can, at one and the same time, support his state and his nation (or at least he could under Benes or Dubcek). However, an ethnic Magyar from Southern Slovakia cannot simultaneously and without contradiction support the Czechoslovak state, whose passport he holds, and the aspirations of the Magyar nation which presumably would desire the eventual separation of Magyar-speaking Southern Slovakia from Czechoslovakia and its reunion with the Hungarian motherland.

Because the practical identification of state and nation occasionally has rested upon some degree of reality in Western history, most Westerners assume that it prevails today throughout most of the world. Actually, it has been, and remains currently, a very exceptional phenomenon. The whole contemporary Western political glossary suffers considerably from the semantic confusion which derives from this misapprehension.

The fallacious assumption that certain Western concepts, which in fact have remained rare and unusual products of a particular historical environment and experience, actually have universal application has led both Westerners and many Western-educated Afro-Asians to think and speak in such terms as "nation building." They have taken it for granted that some exceptional Western historical developments can and should be copied in the Third World and that what, usually, are accidental and artificial Afro-Asian state frontiers (a heritage of arbitrary administrative lines drawn by colonial powers) constitute a suitable framework for the rapid creation of a single nation out of several distinct and antagonistic nationalities, just because something of this sort may have happened two or three times in Western history. (What is forgotten, of course, is that even in the West this process required many centuries and often has remained incomplete.) It is instructive to glance at the case of France and the influence of French thought upon Francophone Africa. From the late eighteenth to the mid-twentieth centuries, it did seem as if the modern French state had succeeded, after more than half a millenium of effort, in creating a single nation out of Germanic Franks, Alemanni, and Burgundians in the north and northeast, Celts in the northwest, a Romano-Celtic-Visigothic-Basque population in the southwest, and a Romano-Celtic population in the south (although, as was pointed out earlier, the unqualified success of the experiment has appeared somewhat in question lately, certainly as far as some Bretons and many Basques are concerned). It is very doubtful, however, if the French example proves very much with regard to the present and future development of former French colonies and protectorates overseas, or whether it is reasonable to expect meaningful and rapid success in an effort to "build" a Congo-Brazzaville, an Upper Volta, a Chad, a Niger, an Ivory Coast, or a Mauretanian "nation" out of quite distinct, ancient, and proud ethnic groups, just because they happen to be contained within some administrative frontier drawn in the nineteenth century by a French civil servant. It rarely occurs to persons educated in the Western tradition that Afro-Asian peoples with a strong sense of national identity and cultural heritage, such as the Yoruba, Ibos, or Hausa-Fulani, should be considered as separate nationalities no less than Bulgars, Serbs, Croats, Czechs, or Slovaks, who struggled for national self-determination for many decades and whose claim to nationhood is no longer seriously contested, even though they lag in numbers behind many of their Afro-Asian counterparts. That does not mean, of course, that a centrifugal process within Afro-Asian (and, for that matter, Western) states should be instigated by outsiders. On the other hand, there is also no justification for outsiders, including Western scholars, to man the barricades against such a process and to resort to invective against what they see fit to term "Balkanization" (as if the population of the Balkan peninsula really was better off living under the ramshackle, multinational Ottoman Empire than under rather more homogeneous, separate successor states during the interwar period).

In any case, what many Western analysts simply do not seem to grasp is that their essentially territorial concept of nationality, according to which citizenship and loyalty to the nation and the state are treated as interchangeable terms, may not be the accepted approach elsewhere and that, both historically and at present, it has been and remains very much a minority view.

In a majority of ancient communities, as of most contemporary nonWestern societies, the criteria determining a person's nationality were derived not from jus soli but rather from jus sanguinis. According to the latter concept, it is not where an individual resides and which state has jurisdiction over him that determines his nationality, but rather who he is — his cultural, religious, and historic identity, i.e. his ethnicity, a heritage received from his ancestors and carried with him, in mind and body, irrespective of his current place of domicile. Consequently, one is dealing here with personal (as opposed to the Western territorial) criteria of nationality.

For instance, following the Germanic invasions of many provinces of the Roman Empire, there lived, side by side on the same territory and under the sway of the same "Barbarian" ruler, ex-Roman citizens and members of one of the Germanic tribal confederations (such as Goths, Vandals, Burgundians, Franks, Lombards, etc.). Yet, in most cases, and over a considerable period of time, the two groups remained distinct entities and, before the law, it mattered <u>who</u> the defendant was and not <u>where</u> he was living. Usually, Romans were judged by Roman law and the new Germanic settlers by their own Germanic customary law. Both groups regarded this practice as proper and, indeed, as a precious safeguard of their respective rights and privileges.

It is from this general model that two current, slightly differing but related, non-Western concepts of nationality are descended – the Eastern (roughly covering Europe east of the Rhine) and the Southern (roughly covering the southern and eastern rims of the Mediterranean, i.e. the successor states of the Ottoman Empire). Both are based upon personal rather than territorial criteria, but the Eastern approach tends to focus upon cultural touchstones of ethnicity (including ancestral language and name), whereas, in the Southern view, religion is one of the primary hallmarks of nationality, so that the existence of a separate religious community frequently is a precondition for the successful development of full-fledged nationhood.

The Eastern concept, of course, long antedates the rise of communist regimes. In the democratic Czechoslovak Republic under Masaryk and Benes (1919 to 1938), for example, Czechoslovak <u>citizenship</u> was quite distinct and separate from <u>nationality</u>. There <u>was no</u> "Czechoslovak nationality." In the Czechoslovak census, Czechoslovak citizens regarded themselves, and were regarded by others, as belonging to one of seven primary nationalities (Czechs, Slovaks, Sudetengermans, Magyars, Ruthenians, Jews, and Poles) and registered accordingly – e.g., citizenship: Czechoslovak; nationality: Magyar; religion: Catholic; marital status: single; etc. The Czechoslovak state, at least in theory and to some extent in practice, recognized the right of each of the nationalities to its own educational, linguistic, and other facilities (in order to preserve its distinct identity), as well as to a reasonably proportionate share of official appointments, particularly in the respective areas in which the population of each of the ethnic groups was concentrated. Again, in the U.S.S.R. today, while there is Soviet citizenship, there is no Soviet nationality. The Soviet census (and the Soviet internal passport or identity card) requires the registration of each citizen as a member of one of the more than one hundred separate nationalities – Great Russian, Ukrainian, Byelo-Russian, Uzbek, Georgian, Armenian, Jewish, etc. Regrettably, in the Soviet case, unlike pre-1938 Czechoslovakia, such identification does not necessarily ensure the grant of the corresponding cultural and national privileges (although these are promised in the Soviet constitution), but, on the contrary, frequently becomes the basis for discrimination. However, the present analysis is concerned primarily with political concepts rather than with the issue of whether these currently are abused rather than implemented. The acknowledgment that there exist various separate nationalities, side by side with a single citizenship, is in line with the historic traditions of the region, dating back many centuries. According to the personal rather than territorial touchstones embodied in these traditions, a Georgian living in Moscow, and perhaps even born there and speaking Russian more fluently than his ancestral Georgian tongue, will still regard and register himself – and be regarded by others – as a Georgian rather than as a Great Russian. What matters is not where he resides nor even necessarily which language he now speaks best, but what his ancestry and cultural heritage is – who he is or rather, who he perceives himself (and others perceive him) to be.(2) In recognition of this aspect, the Soviet census contains a special category comprising members of ethnic groups who no longer speak the ancestral language of their nationality, presumably because they are dispersed, but have adopted another tongue, usually Russian. They are still registered as Ukrainians, Georgians, etc., but, with a comment to the effect that they now command a language other than the mother tongue of their nationality. The percentage of such persons is particularly high among Poles, Germans, and Jews in the U.S.S.R.

The nineteenth century cultural and political history of many of the "revived" nationalities of Eastcentral and Southeastern Europe in all probability reinforced the tendency of the Eastern approach to apply personal rather than territorial touchstones. Peoples whose state had disappeared from the map as a sovereign entity centuries earlier and whose national tongue had degenerated into a peasant dialect without a literature, being superseded as written and spoken forms of elite communication by the language of the conquerors, usually initiated their national renaissance by resuscitating their ancient language in modernized and literary form. In many cases, this cultural thrust, as well as the subsequent moves to ignite the spark of national insurrection, emanated not from the segments of the population that had remained settled on the soil of the old homeland, but rather from individual members of the intelligentsia living abroad, in the Diaspora. Modern Greek language and literature owed much to a few Hellenic writers living in Italy, and the Panhellenic movement originated with the sons of Greek merchants in Odessa and of Phanariotes in Bucharest. The modern Serb language and literature was largely the creation of a handful of Serbs in the Habsburg Empire and the Bulgarian uprising was initiated by members of the Bulgarian Diaspora in Odessa and Bucharest. Similarly, the revival of Hebrew as a modern spoken tongue with a secular literature and the establishment of a Jewish national movement, Zionism, were the products of the Diaspora of Eastern and Eastcentral Europe. In all of these instances, individuals permeated with national sentiments helped to resuscitate an ancient language and culture and then to organize a national movement, thus reviving the nation as a whole, which in turn proceeded to recreate the old national state. In other words, whereas in the West there were some cases in which a state created a nation, in the East individuals sometimes revived nations which then recreated states. It is a reasonable assumption that these factors played a role in accentuating the personal criteria of the Eastern – as opposed to the territorial criteria of the Western – concept of nationality.

In the areas south and east of the Mediterranean, formerly dominated by the Ottoman Empire, a third, Southern view of nationality prevails, bearing close resemblance to the Eastern approach in so far as it lays stress upon the individual's heritage and personal identity rather than his domicile or passport. However, according to the Southern concept, a more significant role in determining national identification is played by religion than by other cultural factors.(3) A very important cause for this phenomenon may be found in the history of the Ottoman institution known as the "millet." For centuries after their appearance upon the political scene, the Ottoman Turks regarded themselves essentially as an army engaged in an ongoing Holy War that had settled down temporarily during one of the truces which interrupted that war, rather than as a normal, permanent state. Consequently, their ideas of governance were rather rudimentary. They were interested mainly in collecting from the conquered peoples financial contributions for the upkeep of the Ottoman armed forces, as well as an occasional tribute of male children, to be converted to Islam and serve as recruits in the elite corps of those forces. On the other hand, as far as administration was concerned, the Ottoman Sultans were content to set up a skeleton framework in which their authority was exerted by nominated representatives (who in remote areas tended to become semiautonomous and even hereditary). Since these representatives dispensed the Sultan's justice mainly in accordance with Koranic precepts, those of the conquered regarded as non-Moslem "infidels" were allowed largely to see to their own internal civil governance in line with their respective religious canons. Since in any case the aristocracy and warrior caste of the various subject peoples often had been decimated during the course of the Ottoman Conquest, the only group left with the necessary literacy and experience to cope with juridical and organizational functions usually was the clergy. Consequently, the limited civil law autonomy of the conquered peoples, de facto became a form of clerical and religious self-government, applying canon law – particularly with respect to matters of personal status, i.e., marriage, divorce, and inheritance. Under this "millet" system (as under the Eastern concept of nationality) what mattered was not where an individual lived, but who he was. Members of the Armenian Orthodox millet (i.e., community) paid certain taxes to its clergy, elected its officials, and were judged by it in civil matters, primarily personal status issues, irrespective of whether they lived in the predominantly Armenian-populated provinces of eastern Anatolia or as a scattered minority in the large Turkish cities. As a result of the millet system, national identity in the regions south and east of the Mediterranean eventually became almost synonymous with religious identity. Thus, the Armenians are simultaneously a distinct nationality and a distinct religion (disregarding the small minority of Armenian Catholics), and the same is true of the Jews, the Druzes, and, to some extent, the Maronites, the Greeks, the 'Alawites, and others.

It is not widely realized that several Middle Eastern states have inherited and incorporated into their system of government various aspects of the millet concept which, for instance, constituted the key to Lebanon's ingenious internal "compromise" (until the recent tragic events and Syria's subsequent domination of the land of the cedars), whereby the president, premier, and speaker of the House were chosen from the Maronite, Sunni, and Shiah millets respectively, and a fixed proportion of members of Parliament represented each of the various millets (30 always being Maronites, 20 Sunni Moslems, 6 Druzes, etc.). The Lebanese electorate complied fully with this arrangement until the conflict with Palestinian Arabs and Syrians destroyed the country's parliamentary structure. Israel, via the British Palestine Mandate, has inherited another aspect of the Ottoman millet system − the exclusive jurisdiction of the various millet religious courts over questions of personal status − marriage, divorce, and inheritance. This constitutes a cherished form of autonomy for the various minorities in Israel, the Druzes, Sunni Moslems, Latin and Greek Christians, etc., and therefore always was included as a specific provision in the various resolutions on Palestine and its future by the League of Nations and the UN, from the foundation of the League until 1947. Granted to the minorities in Israel, this privilege could not be denied to the Jewish community either. Thus, the reason why there is no civil marriage in Israel is due entirely to the exclusive jurisdiction over this topic of the various millet religious courts, derived from the British Mandate and the Ottoman Empire, and has nothing to do with any alleged theocratic tendencies in Zionism (which, in fact, has prided itself from its inception on being a predominantly secular national movement, modelled upon the Italian Risorgimento and the Polish, Greek, and Hungarian national revivals). In other words, one is dealing here with a movement that developed originally in harmony with the ideological overtones of the Eastern approach to nationality, but eventually reached fruition of an area permeated by the Southern view.

Having attempted, thus, to distill some measure of analytical order out of the current confusion in the semantic and conceptual areas alike, it may be useful to add a further dimension to the slightly simplified typology proposed in this chapter. To summarize briefly, it has been suggested here that there are essentially three major approaches to the national question: a Western, territorial concept and an Eastern and Southern personal concept (with East and South respectively emphasizing different − i.e., cultural or religious − criteria of nationality). Some writers, however (mostly from that great experimental laboratory of national conflict resolution − the late Habsburg Empire), and particularly Karl Renner (Das Selbstbestimmungsrecht der Nationen), have proposed a somewhat different analytical schema. In Renner's typology, there are "atomistic" views, according to which the only legally and constitutionally recognizable entities (with the possible exception of the economic field — i.e., corporations and trade unions) are the indivisible, centralistic state as a whole and the various individual citizens who have no collective status, but merely form an unconnected, haphazard, atomized aggregate of persons. There is no intermediate, constitutional entity between these individual parts and the state as a whole. Renner emphasizes that, opposed to these "atomistic" concepts, there are "organic" views which do give legal and constitutional recognition to politically intermediate units (frequently of an ethnic nature) between the state and the individual citizen. According to Renner, "organic" approaches in turn may be divided into those that follow the "territorial principle" and the "personal principle," respectively. Under the territorial principle, autonomy may be granted to a specific administrative area (province, canton or, as in the United States, state), preferably one that has a separate historic identity and tradition of its own or that is populated predominantly by a single ethnic group. These autonomous areas then are constitutionally recognized as legal entities and linked to each other by bonds of federation or confederation. Under the personal principle, individual members of an ethnic group, irrespective of their domicile and without regard to whether they constitute a regional majority or are living as a dispersed minority throughout the state as a whole, are joined together in an autonomous organization (not unlike the millet) that is then also constitutionally recognized as a legal entity.(4) The autonomous organizations of the various nationalities coexist with the central government of the state and its local administration, but have the special constitutional prerogative and duty to carry out certain functions (or to act as monitors and ombudsmen over their implementation by the regular central and local government organs). Such functions presumably would include the establishment, maintenance, and development of the appropriate educational and cultural institutions and facilities, through which the ethnic group in question, irrespective of size, may preserve and enhance its particular linguistic, historical, cultural, and religious heritage. Also involved would be the implementation of measures ensuring that, in their contact with judicial, administrative, and other facets of regular government and in their dealings with general public institutions, no individuals of any ethnic group should be disadvantaged by regulations or practices that take insufficient account of their linguistic preferences and abilities and their cultural and religious customs.

Closer analysis will show that the typology suggested in this chapter and Karl Renner's methodological framework are not in fact incompatible, but can be synthesized without too much effort. The "atomistic" approach, of course, is easily related to the Western concept of nationality, since the inhabitants of an atomistic state, by virtue of their very domicile and citizenship, would be identified nationally with that state irrespective of their true ethnic affiliations, so that all such centralistic polities would regard themselves as nation-states whether, in fact, they were ethnically homogeneous or not. Even Renner's "organic" approach, so long as it follows the "territorial principle" and establishes autonomous administrative areas based upon historic factors rather than ethnicity, can be encompassed within the Western view, as defined in this chapter. On the other hand, that same organic concept, applying some aspects of the "territorial principle," but leading to the creation of autonomous areas based upon ethnic or religious (as opposed to historic, geographic, or economic) criteria, could be compatible with the Eastern or Southern views respectively. (In determining the autonomous areas-to-be, the touchstone in this case would be the cultural identity and individual nationality options of a majority of their prospective populations, rather than some old-established or arbitrarily drawn administrative line on the map.) Finally, Renner's organic approach, if it follows the "personal principle," especially as refined by Bauer, is entirely in line with the Eastern and Southern views of nationality (and is reflected partially by Southern practice, i.e., the millet).

Some contemporary illustrations may help to concretize the Renner-Bauer conceptual framework. A typical example of an atomistic state would be France since the Revolution (which abolished the 36 ancient provinces with their distinctive local institutions, regulations, and traditions, and substituted the 90 lifeless departments that correspond to no historic or ethnic units and lack any genuine autonomy, being mere administrative extensions of central state power in Paris). France does not give constitutional status, at least within her metropolitan limits, to any intermediate territorial or ethnic institution between the centralistic state and the individual citizen. Italy, from her unification in the second half of the nineteenth century to the post-World War II period, had consciously followed the atomistic model of her Great Latin Sister, with a highly centralistic state subdivided into 92 minute provinces without real tradition, autonomy, or life of their own. However, in recent years, Italy has moved away from the French example toward a somewhat more organic approach utilizing the territorial principle, but applying historical rather than ethnic criteria in granting limited autonomy to 20 "regions" (into which the 92 provinces have been grouped). These "regions" in most instances coincide geographically with Italy's old separate kingdoms, duchies, and republics. However, only in a single instance, the (French-speaking) Valle d'Aosta, was a region established with boundaries that follow strictly ethnic lines. In two other cases considerable trouble was taken to gerrymander the regions in such a way as to outnumber a non-Italian nationality with an artificially created Italian majority. Thus the historical and geographical artefact, "Friuli-Venezia Giulia," contains the provinces of Trieste and Gorizia with a considerable number of Slovenes, plus the much larger province of Udine with a huge Italian population. Similarly, "Trentino-Alto Adige" has added the overwhelmingly Italian Trentino to the predominantly German (South Tyrolese) province of Bolzano.

In following primarily historical rather than ethnic lines, Italy's regions are not unlike the Swiss cantons (and for that matter the states of the United States). Of course, Switzerland and the United States are more genuinely organic states since they are federations of intermediate entities established according to the "territorial principle," while Italy still remains essentially a unitary state granting limited autonomy to these entitites. The similarity between these three countries arises only from their mutual disregard of ethnicity as a criterion for delimiting their territorial subdivisions. Not less than four Swiss cantons contain two or more ethnic groups, and another five contain two religious groups that live not intermingled but in geographically separate areas, clearly demarcated on the linguistic and religious maps, on the basis of which it would be simple to create relatively homogeneous new cantons (or half-cantons), as indeed was demanded successfully by the French-Catholic population of the Jura (in the north of the predominantly German-Protestant canton of Berne). However, only once previously, since the establishment of their confederation, have the Swiss responded to a request of this kind, when Appenzell was divided into the Catholic half-canton of Inner-Rhoden and the Protestant half-canton of Ausser-Rhoden.

A number of countries, including Belgium, Yugoslavia and India, although starting, like Switzerland, with an organic approach and applying the territorial principle in accordance with primarily <u>historical</u> criteria, have felt compelled increasingly to resort to <u>linguistic</u> and other ethnic criteria, although not consistently or entirely successfully. The boundaries of Belgium's nine historic provinces have been adjusted recently to follow the Flemish-Walloon language frontier (so that Hainault now has a French-speaking outlier within West Flanders, and Limburg a Flemish-speaking outlier in Liege). However, the existence of the partially bilingual Brussels area, which constitutes a non-Flemish-speaking enclave in primarily Flemish territory (with many of its Flemish-descended inhabitants speaking French much better than their own ancestral tongue and with the city's Flemish-speaking suburbs afraid of being engulfed in a metropolis that is colored by a predominantly French cultural overlay), has rendered a clear-cut linguistic-territorial solution very difficult. Nevertheless, support for a federal scheme based upon linguistic criteria, with a Walloon and a Flemish territorial unit, for a while increased from election to election during the 1960s and early 1970s.

India began with a mosaic of historic provinces and princely states, but under public pressure converted to a system of ethnic-linguistic states. However, the Indian government proved curiously reluctant to implement this conversion consistently and wholeheartedly, leaving such anomalies as Bombay and the Punjab, until further crises and conflicts compelled the regime to divide these two provinces also along linguistic-cultural lines.

The provinces of Yugoslavia, immediately after its creation at the end of World War I, replicated almost entirely the historic units out of which the new state was formed. For a brief period, King Alexander attempted to destroy even these historic entities and to turn Yugoslavia from an organic into an atomistic state following the centralistic French model, by dividing the country into a number of lifeless Governorates, named after geographic features and cutting across historic and ethnic lines alike. However, after his murder, the first steps were taken toward national reconciliation with the 1939 "Sporazum," which not only recreated the historic Croat state, but modified its frontiers in accordance with ethnic criteria by adding to it the Croat districts of Bosnia-Hercegovina. Tito's Yugoslav reorganization, initiated during World War II, ostensibly was not only a move toward a fully organic entity, i.e., a federation, but moreover, toward a state consisting of territorial units based on Yugoslavia's nationalities. However, of the new republics and autonomous regions, only Slovenia, Montenegro, the Kos-Met, Serbia, and to a lesser extent Macedonia, could be considered reasonably homogeneous from the ethnic point of view. Vojvodina was given frontiers which ensured that the Magyar population would be outnumbered by Serbs and Croats, including immigrants that were brought in to replace the expelled German population of the region.   Croatia was left with a sizable Serbian minority, while excluding the Croatian districts of Bosnia-Hercegovina. The latter province became one of Yugoslavia's constituent republics despite the fact that it had no predominant nationality at all, but contained Serbs, Moslems, and Croats alike.

The U.S.S.R., at least in theory, has been established as an organic state, applying the territorial principle in accordance with ethnic criteria which supposedly form the basis of the 15 Union Republics, 20 Autonomous Republics, and 18 Autonomous or National Districts, of which the Soviet Union is composed. In reality, of course, this federal system is somewhat of a hollow shell, since the Soviet Communist Party and state bureaucracy exercise tight centralistic control over every facet of life. Even so, in addition to the substance, the _form_ of ethnic self-determination is not consistently applied either. The frontiers of the Tatar Autonomous Republic, for instance, exclude well over 40 percent of the Soviet Tatars from their "own" state on the Upper Volga, while their southern kinsmen, the Crimean Tatars (deported from their homes to Central Asia by Stalin), have never been permitted to return to the Crimea which has been colonized in the meantime by Great Russians and Ukrainians. The boundaries of the Bashkir Autonomous Republic have been drawn in a manner that leaves the Bashkirs in a minority of less than 30 percent of the state's population. A centrally directed stream of colonization to Kazakhstan's "virgin lands" by Great Russians, Ukrainians, and Byelo-Russians has ensured that the Kazakhs, despite their high rate of natural increase, will constitute only a plurality and not a majority of the Kazakh Republic's inhabitants. In the so-called Jewish Autonomous Region of Birobidzhan, Jews are well under 10 percent of the total population, and only about 0.3 percent of all Soviet Jews live there.   Moreover, in spite of its name, the Region does not contain a single Jewish school or other Jewish cultural institution.

As for organic states following the personal principle, in accordance with the Renner-Bauer conceptual framework, there has been reference already in this chapter to the practices, past and present, of governments employing the millet system (or some aspects thereof). However, it should be emphasized that the Renner-Bauer approach envisaged much loftier status and far broader prerogatives for the constitutionally recognized and guaranteed autonomous representative body of each individual nationality than those enjoyed by the millet or outlined in the provisions of the 1919 peace treaties intended to safeguard ethnic minorities. This approach, of course, contrasts also with British colonial practice which frequently applied the personal principle to the extent of having separate electoral rolls and representation for mutually antagonistic ethnic or religious communities, but confined all representatives to a subordinate role under essentially paternalistic authoritarian colonial government.

The detailed considerations of a conceptual, methodological, and historical nature, to which much of this analysis is devoted, including illustrative references to customary and traditional approaches as well as contemporary practices, are intended to pave the way for a more systematic treatment of the issue of ethnic conflict resolution, unencumbered by some of the current substantive and semantic confusion and misapprehension. The complexities of the national question are such that one-dimensional approaches, relying exclusively upon a single concept – Western, Eastern, or Southern – are likely to prove counterproductive.

In this connection, a further examination of the applicability to ethnic conflict situations of the various categories of the Renner-Bauer typology may be helpful. Atomistic states, however much consideration they might show for the individual, democratic rights and liberties of the citizen and however egalitarian their practices might turn out to be, are averse, by definition, to recognizing intermediate entities between themselves and the individual. Consequently, they cannot deal constructively with the issue that lies at the very core of ethnic conflict – namely group rights and autonomies – whether through application of the territorial principle or the personal principle. In the last resort, the atomistic state, if democratic, is likely to produce majority rule, and, if authoritarian, rule reflecting the concepts of the elite. In either event, it is the interests of the Staatsvolk that most probably will find satisfaction at the expense of other (or minority) nationalities, which will remain unprotected by group autonomy, along territorial or personal lines. The principle of (democratic) majority rule is likely to be fully acceptable only in culturally homogeneous atomistic societies. Otherwise, it cannot but lead to the imposition of one (alien) ethos upon another. (Minorities and majorities exchange positions kaleidoscopically in homogeneous polities so that today's "outs" very well may be tomorrow's "ins." In ethnically heterogeneous countries, however, demographic realities usually keep national minorities frozen in their outnumbered and, consequently, outvoted position so that the democratic ballot can be expected only to legitimize this state of affairs.) As for authoritarian rule in atomistic states, usually it rests upon some degree of identification between the leader and the "national aspirations," i.e., the real or presumed interests of the Staatsvolk. This remains true even when the autocrat himself is an alien, like the Corsican Napoleon, the Austrian (albeit ethnically German) Hitler, or the Georgian Stalin (if in this context one may treat the post-Great Purge U.S.S.R. de facto as an atomistic society, even though, theoretically, it is still an organic federal state). Napoleon pursued French ultraexpansionism as Hitler strove for extreme Pan-German aims; and Stalin, during World War II and afterward, identified with Great Russian Chauvinism, occasionally even at the expense of his fellow Georgians.

To a very major extent, the same objections apply to those organic states that apply the territorial principle according to historic, geographic, economic, or other nonethnic criteria. The autonomy of such territorial units (cantons, regions, states, provinces, etc. in a federation or other noncentralistic system) underwrites group rights, to be sure, but the groups in question tend to be somewhat haphazard entities thrown together by residential factors (which, especially in modern mobile societies, frequently constitute bonds of a very temporary kind at most). The more "natural" and permanent groups of a cultural, linguistic, or religious type, that are the object of much deeper feelings of solidarity and commitment, are not only ignored in such systems but (as examples cited earlier in this analysis demonstrated) often are deliberately fragmented by arbitrary provincial boundaries or diluted by gerrymandering practices intended to ensure that the Staatsvolk will dominate not only the state as a whole, but also most or all of the autonomous territorial units (e.g., the carefully manufactured Italian majority in Trentino-Alto Adige and in Friuli-Venezia Giulia). In other words, from the aspect of ethnic desiderata, such a system of territorial autonomy has few if any advantages over atomistic states, at least so long as it eschews criteria of nationality in delimiting the territorial units. Of course, occasionally the boundaries of historic provinces happen to coincide with ethnic lines.

Many of these serious objections disappear in the case of organic states applying the territorial principle according to ethnic criteria, and doing so fairly and consistently. Regrettably, however, even this approach is not devoid of major pitfalls and shortcomings. The fact is that, within its own area of jurisdiction, each of the autonomous territorial units to be established will, to some extent, constitute a miniature atomistic state. However carefully and equitably it may have been delimited with regard to ethnic considerations, such a territorial entity is almost bound to contain some linguistic, cultural, or religious minorities and, for them, the autonomy granted to this region, province, or canton provides little solace since it ensures merely that they will be subjected to the majority rule of the local Staatsvolk. Moreover, it is precisely the drawing of "ethnically just" demarcation lines between the various autonomous territorial units that constitutes a well-nigh unmanageable task, especially in the absence of some higher authority within the state, magically endowed with superior wisdom, objectivity, and power, yet totally disinterested and acceptable to all the parties. As we pointed out earlier, national antagonisms develop and are fought out particularly in linguistic or cultural frontier areas where two ethnic groups overlap and mingle and where each feels most exposed and threatened, rather than in the compactly settled, homogeneous, and secure heartland of either group. However, these embattled frontier zones are the very areas through which the boundaries between the autonomous regions will have to be drawn — boundaries that will determine under whose local rule future generations will have to live. It is precisely this prospect, of course, that will exacerbate still further the conflict between the ethnic antagonists and spur the efforts of each, in these frontier areas, to achieve numerical superiority linguistically, culturally, or religiously as well as domination over educational and other key institutions, so as to ensure that the contested zones will be included in its own autonomous province or region.

It is exactly within this context that the serious limitations become apparent of proposals to solve conflicts between the Staatsvoelker of two independent countries by means of a federation between them.(5) Frontier struggles, to be sure, are painful enough when occurring on the international scene, but by internalizing them one does not resolve them. Within a federal entity, boundaries still have to be drawn between the respective autonomous regions and, for the reasons enumerated, this means merely that a previously external conflict becomes an internecine one. Yet it is hardly a lesson of history that civil wars are more pleasant and innocuous than clashes between sovereign countries! Nor is it feasible to evade such frontier struggles by the artificial device of "neutralizing" a contested key area, i.e., withholding it from the autonomous regions or cantons of either of the antagonists and declaring it to be a "federal district," "federal capital," "binational" or "international" area. If nature abhors a vacuum, politics certainly does not tolerate a no-man's land (unless, perhaps, it is totally uninhabited).

Within such a neutralized district, there is likely to be total ethnic deadlock, rendering representative government nonfeasible, thus bringing the struggle into the streets, and/or an even fiercer linguistic, educational, communications media, and demographic struggle will be waged to ensure eventual domination over the district by one or another of the contestants. This is painfully evident from the unsuccessful attempt to resolve the Belgian linguistic conflict through the creation of 4½ Flemish provinces – including the Louvain district of Brabant, 4½ Walloon provinces – including the Nivelle district of Brabant, and a "bilingual" Greater Brussels area which as a result has become merely the focus of even sharper struggles between the two ethnic groups. It is apparent, therefore, that all efforts to deal with nationality issues on a purely territorial basis (whether atomistic or organic, territorial-historic, or territorial-ethnic) are subject to grave limitations since territorial solutions all imply some degree of subjection of minority entities to majority rule by the Staatsvolk (whether throughout the country as a whole or within various local autonomous units). The attempt to deal with the problem through the creation of autonomous territorial units, delimited according to ethnic criteria as fairly and consistently as is feasible, should be deemed preferable to the other aforementioned approaches only in as far as it is likely to reduce the proportion of the population having to endure ethnically alien majority rule.(6)

Finally, the application by organic states of the personal principle, in accordance with the Renner-Bauer definition, contains at least theoretically the elements of the most equitable solution, since, in a way, it means that no individual anywhere is relegated to minority status. (All, regardless of domicile, belong to their respective ethnic organizations, and none are subject, therefore, to territorial majority rule, at least with regard to educational, cultural, and religious matters.) The Renner-Bauer approach constitutes, in a certain sense, the complete reversal of the "cuius regio, eius religio" formula of the sixteenth century Treaty of Augsburg — that famous triumph of the territorial principle which "abolished" (religious) minorities by the simple expedient of confronting all subjects residing in a prince's territories with a stark choice between conversion to the prince's creed or expulsion. This formula, or a more brutal version thereof, applied to ideological rather than religious creeds, became the basis for Stalin's division of Europe after Yalta, Teheran, and Potsdam.

However, the application of the personal principle, pure and simple, is not devoid of major problems and difficulties of its own. Modern societies cannot dispense entirely with territorial jurisdiction of one kind or another, if only because contemporary life — at least in such fields as criminal or business law — hardly can function without the existence of a single code of behavior and penalties, equally valid for all and implemented uniformly by the duly constituted and recognized authorities within a given state, province, etc. While it is entirely feasible that persons residing in the same area should be members of different, countrywide ethnic associations, paying dues to them, voting for their representative bodies, benefiting from their assistance, and adhering to their respective educational, cultural, and religious institutions and regulations (or even, as in the case of the millets, being subject to their separate canon laws and rulings concerning personal status questions), it seems inevitable that such a system should have to coexist with some form of territorial government responsible for those issues which affect each citizen as an individual rather than as a member of an ethnic or religious group. With several forms of jurisdiction, personal and territorial, functioning within each state or province, it is difficult to avoid some measure of constitutional complexity as well as grey zones in attempting to delimit the areas of competence of the various authorities concerned. In the absence of an ethnically neutral superior judicial authority, such problems might be difficult to disentangle.

Now it may be possible to simplify this system to a considerable extent but, paradoxically enough, only in states in which a high degree of ethnic polarization exists. For instance, in a country containing two antagonistic nationalities, with a very limited measure of social, marital, and other assimilatory processes at work to blur the lines between them, and where consequently all or practically all citizens, without much hesitation, doubt, or equivocation, would feel and declare themselves to be members of one ethnic group or the other and would opt for affiliation with the corresponding ethnic association, it might be feasible to have one and the same political body serving as a territorial authority in one part of the country and as a personal-ethnic authority in another. The following example may illustrate this point. The population of country X, composed of two ethnic groups, the A's and the

B's (with very few, if any, citizens regarding themselves as A-B's), is allowed to opt for affiliation either with ethnic association A or B. The duly elected representative body of association A may then exercise personal-ethnic authority to promote and protect the culture and institutions of all its members (in effect, probably all A's), wherever in country X they may reside. At the same time, however, association A also might exercise territorial authority over those of country X's autonomous provinces or regions (delimited, as far as possible, according to ethnic criteria), in which nationality A constitutes a majority of the population. The equivalent prerogative, of course, would be granted to the representative body of ethnic association B. The objections voiced previously to the territorial principle, even when applied in accordance with ethnic criteria, would be far less valid in this instance, since the jurisdiction of the territorial authorities would be modified and checked by the personal-ethnic authorities which would be acting as watchdogs and ombudsmen for numerically weak groups.

Thus, in the autonomous regions governed by ethnic association A, its counterpart, ethnic association B, would promote the culture and protect the rights of the scattered groups of B's settled in these areas. In such a case, it might be possible even to constitute the federal government of country X (confined to a relatively small number of central functions) from leading members of the representative bodies of ethnic associations A and B, perhaps chosen in equal numbers, if the numerical ratio between the two nationalities is no greater than 3:2. To prevent ethnic deadlock, there might be a functional division of tasks, with the representatives of A and B, respectively, having the last word in certain fields of central government that are of particular interest to their own ethnic group. To sum up, there would be essentially a three-tier structure. At the lowest level, of municipal and rural councils, the citizenry as a whole, irrespective of ethnic affiliation, would vote and be represented. At the intermediate level, the representative bodies of the various ethnic associations, elected by their respective memberships, would act both as the territorial authorities in the autonomous regions or provinces where their own nationality constituted a majority, and as watchdogs and helpers in areas where their ethnic group was scattered in small numbers. Finally, at the highest level, of central government, leading members of the various ethnic associations' representative bodies would work together with a functional division of tasks between them, leaving each nationality with the last word on those matters which were of particular concern to it. Diagrammatic illustration will be found in Figure 1.1 below. Needless to say, the problem with this solution is that it requires a maximum of mutual good will which is not precisely compatible with a society marked by a high degree of ethnic polarization.

Such a relatively streamlined and symmetrical structure hardly would be feasible in a country in which a process of reasonably successful ethnic assimilation had begun to work at least in some segments of society. In that case there would be a considerable proportion of the citizenry unwilling or unable to opt for A or B, with

C.G.= Central Government (composed of members of the Representative Organs of Ethnic Associations "A" & "B"—conceivably with functional division among them, leaving to each the last word on topics of particular concern to its respective ethnic group).

A.R.= Autonomous Regions (delimited as far as possible according to ethnic criteria and governed by delegates of Representative Organs of Ethnic Associations "A" and "B," respectively).

R.O.= Representative Organs of Ethnic Associations "A" & "B," respectively (elected by all members of the ethnic group in question, without regard to domicile).

D.F.= Functions conferred constitutionally upon Representative Organs of Ethnic Associations "A" & "B," respectively, with regard to the development and maintenance of the educational and cultural facilities required by the ethnic group in question.

P.&I.= Ombudsman functions conferred constitutionally upon Representative Organs of Ethnic Associations "A" & "B," respectively, with regard to the protection of and intercession for scattered "minority" elements of the ethnic group in question (i.e., individuals not residing in their "own" Autonomous Region).

M.-R.C.= Municipal and Rural Councils (elected on a purely residential, nonethnic, basis).

E.G.= Ethnic Groups "A" & "B," respectively (with individual citizens free to "opt" for either, subsequently having the right to elect members of—and the obligation to pay dues to—the Representative Organ of the Ethnic Association in question).

Note: Triangular shapes represent territorial organs of government—central, regional, municipal, or rural; circular shapes represent organs of authority elected on a personal, i.e., ethnic, basis; rectangular shapes represent segments of the citizenry.

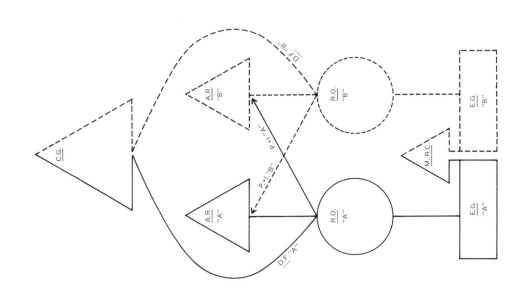

Fig. 1.1. Conceptual model—applicable to ethnically polarized state.

25

many responding "both" (i.e., A-B), or "neither," or "don't know," if asked to identify themselves ethnically. Consequently, in such instances, the structure outlined above (suitable only for countries with a high degree of national polarization, where practically everyone perceives himself and is perceived to be either an A or a B) would be both impracticable and inequitable, since a relatively large number of "others" in effect would be disenfranchised above the municipal level. Therefore, the following rather different model would be required to deal with multi-ethnic states beginning to undergo an assimilatory process.

All territorial authorities would be elected by all citizens domiciled in the territory concerned, voting from a common electoral roll, from the lowest (municipal), through the intermediate (autonomous regional), to the highest (central or federal government) tier of administration. However, the autonomous regions still would be delimited according to primarily ethnic criteria. Side by side with this territorial structure there would be established ethnic associations, constituted of those citizens who wish to express their right to opt for one of these associations, to pay dues to it, to vote for its representative organ, and to enjoy its assistance, guidance, and protection in linguistic, cultural, and religious matters. As under the earlier model, the representative organ of each ethnic association would be entitled to establish the required educational and cultural institutions and facilities for its members, wherever domiciled, and to intercede on their behalf with the appropriate territorial authority in areas where they constitute mere scattered, small groups. However, the representative organs of the ethnic associations would not themselves exercise territorial authority at the autonomous regional or central government levels. A diagrammatic illustration will be found in Figure 1.2 below.

The purpose of these two models is not to present detailed blueprints for utilization in any and all cases of ethnic conflict. In the absence of accompanying case studies in depth of specific conflict situations, with consideration of the gamut of appropriate responses in each instance, such abstract draftsmanship would constitute a fairly useless exercise. Indeed, the author is fully aware that, even as idealized presentations, the models suffer from some serious shortcomings. In each case, one of two elements would seem to be required to make the scheme fully functional. Either there must be some minimal measure of goodwill between the contending groups and sincere desire to make the structure work so that elaborate constitutional safeguards may not be nullified in a clash between incompatible authorities (a goodwill and sincerity that may not be consonant with the very word "conflict" which is the topic of this chapter); or there must be the presence of some absolutist authority with the power to enforce the provisions of the scheme (a power that is not compatible with the assumptions of representative government, upon which this chapter is based).

As may be gathered from the many instances of ethnically centrifugal tendencies in multiethnic states cited earlier on, it is entirely

C.G.= Central Government (elected by the citizen body as a whole).

A.R.= Autonomous Regions (delimited as far as possible according to ethnic criteria, but with their governments elected by all citizens residing in each of the Regions concerned).

R.O.= Representative Organs of Ethnic Associations "A" & "B" respectively (elected by all members who have opted for the ethnic group,in question, without regard to domicile).

D.F.= Functions conferred constitutionally upon Representative Organs of Ethnic Associations "A" & "B", respectively, with regard to the development and maintenance of the educational and cultural facilities required by the ethnic group in question.

P.&I.= Ombudsman functions conferred constitutionally upon Representative Organs of Ethnic Associations "A" & "B," respectively, with regard to the protection of and intercession for scattered "minority" elements of the ethnic group in question (i.e., individuals not residing in their "own" Autonomous Region).

M.-R.C.= Municipal and Rural Councils (elected on a purely residential, non-ethnic basis).

E.G.= Ethnic Groups "A" & "B," respectively (with individual citizens free to opt for either—or neither—subsequently having the right to elect members of—and the obligation to pay dues to— the Representative Organ of the Ethnic Association in question).

G.B.C.= General body of the citizenry as a whole (including those who have opted for Ethnic Groups "A" & "B," respectively, as well as those who opted for neither or for some third group).

Note: Triangular shapes represent territorial organs of government—central, regional, municipal, or rural; circular shapes represent organs of authority elected on a personal, i.e., ethnic, basis; rectangular shapes represent segments—or all—of the citizenry.

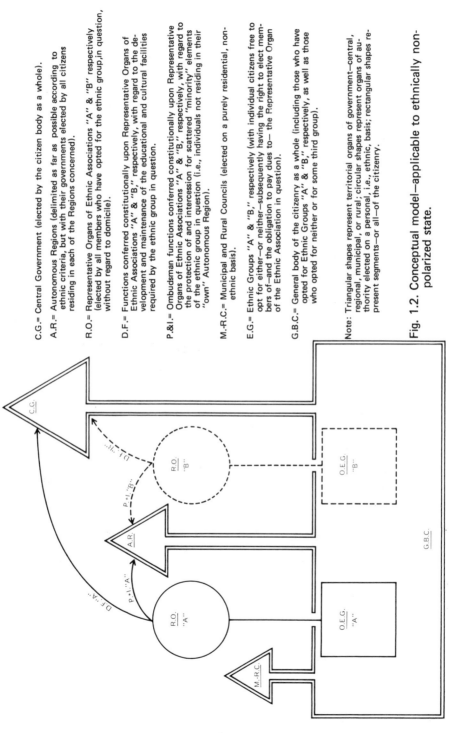

Fig. 1.2. Conceptual model—applicable to ethnically non-polarized state.

27

conceivable that the trend toward separatism may become so strong that relatively few multiethnic societies may survive the next century at all. All these caveats notwithstanding, the models presented here may be helpful in illustrating how some of the concepts defined in this chapter would work in action, as well as demonstrating that the gamut of imagination and innovation has not been exhausted necessarily in this field. Above all, it is hoped that some of the extant semantic and conceptual confusion may be dispelled, at least in part, by the attempt to present two mutually compatible typologies, one of the author's own making and the other distilled from the work of Karl Renner and Otto Bauer. Without minimal theoretical clarity and consistency, practical attempts at ethnic conflict resolution would appear to be foredoomed.

A caveat is in place here. The author is concerned with conceptual and semantic lucidity and no normative implications should be read into the points made in this chapter concerning renewed ethnic self-assertion and accelerating disintegrative trends within existing states. No plea is intended in favor of "redrawing the map" as such. The study attempts merely to discern significant phenomena and to evaluate their impact on the political environment.

NOTES

(1) In this chapter the following terms are employed more or less interchangeably: "nationalities," "national entities," "ethnic units," "ethnic entities," "ethnic groups," "peoples," etc. Similarly, "ethnicity" and "nationality" are used in some contexts with roughly the same connotation. The terms "nation," "constituent nation," and "Staatsvolk" are employed usually to denote an ethnic group that currently controls power in at least one state or has controlled state power in the past.

(2) In current Soviet practice it is, in fact, the bureaucracy implementing the census or issuing internal passports that decides such questions, rather than the individual citizen responding to the questionnaire. There are, for instance, specific official instructions how children of ethnically-mixed marriages are to be registered. Moreover, if a citizen with a typically Jewish or Polish family name or patronymic were to declare himself a Great Russian or a Ukrainian, the bureaucrat filling in the official form probably would register him as Jewish or Polish anyhow, or would request to see the internal passports of his parents to verify how their nationality had been registered.

(3) There is a considerable area of overlap along the frontiers between the Eastern and Southern views of nationality. It must be recalled that, at one stage, Ottoman rule extended to the Carpathians and to the lower Dnieper and Don, embracing not only the Balkans but even portions of the Ukraine (borderland). Under the influence of Panslavism and other eighteenth and nineteenth century ideologies, these regions eventually became "Europeanized" and part of the Eastern zone, as far

as the nationality question is concerned. However, there are distinct remnants of the Southern (Ottoman) approach, focusing upon religion as an important criterion of nationality. For instance, Bosnian Moslems, who speak the same language and are of the same ethnic descent as their Orthodox or Catholic Serbo-Croat neighbors, simply having been converted to Islam under Ottoman rule, are recognized in the Yugoslav census as a separate nationality, Yugoslav Moslems. For that matter, Serbs and Croats are essentially one ethnic group, speaking practically the same language. The main difference is that the Serbs are Orthodox, employing the Cyrillic alphabet (reflecting their Byzantine heritage), while the Croats are Catholic, employing the Latin alphabet (reflecting their Roman heritage). Yet the Yugoslav census and constitution treat them as separate nationalities. Until recent years, the Orthodox Ukrainians and the "Ruthenes," the western branch of the Ukrainian people, of the same ethnic stock and speaking the same tongue, were regarded as different nationalities, because the Ruthenes had become Uniates (Greek Catholics) while under Polish rule. For a long period, the Bulgars and their "Pomak" kinsmen were treated as distinct ethnic groups, merely because the Pomaks, although perfectly good Bulgars, had been converted to Islam during the period of Ottoman domination.

(4) Much of what follows in this paragraph represents not only Renner's approach, but the refinements conceived by his Social-Democratic colleague, Otto Bauer (Die Nationalitaetenfrage und die Sozial-demokratie). Dissatisfied with his party's 1899 nationality program which in paragraph 4 called simply for "national minority rights," Bauer demanded that it be expanded to read: "Within each region of self-government, the national minorities shall form corporate entitites with public juridical status, enjoying full autonomy in caring for the education of the national minority concerned, as well as in extending legal assistance to their co-nationals vis-a-vis the bureaucracy and the courts."

(5) American advocates of this particular solution are misled frequently by the relative success of the eighteenth century founding fathers of this country and are inclined to regard federation as a universal panacea. They tend to forget that the 13 original colonies were largely composed of populations descended from the same or similar ethnic stocks, with a common cultural endowment and political experience and a tradition of mutual respect, tolerance, and reverence for law, strengthened by interaction with the British mother country during the eighteenth century.

(6) A territorial approach, based upon ethnic criteria, can constitute a very positive contribution to conflict resolution and thus be exempted from the criticism and strictures voiced here, provided its implementation is linked integrally to the personal principle, in accordance with the Renner-Bauer concept. (See pp. 23-28.)

2 Immigration and Nationality: A Historical Overview of United States Policy

John P. Roche

Any study of the role of ethnicity in the contemporary world must take into account the St. Bernard that isn't barking, the giant postindustrial society basically unwracked by tribalism. As indicated here, this "American Exceptionalism" is hardly a new phenomenon. In the seventeenth and eighteenth centuries various commentators already noted the essential irrelevance of Old World issues, and that brilliant, underestimated political sociologist, John Adams (in his 1765 <u>Dissertation on Canon and Feudal Law</u>), anticipated by three-quarters of a century Tocqueville's emphasis on the absence of feudalism. Nor can it be entirely a coincidence that shortly after Plymouth Colony was established Governor William Bradford was vigorously denying charges that women and children were voting and otherwise participating in the governance of the plantation!

Geography was crucial, but not definitive. Spanish colonies in the new world were far more remote from their metropole than the British. However, the "Americans" — as they began to style themselves and be styled in the 1730s and 1740s — did initially encounter a seemingly empty expanse of wilderness. As King James I observed in 1620, with characteristic Christian charity, God had sent a "wonderful plague among the savages," a sure sign of His blessings upon the plantations. While medical historians disagree on the nature of the disease (the leading candidate seems to be measles against which the natives had not acquired immunity), the indigenous population had been devastated. But whatever the causes, Americans, like Australians, were confronted with a virtually empty continent, a <u>tabula rasa</u> on which to inscribe their traditions.

Probably the most interesting aspect of "Americanization" over the last 400 or more years is the extent to which it was a social rather than a governmental process. As will be seen, the United States had no organized system for dealing with immigration until the turn of the twentieth century. On one hand this could be extremely congenial —

German regiments fighting in the Union Army distributed orders in German – while on the other it could be condign, considering the fate of Asians on the West Coast. Can one imagine the bewilderment of the highly centralized Japanese government when Theodore Roosevelt's Secretary of State, Elihu Root, informed it that anti-Japanese legislation in California was deplorable, but the Washington authorities had no jurisdiction in the premises? Later President Wilson sent Secretary William Jennings Bryan on a personal mission to plead, unsuccessfully, in Sacramento for repeal of racist legislation. What kind of a way was this to run a country?

This highlights the great paradox in American history – that our society could be open yet intolerant. Indeed, I long ago characterized colonial America as an open society with closed enclaves and this tradition continued well into the twentieth century. Perhaps the paradigmatic case was that of the Church of Jesus Christ Latter Day Saints, or Mormons, who, driven by officially endorsed vigilantism from Illinois and Missouri, finally established their Kingdom of the Saints in Utah – and merrily persecuted all "gentiles" (non-Mormons) in reach. Similarly, in the great cities one found subcultural fortresses where only God would have mercy on the Jew who wandered into Irish turf, or, for that matter, the Irishman who went uninvited into "Little Italy."

Although the legislation of the earlier years of this century asserted federal control over immigration, and the states in the wake of World War I's perfervid chauvinism launched Americanization campaigns, the Depression and World War II clearly were the watershed between the old, essentially locally governed United States and the new Washington oriented nation which most Americans today take for granted. Until 1925 the government kept no statistics on the number of illegal aliens apprehended!

What this essay suggests is the extent, in the area of cultural assimilation and the concomitant elimination of militant tribalism, to which the past worked. Sometimes brutal and sometimes benign, the old order created a community where Chinese street signs in Boston are not blown up by neighboring Irish or Italians and, in a moment of ecumenicism, the Boro President of the Bronx could designate an official "Protestant Day."

The notion of America as a land of liberation probably received its first, and decidedly negative, formulation from John Calvin. Writing in his Commentary on Deuteronomy (c. 1535), the dour reformer expressed the essence of the later "safety valve" theory of the frontier. Justifying capital punishment for blasphemy, he observed, "Some object that since the offense consists only in words, there is no need for such severity. But we muzzle dogs, and shall we leave men free to open their mouths as they please? Those who object are like dogs and swine. They murmer (sic) that they will go to America where nobody will bother them."

What triggered this singular outburst is unknown. Perhaps the voyages of Columbus, Cabot, and Cartier generated an underground myth that beyond the seas lay escape from the torments of sixteenth century Europe. However, this Calvinist vision of America as a proper location for dogs and swine was distinctly a minority opinion. "In the beginning," observed an optimistic John Locke in his Second Treatise, "all the world was America." Of course Locke, one of whose deservedly obscure works was a bizarre "Constitution for the Carolinas," (1669) was Secretary to the Council of Trade and Plantations, with a vested interest in encouraging settlement.

In any case, the view that America was an open society, shared in their different fashions by Calvin and Locke, was by the seventeenth century in wide circulation. And, indeed it had sound basis in fact, providing one understands that this openness was dotted with closed enclaves. The wise Anabaptist steered clear of the Puritan and Anglican colonies, but could find protection in Rhode Island or Pennsylvania. Except for a brief period in Maryland, Catholicism was nowhere officially tolerated, and a record of some sort was set when the Charles Town Anglicans persecuted French Huguenots. By the time the British took over New York (1664), it had already acquired a reputation as Babylon-on-the-Hudson. Laws were severe, but enforcement desultory.

As these new communities grew, the question of membership naturally arose, and presented great difficulties. Only in 1609 did Lord Justice Coke enounce in Calvin's Case that the foundation of English nationality was birth in the King's realm (jus solis). But this did not eliminate the medieval standard that the child takes the citizenship of his father (jus sanguinis). To this day there are elements of both principles in Anglo-American law. If we add the unsettled state of the early colonies to the vagaries of the law, we predictably discover no common denominator.

Without lingering too long in the seventeenth century, let us explore a few of the accepted rationales for membership in the body politic. Since the Massachusetts Bay Colony was technically a chartered company of merchant adventurers, its citizens were the stockholders or "freemen." Because the Puritans had used the chartered company to disguise their intention to establish "Zion in the Wilderness," church membership became the de facto basis for participation. Needless to say, the franchise was limited to males over 21.

Moreover, the Charter (1629) specified that "all and every subject of us (James I), our Heirs and Successors, which shall go to and inhabit within the said lands and premises (and) their children. . .shall have and enjoy all liberties of free and natural subjects within any of the dominions of us (as if they) were born within the realm of England." The Governor and two assistants were further delegated the authority to "naturalize" new members by administering the Oath of Supremacy to emigrants. The oligarchy attempted to restrict full participation to Puritan freemen, but by 1655 the General Court learned from one of its committees that "everyone – Scotch servants, Irish negers (sic) and persons under one and twenty" – was voting.

When Charles II approved the Charter of that "livlie experiment" Rhode Island (1663), roughly the same proviso was included except the King, asserting that "true piety rightly grounded on gospel principles will give the best and greatest security to sovereignty," eliminated the

Oath of Supremacy. The Frame of Government (1681) for William Penn's utopia went even further, providing that anyone who purchased a hundred acres of land ("at one penny an acre") and cultivated 10 acres of it, or a former indentured servant awarded 50 acres and cultivating 20, and "every inhabitant, artificer, or other resident in the said province, that pays scot and lot (a customary contribution based on ability to pay). . .shall be deemed and accounted a freeman. . .capable of electing, or being elected, representatives of the people. . . ."

The emphasis in the seventeenth century was on finding settlers. One widely used system, particularly in the Southern colonies, was indentured servitude. Virginia practice was typical. An individual in England bound himself to the Company, or later a planter, for the term of seven years, was given passage, one year's provisions, a house and tools, and – to compress legalisms – half the crop he produced. Such contracts often included a stipulation that at the expiration of service, he would be made "a free man. . .thereby to enjoy all the liberties, freedoms, and privileges of a freeman."

This is hardly the place to investigate the complex status of early black arrivals – Edmund S. Morgan has explored this superbly – except to note that while they may have initially been legally analogous to white indentured servants, when the term of servitude became 99 years, the system was obviously producing slaves. By the beginning of the eighteenth century, law caught up with reality and in 1705 Virginia enacted a "slave code." Needless to add, slaves were not citizens.

However, there was one legal category that remained in limbo until the passage of the Fourteenth Amendment – the free black. With the usual freakish exceptions that enliven American history (e.g., free black slaveholders), free blacks were denied admission to the political community. According to British precedent, formally unrecognized in American law, they fell into the category of "denizen," a native resident without the prerogatives of citizenship. If any concern was expressed about the legal status of the Indians, it has vanished from the archives.

The ethnic background of the early immigrants was overwhelmingly English and Scots (including Scotch-Irish Protestants). By the end of the century, the net was more broadly cast. Virginia and Maryland, for example, took measures to naturalize – in the modern sense – aliens. Invariably the line was drawn this side of Roman Catholics – particularly the turbulent Irish – whom the British, with some justification, considered agents of foreign powers. To get ahead of the chronology, both Jacobite risings – those of James, the "Old Pretender," in 1715 and "Bonnie Prince Charlie," the "Young Pretender," in 1745 – were mounted from France with substantial Irish Catholic participation. With French Catholic power burgeoning in Canada, the colonists wanted no potential papist conspiracy in their midst.

COLONIAL NATURALIZATION

Between 1700 and 1770 the population of the American provinces, white and black, jumped almost tenfold from 251,000 to 2,148,000. The greatest percentage increase was among blacks as the slavers delivered their wretched cargoes to a booming plantation economy. Between 1740 and 1770 the black population trebled! The bulk of the white arrivals still came from England, Scotland, and Ulster. In 1790 approximately 75 percent of the white populace had its roots in those regions. As the seventeenth century trickle became a stream, demands increased for uniform regulation of non-British immigrants.

The result was an Act of Parliament (1740) "for naturalizing such foreign Protestants, and others therein mentioned, as are settled, or shall settle in any of His Majesty's Colonies in <u>America</u>." After a preamble that puts most travel brochures to shame, the Act provided that foreigners who had spent seven uninterrupted years in a colony would, on taking the appropriate oaths and paying two shillings, attain the status of citizens of the Realm. The process combined civil and religious elements. A judge administered the oaths, but the individual had to demonstrate that he had "received the Sacrament of the Lord's Supper in forme Protestant" within the preceding three months. This was a surprisingly progressive enactment because Quakers were exempted from oaths, the oath was reworded for the Jews to eliminate "upon the true Faith of a Christian," and Jews and Quakers were excused from the Eucharist!

Yet, in another sense, the parliamentary decision was retrogressive – to many Americans seven years seemed like a long time, particularly since naturalized immigrants had already become players in the great game of politics. There was then no uniform residence threshhold, but in operational terms three years appears to be the average. In addition, some legislatures passed out citizenship to substantial numbers by private acts. Thus in effect the Act of Parliament created two levels of citizenship: British or intercolonial, and parochial or limited to one province. For example, a Pennsylvania German given citizenship by the colonial assembly could participate in provincial politics. But he was not a naturalized citizen under the Act of 1740, with the rights of British citizenship everywhere.

In this area, as in every other, the Americans played fast and loose with Royal authority. They considered provincial naturalizations <u>bona fide</u>, conferred land titles on the basis of local citizenship, and generally ignored the Privy Council's concern for legal symmetry. The latter body's efforts became such a nuisance that it rated a line of Jefferson's wrath in the <u>Declaration of Independence</u>: "He (George III) has endeavored to prevent the population of these states; for that purpose obstructing the laws for naturalization of foreigners; refusing to pass others to encourage their migrations hither; & raising the conditions of new appropriations of lands."

The question of fraudulent naturalization cropped up in Pennsylvania in the mid-eighteenth century. Palatine Germans, many from Anabaptist sects, had migrated to Pennsylvania in large numbers. By 1790 they constituted a third of the population. The Proprietary Party, i.e., the Quaker "connexion" in the parlance of the time, was running into trouble, mainly with the frontier Scotch-Irish, who felt the Friends' concern with the "Fatherhood of God, the Brotherhood of Man, and the Neighborhood of Philadelphia" a bit excessive. The Quakers, in quest of allies, welcomed the Germans to their bosom, legally and figuratively. According to well-informed, though perhaps biased contemporary sources, the Germans were naturalized in battalions.

The Anti-Proprietary Party went into a nativist spasm which prefigured many later episodes of the same sort. Among other proposals, it was suggested that election districts be rigged to cut German influence, that Germans be banned from the Assembly, and denied the vote until they were fluent in English. In 1751 Benjamin Franklin put it all in a nutshell: "Why should the Palatine Boors be suffered to swarm into our Settlements, and by herding together establish their Language and Manners to the Exclusion of ours? Why should Pennsylvania, founded by the English, become a Colony of Aliens, who will shortly be so numerous as to Germanize us instead of our Anglifying them, and will never adopt our Language or Customs, any more than they can acquire our Complexion."

The "Palatine Boors" may have been a problem in Pennsylvania, but there was another group that generated mixed emotions – transported convicts. Here it is important – as Abbot E. Smith has shown in his pioneering study – to differentiate political and common criminals. During the English Civil War, for example, Cromwell exiled a number of prisoners of war, notably from his campaign against the Scots, to New England. Later in the century, and after the two eighteenth century Jacobite risings, other prisoners were transported. These able-bodied men were generally treated as indentured servants for seven years and then were absorbed into the population. Many were undoubtedly Roman Catholic in background – the Highlands of Scotland sheltered several strong Catholic clans – but they quietly adopted Protestantism.

But the convicted felons were completely unwelcome. The severity of the British criminal code was notorious. By 1700 there were over 300 capital offenses ranging from high treason to stealing a shilling's worth of goods. In practice it was tempered by "benefit of clergy" and transportation to the plantations. Benefit of clergy to oversimplify, was a holdover from canon law which held that anyone who could read (or pretend to read; memorization of the Psalm employed as the test was common) was a clerk, immune to civil jurisdiction. (This sounds like a convenient escape-hatch, but it was largely closed by the creation of "nonclergyable" offenses. Such improvisations were the life of British law!)

Unlike those taken in arms against His Majesty, these male and female convicts were a thoroughly unsavory lot. Without getting into the esoteric details of the law, since exile was a forbidden penalty, convicts were technically pardoned on the condition that they go into exile for a stipulated period, usually seven years. To the entrepreneurs of the era, they were a likely source of labor for the American and West Indian plantations and shipments began. It seems fair to say that wherever they went, they took trouble with them. In 1670 Virginia passed a law banning them, followed by Maryland in 1676.

In 1717, with jails overfilled, Parliament directed its attention to the problem. In essence, it ordered transportation for all but the most serious offenses and turned to private contractors to peddle this human merchandise overseas. Since this statute clearly superceded the Virginia and Maryland laws, these provinces were opened up and became the destination of most of the eighteenth century convicts sent to North America — 20,000 out of a 30,000 total. A far larger number was shipped to the "Sugar Islands" in the West Indies.

After the War of Independence, the British felt the practice could be resumed and actually landed one shipment in Maryland, but in 1788 Congress, learning another batch was en route, "Resolved That it be and is hereby recommended to the several states to pass proper laws for preventing the transportation of convicted malefactors from foreign countries into the United States." The states immediately implemented this resolution (which leaves the interesting question of the 30,000 malefactors who had arrived earlier; a few may have returned to England after serving their time, but the bulk vanished into the population. They are seldom featured in family trees).

STATE PRACTICE AFTER INDEPENDENCE

Following the outbreak of the War of Independence, the new state governments handled their own naturalization and citizenship matters. On June 6, 1776, the Continental Congress resolved that "all persons abiding within any of the United Colonies and deriving protection from the laws of the same owe allegiance to said laws, and are members of such colony." The rights of naturalized citizens varied. Delaware required a five-year period of probation before a new citizen could hold office, while — in Jefferson's words — "A foreigner of any nation not in open war with (Virginia) becomes naturalized by removing to the state to reside, and taking an oath of fidelity: and thereupon acquires every right of a native citizen."

The Articles of Confederation gave Congress no jurisdiction over naturalization or citizenship except to anticipate the Comity Clause of the Federal Constitution, providing that "The free inhabitants of each of these States. . .shall be entitled to all privileges and immunities of free citizens in the several states; and the people of each state shall have free ingress and regress to and from any other State." The important thing to note is that citizenship in the United States was derived from state citizenship, a point central to the litigation over black citizenship in the Dred Scott Case (1857).

Before moving to the establishment of the General Government under the 1787 Constitution, it might be interesting to note an ironic episode involving French Canadians. Meeting in October 1774, the members of the First Continental Congress were furious at the Quebec

Act (1774), probably one of the few intelligent measures to pass Parliament in that decade. By its terms the Quebecois were allowed to practice the Catholic faith and continue their traditional civil law system. It also included in the province of Quebec substantial tracts of land north of the Ohio River on which various colonies had claims.

In its "Address to the People of Great Britain" (October 21, 1774), the land question was ignored while the Delegates vented their spleen on Popery: "The dominion of Canada is to be so extended, modelled, and governed, as that by being disunited from us, detached from our interests by civil as well as religious prejudices, that by their numbers daily swelling with Catholic emigrants from Europe, they might become...fit instruments in the hands of power to reduce the ancient free Protestant Colonies to the same state of slavery with themselves."

However, on October 26, 1774, this same body in its "Address to the Inhabitants of Quebec" invited the Quebecois to send a delegation to the Congress and join with it in resisting British tyranny! French Catholic Quebec – the French then constituted probably 95 percent of Canada's inhabitants – could have become the 14th star. The "Message," drafted by John Dickenson, was a masterpiece of political warfare, replete with tributes to French culture, quotations from Montesquieu, and a beautiful end-run around the religious question. Moreover, the British had only been in possession for 11 years, so there were good reasons to suspect that Canada could be stabilized. Unfortunately the "habitants," presumably operating on the premise that the known devil was preferable to the unknown, sat out the war. The Americans, reverting to the first track, included a denunciation of the Quebec Act's ecumenicism in the Declaration of Independence.

Benjamin Franklin, who ran the Revolutionary Era equivalent of American covert foreign intelligence operations and was deeply involved in the effort to align the Quebecois with the Continental Army, had another Catholic card to play – Ireland. In 1771 he visited there and struck up something more than an acquaintance with the leaders in the fight for Catholic emancipation. Once the troubles in the New World started, he inspired a message of solidarity from the Continental Congress to Irish Catholics and apparently instigated prompt publication of the Declaration of Independence in two dissenting Irish papers.

Irish Catholics, assigned "to hell or Connaught" by the British, seemingly were emigrating in substantial numbers to America before the War of Independence. The radical Freeman's Journal, whose figures must be treated with some caution, announced that in the five years before 1774 37,000 Irish had emigrated to America – 10,000 a year in 1772 through 1774. As the Ulster Protestants were then strong supporters of an independent Ireland (they were the first to be disarmed as the Rising of 1798 loomed on the British horizon), many emigrants may have been Scotch-Irish. But the majority seem to have been Catholic, and their arrival in the colonies was applauded as an accretion to anti-British sentiment.

Franklin, it seems, never lost hope in an Irish rising to undermine British efforts in America. He directed an "Address to the Good People of Ireland on Behalf of America" on October 4, 1778, and stimulated Sir

Harley Grattan, the official spokesman for the legal Irish nationalists, to urge that "Before you decide on the practicability of being slaves forever, look to America" (1780). In addition, Charles Carroll ("the barrister" to distinguish him from his cousin Charles of Carrollton) from the old Maryland English Catholic family which provided a signer of the Declaration of Independence, an author of the Constitution, and the first American Catholic Bishop, promised in a widely distributed tract that Congress would provide free land and religious toleration to Irish Catholics who joined the cause of freedom in America. The "Protestant Colonies," it appears, could rise above principle to hit a target of opportunity.

An overall profile of the new nation revealed a total population of 2,780,000, of whom 575,000 were black. About three-quarters of the whites came from British, Scots, and Scotch-Irish stock; 8.7 percent German; 3.7 percent Irish; 3.4 percent Dutch; and the remainder scattered or unknown. In the South, the British Protestants were particularly thick on the ground (86.5 percent in North Carolina); the Dutch were bunched in New York and New Jersey; while the Germans clustered in Pennsylvania, Maryland, and the areas that became Kentucky and Tennessee. The Catholic irish, as one might suspect, avoided the Puritan states like the plague, though there was an odd concentration in York County, Massachusetts, later Maine. Blacks, of course, were a massive segment of the Southern population. Maryland alone had more than all the Northern states combined, and Virginia had three times as many as Maryland.

THE FEDERAL GOVERNMENT

So much for the formative years. The time has come to turn to the Constitutional Convention of 1787 to discover the Founding Fathers' views of citizenship. The question has been subjected to microanalysis which can easily be summarized. They virtually ignored the topic. What evidence there is indicates that they considered national citizenship to be derived from state. It was stipulated, for example, that the President of the United States had to be a "Citizen of the United States, at the time of the adoption of this Constitution." Since only the states had conferred citizenship – and, indeed, provided passports for travel abroad – the decision on admission to the new community seemed to remain in state jurisdiction. This hypothesis is strengthened by the Constitutional delegation to Congress to "establish a uniform Rule of Naturalization," which is anything but a substantive grant of power to naturalize.

There was some desultory discussion on the rights of naturalized citizens. Virginia's George Mason "was for opening a wide door for emigrants; but did not chuse to let foreigners. . .make laws for us and govern us." Alexander Hamilton, of West Indian birth, argued (to the contrary) that the strength of the nation would come from immigrants who would be "on the level with the first Citizens." The net outcome of this random rhetoric were the requirements that the President be a "natural born citizen," a Senator "nine Years of Citizen of the United States," and a Representative a citizen for seven years. The first President actually born under the American flag was Martin Van Buren; his predecessors were citizens when the Constitution was adopted. The nine-year Senate rule was used, or rather misused: once in 1794 it was the pretext for voiding Albert Gallatin's election to that body by the Pennsylvania legislature.

The framers, who were working politicians and not members of the French Academy, left these citizenship and naturalization questions unclarified, doubtless confident that their successors in the new federal government could tie up the loose ends. Thus in 1790 the First Congress found itself face to face with the same problem. A naturalization act introduced into the House of Representatives provided naturalization by stages. Any free white alien who had one year's residence was entitled to all rights of citizenship except holding state or federal office; two years was mandated for office-holding.

The states' righters immediately objected. Congress, they held, could only establish a uniform rule for naturalization; the effects of naturalization were for the states to determine. As a Virginia Representative put it, "After a person has once become a citizen, the naturalization power of Congress ceases to operate upon him, the rights and privileges of citizens in the Several States belong to those States." The sour Pennsylvania Senator William Maclay observed, "It is a vile bill, illiberal and void of philanthropy. . . .We Pennsylvanians act as if we believed that God made of one blood all the families of the earth; but the Eastern people seem to think He made none but New England folks."

Congress sidestepped all these issues and passed, on March 26, 1790, a Naturalization Act providing for legal admission of any free white person who had resided for two years "within the limits and under the jurisdiction of the United States." The question of states' rights was neatly evaded by assigning jurisdiction over the act of naturalization to "any common law court of record in any one of the States," i.e., both federal and state courts. The question whether naturalization was a "case or controversy" within the meaning of Article 3 of the Constitution (the jurisdiction of the federal courts is limited to matters in these categories) was not raised until the twentieth century and then given short shrift. Justice Brandeis curtly announced for the Supreme Court (U.S. v. Ness, 1917) that obviously naturalization – though on its face an administrative act analogous to procuring a wedding license – was a "case or controversy." Why? From the outset federal courts had accepted jurisdiction; Q.E.D.

As the country split in the wake of the Jay Treaty (1794), the Federalists moved to increase the residence requirements to five years and to require "good moral character." The Jeffersonians, sensing a blow at their immigrant strength, restored with a demand that all applicants for citizenship be given a loyalty check to guarantee their affection for the "republican form of government." Then Samuel Dexter of Massachusetts, a Federalist who was also antislavery, put the cat among the pigeons. He proposed that all would-be citizens free their slaves and renounce slavery forever. If one recalls that the slavery issue has been deliberately muted in the Constitutional Convention (the word "slave" appears nowhere in the Constitution) and the seeming consensus among the Founding Fathers that if ignored long enough, the problem would vanish, one can put Dexter's action in appropriate perspective.

The debate was bitter, but for the time being the genie was recorked in the bottle. The debate between states' righters and nationalists followed its previous course with the dominant view, that national citizenship was derived from prevailing state status. However, with that unpredictable quality that so unsettles high theorists in search of consistent ideology, Congress in 1795 took a startling tack in the opposite direction. Practical men confronted with a practical problem tend to deal pragmatically with the business at hand and let somebody else worry about principles.

The practical problem was the Northwest Territory, which was in the process of political development. The first state carved from it was Ohio, admitted to the Union in 1802. As a territory the Northwest area was governed by federal authority, but its inhabitants were busy electing territorial legislatures. Who were these inhabitants, i.e., what citizenship did they hold? Under the Comity Clause of the Constitution, a citizen of Connecticut who went to Ohio before statehood could, with a little legal ingenuity, be considered a citizen of Ohio. But what of aliens who wanted to become territorial citizens? A Talmudic mind could work on this for months. Congress simply authorized territorial courts to naturalize aliens! Thus, de facto, we now found citizens of the United States busily creating new states. The anomaly was never noted.

The first surge of nativism in the United States took place in 1798. Using the "Quasi-War" with France as their rationale, the high Federalists, led by Alexander Hamilton, undertook to destroy the "Jacobin faction" in the United States, that is, the emerging Democratic-Republican party led by Vice-President Thomas Jefferson. Central to this design was the Sedition Act of 1798. But, convinced that radical immigrants flooding into the United States were the backbone of Jeffersonianism, the Federalists passed three measures to limit the rights of aliens; the Naturalization Act, Alien Enemies Act, and Alien Friends Act.

The core of the Naturalization Act was a 14-year residence requirement as a prerequisite to citizenship. There was, of course, a ferocious rhetorical brawl in Congress, but in point of fact the Act was of little significance. As Senator Bayard rather wearily noted in debate, "Though foreigners were prevented from becoming citizens of the United States until they have resided 14 years in the country, in many of the States they are entitled not only to vote for filling the offices of the State Governments, but also for filling those of the United States."

The punitive Federalist measure, which was repealed in 1801, had limited impact, but did create another anomaly – state citizens who were not citizens of the United States. Moreover, as the Constitution gave state governments the power to define the federal suffrage, anyone within a state's definition could participate in both state and federal elections. Indeed, if they so chose, states could — and did — permit aliens to vote. This practice was not eliminated until 1921, when the pressure generated by the "Americanization" campaign and the xenophobia generated by World War I led Missouri, the last holdout, to repeal its alien suffrage statute.

The two statutes dealing with aliens constituted the most remarkable delegation of power yet to be bestowed upon a President by Congress and the congressional debates on them prefigure some of the questions raised during the closing months of the Nixon Administration. In essence, President Adams was given absolute, unreviewable authority to deport aliens who "he shall judge dangerous to the peace and safety of the United States."

The Jeffersonian Naturalization Act of 1801 returned to the principles of the 1795 statute. Since, with only slight modifications, the provisions of this law governed United States naturalization procedures for over a century, it may be useful to enumerate the conditions:

1. Five years bona fide residence in the United States by white persons.
2. A declaration of intention filed three years before naturalization in either a state or federal court.
3. Renunciation of any foreign allegiance and titles of nobility.
4. Swearing an oath to support the Constitution of the United States.
5. Satisfying a common law court of record — state or federal — that these conditions had been fulfilled and that the applicant had been of good character throughout the five-year period.

With the obvious exception of the exclusion of nonwhites, this measure provided most liberal terms for acquiring American citizenship. The door was open, the conditions minimal, and the gatekeepers, as scandal after scandal enlivened the nineteenth century, anything but exclusionist in outlook. The administration was less than minimal: if one wanted to discover whether an individual was in fact a citizen, it was necessary to search court records. There was no requirement that this information be filed with the federal government.

In summary, by 1801 the essentials were in place. You could be born a citizen or naturalized. Still obscure, and thoroughly confused by Congress' 1795 improvisation for dealing with naturalization in the Northwest Territory, was the relationship between state and national citizenship. Even more murky was the nationality status of free blacks with, as we shall see, contradictory practice and conflicting judicial decisions. But before moving into immigration and nationality policies in the nineteenth century, a further source of citizenship normally overlooked in studies of the question must be recognized, citizenship acquired under the Treaty Power.

CONTINENTAL EXPANSION

It is hardly necessary here to recapitulate President Thomas Jefferson's wrestling match with his conscience on the constitutionality of the Louisiana Purchase except to note that he won. What is interesting for our purposes is Article III of the Treaty of April 30, 1802: "The inhabitants of the ceded territory shall be incorporated in the Union of the United States and admitted as soon as possible according to the principles of the Federal Constitution to the enjoyment of all the rights, advantages and immunities of citizens of the United States."

The free population of the Territory, estimated at 40,000, was predominantly Catholic, and of French, Spanish, and mixed Creole extraction. Thus it presented problems of absorption absent when Vermont, Kentucky, and Tennessee, populated by British Protestant settlers from the old provinces, were easily admitted to the Union. Jefferson, for example, felt the Creoles were "as yet as incapable of self-government as children," and in 1804 informed Congress that caution was in order in implementing Article III because "the principles of a popular Government are utterly beyond their comprehension."

Jefferson's behavior on this matter defies simple explanation. In an August 23, 1803 letter to Treasury Secretary Albert Gallatin, he suggested a Congressional enactment: "Louisiana, as ceded by France to the US, is made a part of the US. its (sic) white inhabitants shall be citizens and stand, as to their rights & obligations on the same footing with other citizens of the US...Florida also, whensoever it may be rightfully obtained, shall become a part of the (US) its white inhabitants shall thereupon be citizens...."

However, the Act of March 26, 1804, organizing the Territory of Orleans, can only be described as colonial legislation. The governor, appointed by the President and holding office at his pleasure, was to rule with a legislative council, also appointed by the President. Nothing was said about the citizenship of the inhabitants, whose only role − if free white householders with one year's residence − was to serve on grand or petty juries. In short, the government of the Orleans Territory was analogous to that of a British Crown Colony.

This did not end the matter. Space limitations prohibit thorough exploration of the continuing debate except to note this crucial issue. As the United States expanded, were new territories to be treated on the model of the Northwest Ordinance? Or were they to be established as colonies? The argument crossed party lines. High Federalists such as Gouverneur Morris agreed with the colonial solution, while another voice from the Federalist camp deplored making "the modest Jefferson despot of Louisiana." On the other hand, some Jeffersonians were appalled by the statute, and petitions began to arrive from New Orleans bitterly complaining about the violation of the Treaty.

A year later Congress revised the law providing the people of Louisiana the same standing as those ruled under the Northwest Ordinance − with one significant exception. Slavery was permitted. A territorial Assembly was to be elected as a lower house with the appointed Council remaining in place. The essential section in precedential terms was "that whenever it shall be ascertained. . .that the number of free inhabitants (in the Territory) shall amount to sixty thousand, they shall be thereupon authorized to form for themselves a constitution and state government, and be admitted into the Union upon the footing of the original States. . . ." Citizenship was taken for granted, and, on the model of the Northwest Ordinance, two years' residence qualified a freeholder to vote.

To pursue this topic further, the question again arose in the wake of the Treaty of February 22, 1819, (in which Spain sold Florida) which contained a provision virtually identical with Article III of the French Treaty of 1803. In this instance, the question of citizenship was explicitly raised May 21, 1822, when the Acting Governor of East Florida, W.G.D. Worthington, wrote Secretary of State John Quincy Adams. General Andrew Jackson, a man of direct action, had issued an ordinance providing free white aliens could obtain citizenship by taking an oath of allegiance before an American official. Worthington objected in principle, writing Adams: "I am of opinion that a Treaty cannot Naturalize Aliens,. . .but the only mode is under the Constitution, prescribed by Congress." He seems not to have complained to Jackson.

Adams' reply, if any, is not on record, but that well-known later strict constructionist, Secretary of War John C. Calhoun, wrote to Colonel Abraham Eustis at St. Augustine six months later and, inter alia, informed him that "The Spanish or other foreign inhabitants. . .are to be considered de facto citizens of the United States, after they have taken the oath of Allegiance, without passing thro' the formalities of the naturalization law."

To complete the story of continental expansion, Texans became citizens when the Lone Star Republic entered the Union, and the Mexican Treaty of February 2, 1848 provided an option for Mexican citizens. Within one year they could opt to retain their native nationality. However, failure to take positive action was construed as rejection of Mexican status and they were then to be admitted to "an equality with that of the inhabitants of the other territories of the United States." The Russian Treaty of 1867 by which we purchased Alaska gave Russians three years to repatriate and conferred citizenship on all but Indian and Eskimo natives. In 1867 this problem vanished but reemerged under very different circumstances after the Spanish-American War. These will be examined later in appropriate context, i.e., that of extracontinental expansion and the question of whether "The Constitution follows the Flag."

CITIZENSHIP, IMPRESSMENT AND THE WAR OF 1812

To return to the chronological narrative, issues of citizenship first became involved in the international arena during the Napoleonic Wars. For background, neither British nor American law recognized any right of expatriation, adhering rather to the doctrine of indefeasible allegiance. As in the instances discussed earlier, nationality could be transferred by treaty, but not by individual option. Specifically, the British government claimed the power to impress any birthright Briton for service in the fleet – essentially the naval version of the militia power. As the United States became a growing commercial power, its ships became ideal targets for a "hot press." They would be halted and any seamen who could not demonstrate American birth was promptly drafted into the Royal Navy.

Given the appalling conditions and barbaric discipline of the King's ships, any sensible foretopman took the first available opportunity to desert. Since it was rather difficult for a Cornishman, for example, to pretend to be a Spaniard, they would bootleg themselves into the American merchant marine, and with a bit of skulduggery obtain a forged certificate indicating birth in Vermont. The basis for this thriving industry in false papers was an American law providing for a seaman's certificate of citizenship to be issued by a customs collector. The Act indicated that the applicant provide evidence of his citizenship to the collector "in a manner hereinafter directed," but Congress never got around to defining this manner. A British investigation, doubtless a bit biased, indicated that around 100,000 such certificates had been issued – at a time when the full complement of the British merchant marine (thrice the tonnage of the United States) was roughly 120,000!

The British conclusion, which understandably should be doused with saltwater, was that perhaps 1,000 authentic Americans were in the Royal Navy, while there was a net loss of some 40,000 British runaways with falsified American certificates in their pockets. We do know that when the War of 1812 broke out, 2,548 Americans in the British fleet refused to fight – a singularly courageous act – and were imprisoned in Dartmoor. The argument simmered at a low boil until June 21, 1807, when it hit the front burner with a vengeance. The Royal frigate Leopard stopped and boarded the American frigate Chesapeake, and removed three alleged British deserters (one a Massachusetts-born black!). There was nationwide fury, but the issue was defused by a British disavowal of the attack and recall of the officer responsible.

Impressment has often been listed as one of the causes of the War of 1812, though paradoxically the maritime states were the least militant on the subject. Indeed, in Massachusetts the General Court took testimony from leading shippers, employers of 18,700 hands, and discovered only thirty-five bona fide instances of impressment of Americans. The legislative report severely downplayed the matter as "so small that it scarcely excites (American seamen's) attention or regard." In contrast, the "War Hawks," westerners with their eyes on the seizure of Canada, played impressment for all it was worth. However, with the end of the Napoleonic Wars, the press gangs lost their utility (the issue was not mentioned in the Treaty of Ghent, ending hostilities with Britain) and vanished into the history books. In 1870, by Convention, the United States and Britain agreed to the right of individual expatriation.

THE GREAT SURGE OF IMMIGRATION
AND EARLY REGULATION

Whether their sovereigns recognized the right of expatriation or not (and most did not), the common people in Europe voted for it with their feet. Immigration statistics before 1892, when the Bureau of Immigration was established, have an existential character. The Federalists, with their passion for order, had included in the 1798 Naturalization Act a proviso requiring all ships' masters to send a list of immigrants to the Secretary of State, but this was dropped by the Jeffersonians. It was reenacted in 1819, covering Atlantic and Gulf ports, but not establishing any statistical basis for dealing with overland arrivals. Moreover, the manifests submitted by skippers to port authorities did not necessarily indicate the country of origin.

To take a classic example, immigration by ship from Canada jumped radically in the late 1840s. On its face, this is inexplicable unless one is acquainted with Irish-American folklore in which the reference to an Irish immigrant, or his descendants, as a "two-boater" was a casus belli. "One-boaters" were considered aristocrats who made it from Liverpool to the United States in one voyage; "two-boaters" only had the fare to Halifax (generally) and had to work in Nova Scotia a while to earn enough to make it to Boston, New York, or Baltimore. 'Twas said they were a distinctly inferior lot, but however evaluated, they were not "Canadians."

The estimate employed by the Census Bureau for the period prior to 1820 indicates that between 1783 and 1820, 250,000 immigrants arrived on these shores. The annual total rose incrementally — with two bad years in the wake of the depression of 1837 — and topped the 100,000 mark in 1840. Over 90 percent came from Western Europe, overwhelmingly from the British Isles with Germans providing the remainder. At no point in the nineteenth century did the percentage of males fall below 50 percent (it generally ran between 55 and 60) and since, as one might expect, only a handful were over 40 years old, there was a marital bonanza for American women.

Although, comparatively speaking, the immigrants were well off (they had been able to raise the money for their passage), their arrival in the principal ports of entry created a number of difficulties. First of all, they had little money left; second, after a month or more in steerage on what the Irish called the "coffin ships," they were literally and figuratively a scurvy lot; and third, they were often "plague bearers," with cholera the most common disease. These were serious social problems, but in addition prejudice entered the picture, particularly against the Catholic Irish and less so against the German Catholics. The impact of the Irish tsunami is reserved for separate treatment; our immediate concern is the effort of the states and cities directly affected to cope with the burdens on public services created by the immigrants.

As background, it might be noted that some efforts were made in the colonial era to bar "paupers" from various provinces. Essentially the model was the Elizabethan Poor Law, which settled a pauper in his parish and held the parish responsible both for rudimentary welfare and for his movements. If he turned up, for example, in another parish and tried to "go on the rates," he could be shipped back at the expense of his own parish. However, in seventeenth century Massachusetts Bay it was a bit hard to ship a pauper back to Sussex, and so an alternative was devised. One suspected of being a potential "welfare-chisler" was allowed to settle but "warned off." This meant he could remain indefinitely but never be eligible for relief.

In a leading nineteenth-century case the state of New York in 1824 devised a new variation on the Elizabethan theme. "Every master or commander of any ship. . .arriving at the port of New York from any country out of the United States (or other state) shall within twenty-four hours. . .make a report in writing. . .to the mayor of the city of New York. . .of the name, place of birth, and last legal settlement, age, and occupation (of every passenger)." This would at least have provided New York with vital statistics. The statute was challenged as a state intrusion into interstate and foreign commerce, but in New York v. Miln (1837) the United States Supreme Court held it a valid exercise of the state's police power, noting that "We think it as competent for a State to provide precautionary measures against the moral pestilence of paupers, vagabonds, and possibly convicts, as it is to guard against the physical pestilence which may arise from unsound or infectious articles imported, or from a ship, the crew of which may be laboring under an infectious disease."

Emboldened by this support from the high Court, various port cities moved to enlarge and tighten their control over immigrants. New York, for instance, imposed on each shipmaster a fee of $1.50 for cabin and $1 for steerage passengers (which he in turn could recover from the immigrants) for the support of a marine hospital. Massachusetts went further, requiring shipmasters to pay the city of Boston $2 an immigrant for the support of foreign paupers. Naturally these laws were appealed, but by the time the litigation reached the Supreme Court in The Passenger Cases (1849), the interrelationship of slavery and the commerce power (e.g., could Congress prohibit the movement of slaves into the territories?) had utterly fragmented the Court. There were eight opinions covering 181 pages. The state laws were voided 5-4; but there was no majority rationale!

Without examining the legal chaos which surrounded the issue of state regulation of the entry of immigrants (New York's legislation of 1855 was the most enlightened and effective), the important thing to note is that the whole process was thoroughly decentralized, with the federal government virtually out of the picture until the Bureau of Immigration was established in 1892. All the screening, whether medical or for pauperism, was handled by officers appointed by the state or city.

The Department of State collected statistics from 1820 to 1870. (Under an 1855 Act of Congress United States customs collectors were required to submit quarterly reports which were compiled into an annual report to Congress.) The Treasury's Bureau of Statistics got into the game from 1867 to 1895. Finally, the Office, then Bureau of Immigration and now incorporated into the Immigration and Naturalization Service, inherited the task.

But, as indicated earlier, until the 1890s the statistics have an "Alice-in-Wonderland" quality. In 1833, to take one example, a solitary Pole was registered, but 159 Russians. In 1834, 54 Poles poured in, but only 15 Russians. Of course, there was then no Poland! Or, there were three: German, Austrian, and Russian. But when the time came to prepare the figures necessary for the operation of the "quota system" — a racist policy enacted in 1924 — some poor clerk had to work out the appropriate niche for, say, a Jew born in Russian Poland ("a Russian") who emigrated to New York from German Poland ("a German"). There is doubtless macrovalidity in the Census data, but one would like to know more about that lonesome 1833 Pole.

THE IRISH TIDAL WAVE

Whatever statistical margin of error one assumes, nothing in the history of American immigration to that time approximated the Irish tidal wave that began in 1847. The travail of the Irish has been detailed at length elsewhere. Our concern here is with the broader impact on American society of the arrival of over a million Irish Catholics in a decade. It was a distinctive migration. Like the Jews, the Irish were not paranoids — they had enemies whose policies, either deliberately or accidentally, amounted to genocide. The matrix of their world view was Catholicism — Irish Catholicism, a puritanical, disciplined, fighting faith. It was strongly antiintellectual and antihumanist; but, in fairness, a community in a state of siege has little time for dreamers or elaborate ratiocination.

Furthermore, unlike other Catholic immigrants, the Irish spoke English and could not be tucked away indefinitely in an ethnic cocoon to babble some foreign tongue. (By the beginning of the nineteenth century, largely as a consequence of savage British retribution against "hedge priests" and teachers, Gaelic was largely limited to the wilds of Connaught and the Islands.) In other words, the Irish had the threshold skill — the language — and set to work in America to establish the political base denied them in their homeland. The first step was building the fortress, otherwise known as the Parish and its churches. The nativists early realized the true character of the Irish church. In the ferocious Philadelphia riots in 1844, an Irish church was obliterated. A German Catholic one, a few blocks away, was undisturbed.

To look at the issue from a different perspective, the Irish Catholics were qualitatively different from other major immigrant groups. Their religion and cohesiveness set them apart from other English-speaking arrivals. And, unlike non-English speakers, they were prepared to take an active hand in the political game. By the early 1840s, for example, Bishop (later Archbishop) John Hughes was a political potentate in the politics of New York State and City, working hand-in-glove with Governor William Seward. Critics have argued with justice that Irish bloc tactics contributed to the growth of nativism, but for better or worse that was the way they conducted the exercise.

If you were a nativist, then, what you saw was the seemingly endless growth, both by immigration and reproduction, of huge urban aggregations of extremely aggressive "aliens" – in the true sense of the word. Allegedly addicted to medieval superstitions; dominated by an undemocratic clerical hierarchy; loud, brawling, and heavy on the poteen; they seemed ideal candidates for "paddy wagons." (New York City statistics for May through July 1858, show 10,500 Irish arrests on a total of 17,000 – mostly on the familiar charge of "D&D," drunk and disorderly.) In fairness, given their premises, the nativists had a case. The Irish were simply not about to assimilate and behave like good little immigrants. They even had the gall to demand an end to Bible reading in public schools, claiming that the King James Version was heretical!

Moreover, because of their political compulsions, the Irish began to constitute more of a political problem to the Old Order than the statistics might suggest. Between 1840 and 1860 about 1,700,000 Irish (including those bogus "Canadians") emigrated to the United States. If you include earlier arrivals, the count may reach 2 million. Now 2 million on a white population base of roughly 23 million (1860) does not sound overpowering, but two other considerations must be added. First, only about 50 percent of the natives were males, while the ratio among the Irish may have been as high as 2:1 male. Second, the Irish were not scattered all over the countryside, but clustered in the big cities of the Northeast.

There had been scattered acts of violence against the Irish going back to the 1820s. In August 1835, in the words of the French visitor Michael Chevalier, "the intolerant spirit of a part of the Protestant population (of Boston and Charlestown) was offended by the sight of the Ursuline Convent...on the Night of August 12, the convent was surrounded and attacked...the sisters were driven from the convent with violence; everything was plundered; the tombs of the dead were forced open; the building then fired...Boston firemen hastened to the spot, but were repulsed by the populace by main force." In 1844 Philadelphia was for weeks in a virtual state of siege. Organizations dedicated to "No Popery!" began popping up like mushrooms, though – as suggested earlier – their real target was Irish Popery.

THE NATIVIST SPASM

In the early 1850s the nativist mass became critical. Almost overnight a secret society, the "Know-Nothings," burgeoned into a mass movement in the Northern and border states. Organizationally, its background remains to this date astoundingly obscure, but clearly the fact that the immigrant vote allegedly put Democrat Franklin Pierce in the White House in the election of 1852 led Whig politicians to mediate on immigrant restrictions and form unofficial links with nativist organizations. Beginning locally in 1852, with surprising success, the Order of United Americans went national in 1854 with the formation of the American Party.

The objectives of the movement were set out in the charter of one of its constituent elements: "The object of this organization shall be to protect every American citizen in the legal and proper exercise of all his civil and religious rights and privileges; to resist the insidious policy of the Church of Rome, and all other foreign influences against our republican institutions in all lawful ways; to place in all offices of honor, trust, or profit, in the gift of the people, or by appointment, none but native-born Protestant citizens, and to protect, preserve, and uphold the Union of these States. . . ."

While much of this proclamation reflects the demagoguery of frustrated politicians, nativist intellectuals found an unwitting supporter in the Vatican, Pope Pius IX. Greeted on his elevation (1846) as the "Pope of progress," Pius found himself deeply embroiled in the Italian War of Independence of 1848 to 1849 and was a thoroughly embittered exile when on February 9, 1849, Mazzini proclaimed the Papal States the "Roman Republic." When the independence movement was suppressed by French and Austrian forces, Pius returned and dedicated the rest of his long career (d. 1878) to excoriating liberalism in all its manifestations and asserting the power of the Church over secular affairs in a manner reminiscent of Boniface VIII's universalist claim of 1304, Unam Sanctum.

In 1854, assuming Papal infallibility, he proclaimed the "Dogma of the Immaculate Conception." A decade later, in his famous Syllabus of Errors, he included among them any belief that the "Roman Pontiff can and ought to reconcile himself to, and agree with, progress, liberalism, and contemporary civilization." With Pius as their shepherd, American Catholics, struggling to define their role in a secular, liberal, and decidedly contemporary civilization, found wolves no problem. Their interest in the "Dogma of the Immaculate Conception" was minimal (indeed, most probably assumed it referred to the birth of Jesus, not Mary), but the Pope's pretensions made it hard to escape the charge of subservience to a foreign power.

The point of this trans-Atlantic interpellation is to emphasize that events in the United States did not occur in a vacuum. On an entirely different level, for example, the diversion of the best British passenger ships as troop transports in the Crimean War (1854-1856) and the subsequent Indian Mutiny (1857) undoubtedly exacerbated the toll of death and disease among American immigrants, consigned to marginal craft, if not hulks. And how would one tempted to nativism react when he learned in 1849 that the outstanding British philanthropist Anthony Ashley Cooper, later Lord Shaftsbury, met with 200 of London's leading thieves to encourage their entrepreneurial emigration to America?

The American Party, to return to the central narrative, was able to draw both on public prejudice, fanned by wild tales about orgies in nunneries, and on intellectual arguments about the antinomy of democ-

"I AM NOW INFALLIBLE."

Ill.   2.1.

Source: Thomas Nast, Harper's, 1871.

racy and Catholicism, based on tracts by the Rev. Lyman Beecher and Samuel F.B. Morse. Also, without digging too deeply into the notion of a collective unconsciousness, there was a sense in which anti-Catholic agitation was politically functional. It took people's minds off the metastasizing issue of slavery and united the Old Order, North and South, against a common enemy. Liberal German refugees from the failures of 1848 could also demonstrate their Americanism. A historian feeling his way through the 1850s is inevitably reminded of El Greco's ominous, somber masterpiece, "A View of Toledo." There was a sense that the Republic was coming apart at the seams and Know Nothingism, like the great religious revivals of the decade, could be considered symbolically as a restorationist phenomenon.

Between 1852 and 1855 the American Party seemed to be taking the country by storm. The Massachusetts state election of 1854 was the blockbuster. The Know Nothings elected the Governor, all state officers, the whole Senate, and 376 of the 378 members of the House of Representatives. Similar though lesser triumphs were registered elsewhere and were reflected in the nation's capital – which had an elected Know Nothing Mayor and perhaps a hundred resident Know Nothing Congressmen. (Exact figures are elusive because in many areas members of the old parties, particularly Whigs, climbed on the American Party bandwagon.) The American Party was widely predicted as the probable winner of the 1856 presidential election.

Then, almost as suddenly, the American Party was dead. The failure of the Compromise of 1850 and the Kansas-Nebraska Act (1854), and the outbreak of civil war in "bleeding Kansas" restored the primacy of the slavery question. The American Party had taken a nonposition on slavery – its Massachusetts ranks were filled with Free Soilers, its Mississippi cadres with slaveholders. But it could not avoid the reef which shattered it, like other institutions, on North-South lines. In the election of 1856, its presidential candidate, Millard Fillmore, carried only Maryland.

As far as restricting the political role of Catholics and immigrants was concerned, there was a great deal of shouting but, in statutory terms, there was virtually no residue except Prohibition where state after state followed Maine's example (1854) in attempting to reform this "noisy, drinking, brawling rabble." To say this is not to suggest that a number of Catholics were not molested in person and property – there were shameless displays of hysterical violence. But the immigration and naturalization laws remained intact, and shortly the Catholic immigrants were to be permanently annealed to the American polity in the fiery furnace of war.

BLACK CITIZENSHIP AND DRED SCOTT

We have already cursorily examined the status of the free blacks in the colonies and early Republic. Given the extensive recent scholarly coverage of this long neglected topic, brevity is in order. Suffice it to say that in the slave states they occupied a position between their enslaved compatriots and free whites. Initially there was a good deal of legal sloppiness, but as the century progressed and the South developed more and more of a siege mentality, laws were tightened up. For one thing, as the black elite they were automatically suspected of subversion, of fomenting slave revolts. Thus efforts were made to limit their education, mobility, occupations, and even manners. Municipal ordinances (the free blacks were mostly urban) on occasion even banned them from carrying canes! Needless to say, they were excluded from the political process.

In the North, there was diverse treatment, varying from state to state and even from town to town. The southern sections of Illinois and Indiana, for example, were Southern in attitude. Indeed, Northwest Territorial records indicate that in the eighteenth century slaveholders, crossing the Ohio into presumably free jurisdiction, simply went before a sympathetic justice of the peace and converted their slaves into long-term indentured servants.

Cities such as Philadelphia, New York, or Boston featured strong Irish Catholic resentment against free blacks, but the "separate but equal" doctrine was formulated in 1850 by an eminent Protestant, Chief Justice Lemuel Shaw of the Massachusetts Supreme Judicial Court. Only two of Boston's 161 grammar schools were open to blacks. Benjamin Roberts, the father of a black child, went to court to get little Sarah admitted to a lily-white neighborhood school; the Justices in their wisdom endorsed racial segregation and told her to travel daily to an open school. (In fairness to the Irish, it should be noted that this practice dated back to 1798.) Inadequate records indicate that in the New England states blacks, by and large, could participate in politics de jure, though community pressures, which increased in urban areas during the 1840s and 1850s, may have inhibited their voting. One of President Lincoln's more embarrassing moments occurred in 1863 when Connecticut passed a provision barring black suffrage!

With this as a background, we can turn to the murky subject of black citizenship. If we begin with the proposition taken for granted by the Founding Fathers that national citizenship was derived from state, a black citizen of Massachusetts was automatically a citizen of the United States. Under the Comity Clause of the Constitution he would then be theoretically entitled to the privileges and immunities of the citizens of other states, i.e., he could go to South Carolina and be treated as a citizen of that state.

However, in 1822 South Carolina passed a Negro Seaman Act which required that free Negroes or persons of color employed on incoming ships from ports outside the state be jailed until the ship's departure. Virginia and other slave states had similar statutes, and Florida included the stipulation in her Constitution of 1845. Shipowners, who had to pay the cost of this bizarre quarantine, promptly objected and the British government officially protested. A test case soon arose in Charleston involving a Black British seaman named Henry Elkinson who was pulled from his ship and jailed.

Elkinson promptly appealed to Supreme Court Justice William Johnson, a South Carolinian, who was riding the Southern Circuit. Chief Justice John Marshall, on similar Circuit duty in Virginia in 1820, had circumspectly avoided the merits of Virginia's law, observing that "as I am not fond of butting against a wall in sport, I escaped on the construction of the act." But Johnson was made of less pragmatic stuff. In 1823 in Charleston he granted Elkinson habeas corpus and flatly declared the state law an invasion of Congress' authority of interstate and foreign commerce. The decision touched off a furious assault upon him in the press and he wrote a ferocious reply under the nom de plume "Philonimus."

Unfortunately Johnson's bold assertion of national power was frustrated. The Charleston authorities simply ignored it. In Washington, President Monroe asked Attorney General William Wirt's opinion in the matter and Wirt agreed with Johnson. Monroe then wrote the Governor of South Carolina requesting repeal of the law; he too was ignored and subsequently, with the imprimatur of President Jackson, the quarantine on free persons of color was enforced until the Civil War. There was one interesting sequel. In 1846, the Commonwealth of Massachusetts officially dispatched Rockwood Hoar to Charleston to challenge the application of this statute to a free black citizen of Massachusetts. The quasi-ambassador was promptly deported on the ground that if he remained he would be lynched!

The Elkinson case involved nationality only by implication; he was undeniably a British subject and so Johnson's rationale for his decision was the Commerce Clause. However, President Monroe, in a different context, asked Attorney General Wirt "were free Negroes living in Virginia citizens of the United States?" The gist of Wirt's reply was "the Constitution by the description of 'citizens of the United States' intended those only who enjoyed the full and equal privileges of white citizens in the State of their residence. . . .Then free people of color in Virginia are not citizens of the United States." "White" has been emphasized because it was an addition to states' rights doctrine; in 1787 some states had nonwhite citizens.

Before we get to Dred Scott's case, in which the issue of black citizenship was jurisdictionally essential though it was the tip of the iceberg, contrary precedents should be noted. As early as 1798 a federal judge on Circuit in the Illinois Territory held, in essence, that "free soil made free men." Judge Symmes ruled that a former slave and his wife brought there by their master were citizens of the United States entitled "to enjoy all and every privilege and franchise with relation to their personal liberty and protection of property, unmolested, subject only to the laws of the land." A thorough search of judicial records would undoubtedly reveal a number of similar decisions.

Yet the decisions of territorial judges and others on the inferior judicial echelons were hardly compelling. What was important – and for some reason totally neglected by talented and industrious Abolitionist lawyers – was John Marshall's own Supreme Court decision, Gassies v. Ballon (1832). The question was highly technical in character, but the decision reached the heart of matter. Asked whether a naturalized alien living in a state was a citizen of that state, Marshall replied: "This (fact of domicile in Louisiana) is equivalent to an averment that he is a citizen of that state. A citizen of the United States residing in any State of the Union is a citizen of that State." Marshall, in other words, made state citizenship derivative of national, but did so in one paragraph without any documentation.

Probably the most outspoken denial of state jurisdiction over national citizenship was made the year before Dred Scott by Attorney General Caleb Cushing. "What constitutes citizenship of the United States cannot," he informed President Pierce, "be determined by the several States. If they were to undertake it, they would be found to differ radically and irreconcilably in the matter. . . .When Congress enacts that only citizens of the United States are competent to do certain things, it may well proceed to say, if it chose, who the persons thus designated are, and to define them." Cushing of Massachusetts, normally considered the paradigmatic "dough-face" (Northern man with Southern principles), here enounced the most far-reaching definition of national power. It was not cited in the Dred Scott decision!

To understand the full dimensions of Dred Scott, one must realize that for years Congress and the President had been trying to get slavery out of politics. The collapse of "squatter sovereignty," the effort to leave the decision in the hands of the locals incarnate in the Kansas-Nebraska Act, left few options. One was the judiciary, for as Tocqueville pointed out, American policy-making usually eventuated in litigation. The thought that the Supreme Court might exorcise the shade of slavery had surfaced in Congress on several occasions, notably in the debates over the Compromise of 1850. Indeed, on one occasion the effort to pass the buck to the courts was so apparent that the ironic Senator Tom Corwin of Ohio congratulated his colleagues on divising not a law, but a lawsuit.

The Abolitionists were also trying to be helpful, figuring that whichever way the Supreme Court went, they would win. If it endorsed slavery, they could accuse it of betraying American principles. If it for example supported Congress' right to bar slavery from the territories, their cause would advance. The test case that emerged, however, has to be studied in detail to be believed. The status of Dred Scott had been subjudice in various courts for a decade, but in 1855 to 1856 it came before the Supreme Court. Closely divided, and with a presidential election looming up, the Justices ordered reargument at the next term. In March 1857, the Court — in thorough disarray — handed down its judgment.

The temptation to enter the legal labyrinth must be resisted. From the vantage point of the student of American nationality, the simple issue was: Could a black man obtain citizenship? In Dred Scott Chief Justice Roger B. Taney put the question this way: "Can a negro whose ancestors were imported into this country, and sold and held as slaves, become a member of the political community formed and brought into existence by the Constitution of the United States. . .?" His answer was "no," but paradoxically it was based on a denial of states' rights. The states could create state citizens, he argued, but only the federal government could define national citizenship. Employing historical hocus-pocus, he determined that blacks were not American citizens at the formation of the Union and had been barred from naturalization. They were simply left in legal limbo.

Justice Benjamin Curtis dissented, upholding Scott's citizenship, but ironically he utilized the logic of states' rights! The states, he held, had traditionally exercised the right to admit whomever they chose to membership in the body politic, and a state citizen ipso facto became a citizen of the nation. Congress' only power was to remove the disabilities of foreign birth by naturalization and thenceforth individual status was state defined.

The Dred Scott decision, while legally confusing (there were nine separate opinions), was a political bomb, exploited to the hilt by the Abolitionists and, in a lower key, by the new Republican Party which wanted to hold its ex-Whig supporters in the South and border states. The decision clearly did not settle the matter of black citizenship. In fact, in 1862 Attorney General Edward Bates, replying to an inquiry from Treasury Secretary Chase whether free Negroes were citizens, provided a concise historical summary with the following rhetorical questions. "Who is a citizen? What constitutes a citizen of the United States?"

The answer was:

I have often been pained by the fruitless search in our law books and the records of our courts, for a clear and satisfactory definition of the phrase citizen of the United States. I find no such definition, no authoritative establishment of the meaning of the phrase. . . .For aught I see to the contrary, the subject is now as little understood in its details and elements, and as open to argument and speculative criticism, as it was at the beginning of the Government. Eighty years of practical enjoyment of citizenship under the Constitution have not sufficed to teach us either the exact meaning of the word, or the constitutional elements of the thing we prize so highly.

The Union victory in the Civil War solved the question once and for all. The Civil Rights Act of 1866 provided that "all persons born in the United States and not subject to any foreign power (e.g., children of diplomats) excluding Indians not taxed, are declared to be citizens of the United States." This was enlarged and set in concrete by Art. I of the Fourteenth Amendment: "All persons born or naturalized in the United States, and subject to the jurisdiction thereof, are citizens of the United States and of the state wherein they reside."

THE CIVIL WAR

If the Civil War solved the legal dilemmas of citizenship, it also played an important role in the acceptance of immigrant groups in the body politic. Most Irish, for example, settled in the North (New Orleans was the only southern port with a sizeable intake) and without going into the statistics it is obvious that the eleven states of the Confederacy were the bastion of Anglo-Saxon Protestantism. One odd aspect of Southern political life merits brief discussion — the white united front against the blacks inhibited nativism. In the Thirty-sixth Congress (1859 to 1861), for example, Florida's two senators were Stephen R. Mallory and David Levy Yulee. Mallory was an Irish Catholic who went on to be the Confederate Secretary of the Navy; Yulee was Jewish, the son of Moses Levy who was summarily naturalized by General Andrew Jackson in the latter's earlier discussed action. Similarly, Louisiana's senior senator was Judah P. Benjamin, a Jew who later had the distinction of serving Confederate President Jefferson Davis as Attorney General, then Secretary of War, and finally Secretary of State.

But these were individual cases drawn from a small immigrant population. In the North great masses of immigrants — unrepresented in the Cabinet or Senate — rallied round the flag. Carl Schurz and other German "Forty-eighters" (including Karl Marx's associate George Wedemeyer) moved immediately to organize regiments in the German communities. The Irish also established ethnic regiments, several of which were grouped in the famous "Irish Brigade" whose exploits created the myth of the "fighting Irish." The Brigade's reputation was deserved, but in fairness to other soldiers, regimental desertion records suggest there were also "running Irish."

The distinctive aspect of Irish regiments was the extent they considered themselves in training for the liberation of Ireland from the British. The United States had become the sanctuary for the Fenians, Irish radicals who (like later Zionists) dreamed of a liberated homeland. Few of them lived to participate in the desultory postwar raids on Canada or in the abortive Irish rising of 1867. General Ambrose Burnside, not the British, was their undoing. At Fredericksberg he marched them through the open field against Confederate entrenchment in the sunken road and Longstreet's cannon wheel to wheel. The Stars and Stripes and the Green Flag went down in gore together. Viewing the carnage, Lee turned to Longstreet and said, "It is well that war is so terrible; we should grow too fond of it."

The Fenians never achieved their mission, but the behavior of the immigrants — Protestant and Catholic alike — on the battlefields muffled nativism for almost half a century. And the American Fenians did manage one magnificent deed, the Entebbe Raid of its day. They arranged for the rescue of transported leaders of the Irish revolt from western Australian penal settlements. It was beautifully laid out with agents going ahead to make contact, a ship ostensibly equipped as a whaler, and then a night rendezvous and rescue on a beach near Perth.

The Confederates constantly complained that the Union was recruiting mercenaries in Europe, notably Germany and Ireland. One-third of the Union army was foreign-born, but there was no noticeable jump in immigration statistics during the war years. However, given the crazy 1863 draft system which permitted the rich to purchase substitutes, it is probable that many poor laborers took that option. There is a contemporary postcard with a poem and a drawing. The poem, no irony intended, is "Wanted: A Substitute," and it praises the virtues of these brave chaps. The drawing shows a stereotypical "Paddy" in uniform.

The Confederate view was expressed in the ballad "Old Unreconstructed":

> We whupped the best they sent us; we whupped them fair and
>   true;
> We whupped their German immigrants and the Italians too.
> We whupped the Frogs and Squareheads, and all their furrin
>   might;
> But when they went and got the Micks, we knew we had a fight.

Warming to the Irish-American ego, it is hardly a just description of the valor displayed by young men of all backgrounds in a holocaust which, proportionately, killed a higher percentage of young American males than the British, French, or Germans suffered in World War I. As a final footnote, the balance sheet on the Irish must include their responsibility for the sanguinary 1863 Draft Riots in New York City and antidraft violence in the Pennsylvania mining region.

POST CIVIL WAR PATTERNS

A few may have emigrated from the British Isles and Europe to take a hand in the Civil War, but the essential motivation was the dual quest eulogized in Goethe's "Faust" – for freedom and land. After the failure of the liberal revolutions of 1848 in various of the Germanies (to use contemporary usage), German immigration jumped from 60,000 in 1849 to a peak of 215,000 in 1854. It then fell off until the end of the Civil War, and had its ups and downs through the remainder of the century. Roughly five million Germans arrived in this time frame. Scandinavian immigrants were also thick on the ground, perhaps a million by 1900.

This immigration was vigorously stimulated by western state governments and the federal government, once the Republicans gained control. After 1850, when the Congress made its first public land grant to Illinois for the encouragement of railroads, the lines went into the immigration business in a big way. Customarily railroads had followed lines of settlement; now, particularly on the transcontinental route, they faced the task of creating settlements. For one thing, they wanted the money from land sales, and second, they wanted passenger and freight business. The Union Pacific Railroad, for example, created the town of Cheyenne two years or more ahead of the road builders! After

1862, the government's alternate sections were — theoretically at least — to be assigned to small holders (American-style) under the terms of the Homestead Act and aliens who had declared their intention to become citizens were eligible for grants.

The ubiquitous Fenians, for instance, recruited Irish for settlements in Nebraska designed as jumping off points for the invasion of Canada and thus, by the 1870s, Europe was being scoured for potential Americans. Railroad pressures in three western states, for example, got religious pacifists exempted from the militia to successfully encourage Mennonite settlements. Agents for the railroads, state governments, and plain old-fashioned speculators met every ship from Europe. In the 1850s Wisconsin even appointed a Commissioner of Immigration to live in New York where, with the aid of a public relations man, he was soon glorifying the beauties of that state in papers here and abroad.

All in all, it was a wild and chaotic scene, but our concern must focus on the reaction of various European states to the disappearance over the horizon of substantial, generally youthful segments of their populations. Curiously, there had been few objections early in the nineteenth century, apparently based on the general acceptance of Malthusian doctrine that population was rapidly outpacing food supplies. As a leading American journal, Banker's Magazine, noted in 1876: "But for the theory of Malthus and its influence in shaping the policy of the British and their governments in favor of emigration, we should have lacked a very powerful agency in our national development which European emigration supplied."

However, after the levee en masse of the French Revolution became institutionalized as mandatory military service on the Continent, particularly with the expansion of Bismark's Prussia, governments had second thoughts about shipping potential cannon fodder overseas. And naturalized Americans returning to visit their homeland found themselves drafted into the French and Prussian armies. As might be expected, some Fenians, naturalized Americans, highlighted the issue by taking a hand in the botched 1867 Irish uprising and winding up in Her Majesty's courts charged with high treason. The Democrats, with a very substantial Irish-American constituency, bitterly assaulted the Andrew Johnson administration for its passiveness. The Republicans, who were no admirers of the Irish, got worried about the extent to which this issue could be used against them, notably among their big German-American following, in the presidential election of 1868.

In 1867 President Johnson attempted a preemptive strike by asking Congress to take a firm position on the right of expatriation, noting that his protests to various powers had been stymied by the fact that American law did not recognize the right of our citizens to assume another nationality. What ensued in Congress resembled three-dimensional chess. The outcome was an 1868 statute which piously endorsed the "natural" right of expatriation (in the preamble, which had no legal force) and provided that native-born and naturalized citizens should receive identical protection when traveling in foreign states.

In essence this was no protection at all unless the sinning sovereign cooperated. We were not, after all, going to blockade France to rescue some draftees or Britain to save the necks of some Fenians. However, in the same year the historian-statesman George Bancroft undertook to alleviate the conflict employing the treaty route. The first "Bancroft Treaty" with the North German Confederation provided that "Citizens of the North German Confederation, who shall become naturalized citizens of the United States of America and shall have resided uninterruptedly within the United States for five years, shall be held. . .to be American citizens." Similar treaties were enacted with Bavaria, Hesse, Wurttemberg, and Baden, and an 1870 Convention with Britain achieved the same end.

Unfortunately this was only one side of the coin. The abstract right of a Bavarian to become a naturalized American was affirmed, but in practice there was a thriving business in bogus naturalization papers. For the rest of the century the State Department was plagued with specific cases of this sort, and – with no help from Congress – had to wander around in an administrative maze. (Remember, there was no central record of naturalizations.)

THE REVIVAL OF NATIVISM

With the advent of the 1880s, we find the beginnings of the exclusionist movement which reached its apogee in the act of 1924. Historians have explored its sources – the rise of Social Darwinism, the Progressive distaste for urban immigrant squalor, trade union objections to the employment of immigrants as strikebreakers, and pragmatic political complaints about ethnic power politics, among others. So we shall focus on the bottom line, the implementation of restrictive measures.

The first to feel the crunch were the hapless Chinese who like the blacks had distinctive pigmentation to distinguish them among ethnic groups. The Census lists one Chinese debarking in 1820 to be joined by two compatriots by 1830. (Japanese were not counted until 1861, when one hit the beach, perhaps returning Commodore Perry's recent visit.) Chinese immigration remained in single digits until 1854, when it leaped to 13,100, and thenceforth remained in the 3 to 5,000 annual range for fifteen years. After the Burlingame Treaty of 1868, opening diplomatic relations with the Chinese Empire, the flow increased until the crucial year 1882. This year registered 23,000 arrivals. In 1882, to beat the deadline of the Chinese Exclusion Act, almost 40,000 entered the country.

This was a drop in the bucket, or so it would seem, unless one understands the pathetic position of the Chinese and their geographical concentration on the West Coast, overwhelmingly in California. California politics in the 1870s featured a savage, no-holds-barred, confrontation between anarcho-populists and the railroad barons. There was a strong trade union movement which dominated the city government of San Francisco and with its allies enacted the California

Constitution of 1879. When you realize that one provision (Art. XIX, Sect. 2) of the Constitution forbade corporations to employ Chinese, another barred banks from any function but storing specie, and two devastating antirailroad weapons were in the package, you get the smell of the battlefield. And the Chinese were firmly situated in no-man's-land.

Brought in as contract laborers to build the railroads, they were viewed by California radicals as dirty yellow scabs. From the vantage point of Leland Stanford, Collis P. Huntington, and the other rail and mining magnates, they were useful pawns on the board who had to be protected from the wrath of the radical upstarts. All hands were, of course, racist, but the radicals set to work passing laws and municipal ordinances to demean the tragic victims – one required that Chinese cut off their queues!

The Workingmen's Party may have had a majority, but the railroad barons had the federal judges, notably Justice Stephen J. Field of the Supreme Court, whose bailiwick was the Ninth Circuit. Utilizing a constitutional anomaly too complex to explain, Field and his associates on the federal bench knocked down one anti-Chinese measure after another, ranging from the California constitutional provision barring corporate employment of Chinese to the "Queue Law." The weird result was that Chinese aliens in California had far better civil rights protection than American blacks in Alabama!

The Chinese may have won some reprieves in California, but when the exclusionists took their case to Congress, they got a very sympathetic ear. Twice Congress passed exclusion acts, only to have them vetoed by Presidents Hayes and Arthur. In 1882, however, a measure was at last passed and signed which avoided the flagrant treaty violations of its predecessors. It suspended Chinese immigration for ten years. It is interesting to note that this bill received strong support throughout the nation. More Northern Congressmen voted for it than Southern and Western combined. A side issue was taken for granted; the Chinese, being neither white nor black (an 1870 act made "Africans" potential citizens) were ineligible for naturalization.

Thus entered into American law the category "aliens ineligible for citizenship," which was employed with Supreme Court imprimatur (Ozawa v. U.S., 1922) to prevent Chinese, Japanese, Koreans, and other Asians from owning land, engaging in certain occupations, and other harassments. (cf., O'Brien v. Webb, 1923) Fortunately, in 1898 the Supreme Court did limit the field by ruling in U.S. v. Wong Kim Ark that native-born children of aliens ineligible for citizenship were, under the terms of Art. I of the Fourteenth Amendment, citizens of the United States.

Also in 1882 Congress passed an immigration measure virtually forced upon it by the Supreme Court. In 1876 the Court held all state regulations of immigration to be a violation of federal authority, thus ending the ambiguity created by the early Passenger Cases. The cities which were ports of entry – in particular New York, which probably handled close to three-quarters of the immigrant load – demanded action. It took six years, but finally the Secretary of the Treasury was given jurisdiction over immigration with the right to collect a fifty cent head tax for a welfare fund. Convicts, lunatics, idiots, and potential welfare cases were barred entry; and existing state agencies were delegated the authority to administer the rules.

Regrettably, space does not permit adequate exploration of the background of the nativist and exclusionist spasm which hit the country in the 1880s and 1890s. A study of immigration can too easily expand into a history of the United States! Again there was a strange diverse coalition which included the American Protective Association (1887), convinced that the Catholics (read Irish) must be prevented from taking over the country; Terence Powderly's Knights of Labor, a formerly "secret" (in the Masonic sense) labor organization which went public in 1881 and objected to the importation of strikebreakers and contract laborers; progressives and conservationists such as Madison Grant, Frederick Law Olmstead, and Henry George who preferred trees and open spaces to people; and superpatriots, triggered by the Haymarket bombing of 1886, attributed to German anarchists, who wanted the nation protected from subversion. Then there was the Immigration Restrictive League (1894) which – doubtless influenced by the Harvard background of its founders – launched a major campaign for the literacy test, a class rather than a racial restriction.

Even the Populists, generally considered a progressive force in American politics, included a nativist footnote in their notable 1892 Omaha Platform. After announcing that "The land, including all the natural sources of wealth, is the heritage of the people, and should not be monopolized for speculative purposes," they urged the government to seize "all lands now owned by aliens."

THE NEW IMMIGRATION

This nativist surge is often attributed to the rise of the "new immigration," that is arrivals from Eastern and Southern Europe with a heavy proportion of Italians and Jews. Once again, as with the Chinese in California, we are faced with a special problem. Before 1900 (the first year Italian intake reached 100,000), those arriving from these areas were statistically insignificant by comparison with the "old immigrant" Germans. But they were highly visible. Instead of heading for an isolated homestead in South Dakota, they remained in the cities, notably New York.

Some have thought it odd that Italians, largely peasants, would not have moved into the still (Frederick Jackson Turner notwithstanding) largely empty West, overlooking the Italian tradition of the contadini (the urban farmer), who lives in an often sizeable community and goes out every day to work his field in the countryside. In short, unlike Scandinavian, German, and British immigrant farmers – whose dream was an individual small holding – the Italians were accustomed to a high level of concentrated community life. Thus, probably quite unconsciously, they preferred menial urban employment to what Marx (using the Aristotelian sense of "idiot" as one who could live outside a community) called the "idiocy of rural life."

As chronicles or novels (such as Ole Rolvaag's) of farm life on the frontier demonstrate, it was a back-breaking business. And, as one Swedish joke from Minnesota noted, men were dying of starvation at the entrance to wolves' caves — but largely beyond newspaper and camera range. The urban slums, with New York's lower East Side featured, were news. Jacob Riis's How the Other Half Lives (1890) was the first great expose of tenement squalor. Riis himself was sympathetic to the plight of the newcomers, but his vivid prose provided ammunition alike to the just and the unjust, to those who wanted conditions improved and to those who felt there was no place in the United States for (in Kipling's words) "lesser breeds without the law."

The Jewish arrivals from the Russian "Pale of Settlement" were also urban people, but not usually by choice. With a handful of exceptions (including Lev Davidovich Bronstein, a parent of Leon Trotsky), Czarist edicts banned the Jews from farming. Moreover, they constituted a new variety of Jews. The earliest synagogue in North America at Newport, Rhode Island was formed by Sephardim, descendants of Iberian Jews expelled from Spain in 1492 for their alleged complicity with the Moors and rejection of forced conversion to Christianity. Basically skilled and learned (with their own language, Ladino), they presented no assimilation problems, particularly since they were so few in number.

Next on the scene was the Jewish segment of the German immigration, which was thoroughly assimilated in German culture. They constituted, and indeed today still claim to constitute, the aristocracy of American Jewry. In ethnic terms, they were German-Americans who happened to attend a Jewish "church." (Standing on this side of the Nazi abyss, it is difficult to realize the nineteenth-century German Jews were considered, and considered themselves to be, essentially liberated from the curse of anti-Semitism.)

Finally, beginning in the 1880s, increasing in the 1890s, and turning into a flood after the savage anti-Semite von Plehve was appointed Czarist Minister of the Interior in 1902 and the Russian state increasingly encouraged pogroms by the paramilitary "Black Hundreds", came the Ashkenazim, Yiddish-speaking refugees from "The Pale of Settlement" in Russia and Russian Poland.

They were qualitatively different from every previous mass immigration. The Swedes came from Sweden, the Irish came from "occupied Ireland," but the East European Jews had no homeland. They were not "Poles," "Lithuanians," or "Russians," even though they had physically grown up in these areas. They were considered alien enclaves by the Christian natives of these regions. In other words, when they arrived on the "Golden Shore," they were not Polish- or Russian-Americans who attended a Jewish "church"; they were Jews straight from a medieval tapestry.

These "new immigrants" were to trigger demands for restrictive measures, but despite much sound and fury Congress was painfully slow to take the necessary prophylactic action. For one thing, politicians facing substantial constituencies (e.g., presidents and senators, who were still indirectly elected) were leery of alienating what they perceived as monolithic voting blocs. The lesson of "Rum, Romanism, and Rebellion," a quaint characterization of the principles of the Democratic Party propounded by a pro-Blaine preacher on the eve of the 1884 presidential election which Blaine later said cost him the New York Irish, New York's electors, and made Grover Cleveland president, was not quickly forgotten.

THE GROWTH OF RESTRICTIONS

Thus far the emphasis of legislation on immigration and naturalization has been on the quality of the individuals concerned. With the exception of the Chinese, the number of arrivals was irrelevant. The Contract Labor Law of 1885, for example, was designed to exclude people deliberately imported into the United States to depress wages (particularly in the coal fields); it did not bar Welsh coal miners who came on their own. This tradition was continued in the statute of 1891, which brought together the early categories of exclusion (idiots, paupers, etc.) and added polygamists, persons convicted of crimes involving moral turpitude, and – as a further buttress to the Contract Labor Act – those whose passage had been paid by others. However, persons convicted of political offenses were excluded from the criminal category.

Far more important was the federalization of the regulation of immigration by the 1891 measure. The office of Superintendent of Immigration was established, and national officials took over the management of the arrival process, inspecting immigrants to assure that they met standards set by law. At this point Ellis Island entered American history as the inspection station in New York where most immigrants debarked. To emphasize the obvious, it is quite amazing that until 1891 the whole immigration and naturalization process was virtually ignored by the federal government, and – as will be seen – the assertion of full authority did not occur until World War I.

There were a few more additions to the categories of exclusion (anarchists after the murder of President McKinley, prostitutes, and potential prostitutes – girls brought here with a view to their debauchery!) and various attempts to tighten administration, but with the exception of the earlier Chinese Exclusion Act and President Theodore Roosevelt's 1907 "Gentlemen's Agreement" which forestalled a "Japanese Exclusion Act" by voluntary arrangement with Tokyo limiting the number of Japanese immigrants, the laws remained nonracist in character.

What is surprising in retrospect is that this tradition lasted as long as it did. Nativist pressures, growing in the late 1880s, became enormous in the next three decades. Congress became the focus for exposing the evils of unlimited immigration. In 1888 the House appointed a select committee, chaired by Melbourne H. Ford of Michigan, to investigate the state of our immigration laws. The Committee turned in a damning report, suggesting that idiots, paupers, criminals, drunks, and other riffraff were annually slipping in by the thousands. Indeed, foreign states were deliberately shipping their poor and emptying their prisons on boats to America.

Ford's defeat in the election of 1888 may have calmed congressional opinion a bit, but in 1889 both the Senate and House created Committees of Immigration and Naturalization. These bodies pretty well eschewed the inflammatory rhetoric of the Ford inquiry, but set to work on what became the Act of 1891. However, the singular coalition of nativists received an immense impersonal boost from the Depression of 1892, which led both the Democratic and Republican parties to include in their political platforms planks calling for legislation restricting immigration. Thus we come to the new standard that American immigration policy should regulate both quality and quantity, a standard accepted by Irish Catholic unionists (in defense of their jobs) and the American Protective Association which, inter alia, condemned the power of the "immigrant vote, under the direction of certain ecclesiastical institutions."

It would be tedious to catalog the seemingly endless congressional investigations into immigration which enlivened the pre-World War I period. It is enough to say that this era saw the enthronement of racism in American public policy (the "separate but equal" doctrine, confining blacks to the "Jim Crow" car, was formulated by the Supreme Court in Plessy v. Ferguson, 1896) and in "social science."

Columbia's distinguished political scientist, John W. Burgess, announced in a widely used textbook that

> the Teutonic nations. . .are intrusted (sic), in the general economy of history, with the mission of conducting the political civilization of the modern world. The further conclusions of practical politics from this proposition must be, that in a state whose population is composed of a variety of nationalities the Teutonic element, where dominant should never surrender the balance of political power. . . .Under certain circumstances it should not even permit participation of the other elements in political power.

There were certain problems defining the "master race." "Teutons," "Aryans," "Nordics," and even a few "Celts" argued the issue among themselves. But if there was no full agreement on who belonged to the club, there was unanimity in spotting the untermenschen – the Asians, dark Southern and Eastern Europeans, and the Jews. Those interested in this anthropological witches' sabbath are referred to the 42 volumes published in Washington in 1911 by Senator William P. Dillingham's official Immigration Commission. Although the towering Italian social theorist Gaetano Mosca had deductively demolished the concept of "race" in his Elementi (1893), and 1911 saw the publication of the immigrant anthropologist Franz Boas's savage excoriation of racialism, The Mind of Primitive Man, the pack was loose in the land.

Sometimes the logic was a bit exotic. An Italian could resent being stereotyped as inclined to crime and violence, but what was a Jew to do when accused of communism and, particularly by the Populist reformers, of plutocratic greed? (Frank Norris's standard oppressor of the poor in his anti-capitalist protest novels was a "Rothchildean" Jew.) At a deeper level, perhaps many advocates of the "Old America," that Jeffersonian dream of the bucolic utopia of farmers and artisans, found in the Jew the amalgam of those forces of industrial society which made them obsolete. The capitalist and the communist are, after all, opposite sides of the same coin, creatures of a new order undermining the Jeffersonian ideal. This was, however, not particularly comforting to the average East European Jewish immigrant. It was all very well to be an archtype in the mind of, say, Henry Adams, or maybe even an honor. However, you may be neither a capitalist nor a communist, but just a man looking for a job and a decent life.

In statistical terms, from the nativist standpoint immigrants from Southern and Eastern Europe outnumbered the "nordics" in the 1890s by about 2 million to 1.5; however, in the first decade of this century the floodgates broke. The respective figures jumped to 6.25 million to about 2; and in the teens, before the War turned off the tap, the ratio was approximately 4 to 1. In net terms over this 30-year period, 3.5 million "Nordics" were swamped by 11.5 million alleged "untermenschen."

A FOOTNOTE ON NATIVE AMERICANS

As the sentiment that the new immigrants should "go back where they come from" coagulated to reach a critical mass after World War I, there is the question of the Native Americans, the Indians, who in theory at least had the right to issue this injunction to immigrants old and new. For most of the nineteenth century their legal status remained in a limbo established by Chief Justice John Marshall in Cherokee Nation v. Georgia (1831). The Cherokees were attempting to defend their treaty rights against Georgia (supported by President Andrew Jackson), but Marshall held they had no right to bring suit in a federal court.

The Chief Justice, as his subsequent decision in Worcester v. Georgia (1832) which brought a thunderbolt from Jackson indicated, was not unsympathetic to the tribe. But he could find no basis for federal jurisdiction under the terms of Article III of the Constitution and baptized the Cherokees, and by the principle of fungibility all other Indian tribes, a "domestic dependent nation." This may have paid off occasionally. Indian tribes allied with the Confederacy made separate peace treaties with the United States in which they were reimbursed for their slaves. But in general it was thoroughly unjust and unjustified, particularly as Indians left reservations and joined the population at large.

In 1884, such an individual (John Elk – a detribalized or "civilized" Indian resident of Omaha, Nebraska) was denied the right to vote. He took his case to the Supreme Court which in Elk v. Wilkins (1884), following Marshall's lead, found that he had not been born a citizen under the Fourteenth Amendment. He was born in the United States, but not "subject to the jurisdiction thereof." The Justices added that an Indian who "wanted to take the white man's road" would have to get Congressional sanction. Only Congress would determine whether he qualified to be "let out of the state of pupilage."

In 1881 Congress voted down a provision granting citizenship to "civilized" Indians – those who left their tribes to take up private agricultural allotments. Following Elk v. Wilkins, Congress returned to the matter and, in 1886, passed a measure providing individual plots and granting citizenship (in the words of its Senate sponsor) to "those Indians and those only who have taken allotments under this bill, and those born within the United States who have taken up residence separate and apart from any tribe of Indians therein and have adopted the habits of civilized life."

In practice, "civilized" Indian citizens were subject to roughly the same pernicious legal discriminations as free black citizens, a policy that continued even after a 1924 statute granted citizenship to all Indians.

THE CONSTITUTION AND THE FLAG

Finally, before moving to the great transformation in immigration policy, brief attention should be paid to the status of the inhabitants of Hawaii and, subsequently, the islands acquired from Spain at the end of the Spanish-American War. Here the problems fell under the headings of citizenship and civil rights. Without investigating the arcane details, suffice it to say that the Supreme Court in an orgy of improvisation known as The Insular Cases (leading cases: Downes v. Bidwell, 1901, and Hawaii v. Mankicki, 1903) differentiated between "incorporated" and "unincorporated" territories. The basis of distinction became esoteric at times, but the outcome was that "the Constitution followed the flag" to incorporated territories, while only the "spirit of the Constitution" made a landfall in unincorporated ones.

Here we can contrast the rights of a citizen of the territory of Alaska (Rasmussen v. United States, 1905) and of the territory of Porto Rico – Puerto Rico after 1932. Did they both have the same constitutional rights? The Supreme Court said no (Balzac v. Porto Rico, 1922). The evidence did not indicate that Congress in the Organic Act of 1917 (which conferred citizenship on Puerto Ricans) intended to create an incorporated territory. Thus while an Alaskan under the auspices of the Sixth Amendment was entitled to Anglo-Saxon jury trial, a Puerto Rican – as long as his fundamental right to justice was respected – could be tried without a jury. The Court was never persuaded precisely to define the outward and visible manifestations of incorporation.

THE GREAT TRANSFORMATION

With these odds and ends out of the way, we can turn to the great transformation, the shift to a restrictive immigration policy that accompanied the xenophobia of World War I and was set in concrete in the early postwar years. The nativists had been attacking the loyalty of the newcomers for decades, but were frustrated by the absence of a catalyst. To put it differently, as long as American foreign policy incorporated continentalism, or hemispherism, European immigrants faced no conflicts in allegiance.

French immigrants (of whom there were few) could, for example, be outraged at German-Americans over the Franco-Prussian War, but since the United States had no policy on the issue – and indeed was foreclosed by the Monroe Doctrine from intervening in the affairs of the "Old World" – their fury was of no consequence to the American authorities. It was true that during the Mexican War a few Irish-American soldiers had been persuaded to desert to the Catholic side, but the members of this San Patricio Battalion were captured and summarily hanged by General Winfield Scott and obliterated from the sagas of the Irish in America.

In short, membership in the Irish Republican Brotherhood, or the Sons of Italy, or any of the hundreds of immigrant organizations reflected no failure of American allegiance. As long as the United States followed President John Quincy Adams's dictum that we are "the friends of liberty everywhere, but custodians only of our own," there could be no pressure on adopted citizens to choose between their mother country and their new homeland. This was not entirely an accident. There is reason to believe that Adams, as Secretary of State and chief architect of the Monroe Doctrine, wanted to keep European broils (notably the hot issue of Greek independence) out of American politics. Hence the self-denying ordinance incorporated in the Doctrine.

World War I changed this background and, as the Wilson administration moved further and further from neutrality towards intervention, provided the nativists with their weapon. Once the United States declared war in April 1917, it was open season against "hyphenates" (see the cartoon below), immigrants who retained even the slightest affection for enemy lands. This was a significant chunk of the population that included first and second generation German-Americans, and, on a different axis, segments of both Irish and Jews. The latter groups were not so much pro-German as anti-British and anti-Czarist, respectively. The brutal British suppression of the Easter Rising of 1916 alienated Fenian element in the Irish-American community, but their agitation was effectively muffled by the powerful and conservative Catholic Church, which ordered automatic excommunication for members of the Sinn Fein. Similarly, the Russian Jews' opposition to Czarist anti-Semitism was alleviated by the Russian Democratic Revolution in March 1917.

The amount of actual disloyalty in the immigrant population was trivial, but there was enough symbolism to provide Theodore Roosevelt,

The Hyphenated Americans—" By hier iss Neutral!"   (65)

Ill. 2.2.

Source: Boardman Robinson, <u>Cartoons on the War</u>, New York, 1915.

a roaring nativist and Anglophile, with ammunition for hundreds of furious speeches. After all, what had America come to when in 1914 and 1915 Germans and Irish gathered in Brooklyn parks for picnics celebrating British defeats? How could that spineless Woodrow Wilson (who was in fact a Southern racist) tolerate pro-Kaiser parades and public attacks on the righteousness of Britain's cause by German-American spokesmen? Theodore Roosevelt and his adjutant, Elihu Root, were in a continuous state of apoplexy. Indeed, careful analysis of returns in the presidential election of 1916 has suggested a cosmic irony. Theodore Roosevelt's readmission to the Republican Party after his 1912 safari as the Progressive candidate for president probably led German-American voters to opt for Wilson ("He kept us out of war!") over Charles Evans Hughes, the astute Republican who correctly viewed T.R. as a loose cannon on the gun deck.

The nativist and particularly anti-German excesses of the War years have been chronicled in detail. Suffice it to say that the country was swept by temporary insanity which led to barring German from school curricula, renaming streets, parks, and German-Americans, and converting sauerkraut to "Liberty cabbage" and Hamburgers to "Liberty-burgers." The national government played a minimal role in this vigilantism — President Wilson considered it in poor taste — but state and local governments more than took up the slack. What occurred, including the summary deportation of "radicals" during the "Red Scare," was the most disgraceful episode in the history of American pluralism.

In legislative terms, nativism came to a head in February 1917, when Congress changed and codified all nationality statutes. There were two key additions to existing law and practice; the requirement that immigrants over 16 be literate, and the formal creation of the "barred zone" designed to cut off entry by "Asiatics." The definition of Asiatics was a bit bizarre. There was a hole in the exclusionary zone to accommodate such presumed "Aryans" as the Persians and their mountainous neighbors in Afghanistan and the Russian Caucasus. This enactment launched a flood of litigation in the course of which high caste Brahmins, Parsees, and others technically from the barred zone were held by federal courts to be admissable whites.

President Wilson was no admirer of the immigrant masses welcomed by Emma Lazarus and the Statue of Liberty, but he knew where the Northern Democracy got its votes and vetoed the bill because of the literacy test. His first veto, like those of Presidents Cleveland and Taft before him, stuck, but on the second round Wilson's veto was overruled by Congress. The literacy test alone was the point at issue; nobody seemed disturbed by the barred zone, presumably because few voters hailed from Java, Burma, or the other excommunicated areas. The period from 1917 to 1920 also saw the passage of a number of punitive measures aimed at aliens and sedition mongers, but the repressive spasm ended as quickly as it flared up when Harding was elected.

THE QUOTA SYSTEM

In the immediate aftermath of the War, Congress was quite disturbed by the possibility of Europeans fleeing the ravaged countries to succor in America. The House aimed at an immigration moratorium and, after a number of periods were debated, settled on two years. The Senate took a different route and produced a bill limiting immigration to three percent of the 1910 foreign-born population. This the House accepted, but in the dying days of his administration Wilson pocket vetoed the measure. A month later Warren G. Harding was in the White House, a man who on both personal and political grounds took seriously the dire warnings from Congressional committees that eight million Germans and every Jew in Poland were looking for steamship tickets. The barred zone would not suffice and most were literate in German or Yiddish. A new exclusionary mechanism had to be devised.

Initially, as a stopgap, the three percent law was reenacted, with Harding's approval in 1921. This time, rather than dealing in macro-statistics, the lawmakers limited the three percent to members of the appropriate nationality group. For example, no more than three percent of the foreign-born Italians resident in 1910 could be admitted. In 1910, there were 1,343,125 residents in this category. There was almost an identical number of Irish and 2,311,237 Germans. More broadly, in 1910 there were over four million in the census category "Northwestern Europe," but only a million and a half from "Southern Europe." The dice were loaded in favor of "old immigrants" and, in fact, most of the 350,000 aliens who entered yearly under this act were from "North-western Europe."

As far as the Polish Jews were concerned, a fictive "Polish" resident figure of 937,884 was established for 1910. As the Census footnote put it, "Persons reported in 1910 as of Polish mother tongue born in Austria, Germany, or the U.S.S.R. have been deducted from their respective countries and combined as Poland." Since most Polish Jews spoke Yiddish and stubbornly rejected Polish and Russian, one can only wonder in what statistical secret drawer they were hidden.

The three percent proviso would seem on its face an adequate barrier to any massive influx of untermenschen but one should not underestimate the sense of panic or the inventiveness of the nativists, now in full control of the government. From 1921 to 1924 the Northern Democrats, deserted on this issue by their white supremacist Southern colleagues, fought a desperate holding action against still another change in the statistical base. Without questioning the sincerity of those desperately holding off what was in their view the "mongreliza-tion" of the American population, the Congressional debates still make disconcerting reading.

The dissenting Democrats were in fact on solid scientific ground when they stated that "The obvious purpose of this discrimination is the adoption of an unfounded anthropological theory that the nations (favored by the quota system) are the progeny of fictitious and hitherto unsuspected Nordic ancestors. . . .No scientific evidence worthy of consideration was introduced to substantiate this pseudo-scientific proposition. . . .It is pure fiction and the creation of a journalistic imagination." However, the nativists could deal easily with this. After all, Representative Adolph Joachim Sabath, author of the Minority Report opposing the 1924 proposal, was a Czech-born ward heeler from Chicago, precisely the type of person their measure was designed to exclude.

The measure of their inventiveness appears in the replacement of the 1910 resident base for employment in tandem with the quota by the flagrantly existential concept of "national origin." John Jacob Rogers, Representative from Massachusetts, obviously felt that 1910 or even 1890 (another cutoff date frequently discussed) was too lenient. Quotas should be determined on the basis of national origins, presumably running back to 1607. To make a long and windy story short, in 1924 Rogers's formula won the day. The 1924 Act, though not fully implemented until 1929, provided that the annual quota for any nationality "shall be a number of inhabitants in continental United States in 1920 having that national origin, bears to the number of inhabitants in continental United States in 1920."

Thus in 1920 there were 106,466,000 Americans. If 75 percent of them were however remotely descended from "Northwestern European" stock, 112,000 immigrants would be admitted from these nations. The rest of the old world could divide up the remaining 38,000 (Western hemisphere nations were exempt) in similar fashion except that Rogers did, in a generous moment, provide a minimum quota of 100 for any nationality (excluding, of course, those hailing from the barred zone and other Asians). With minor modifications — during World War II our Chinese, Filipino, and Indian allies were awarded token quotas and the right to citizenship — this remarkable statute remained in effect until 1965, when the national origins system was phased out effective July 1, 1968. How the Census Bureau determined the national origins of our 1920 populace remains a state secret.

The implementation of the national origins system coincided with the advent of the Great Depression. Thus, for some time its impact was hardly noticeable. Indeed, during the depths of the Depression the intake of immigrants was for three years in virtual equilibrium (at around 35,000) with disappointed returnees. In cold-blooded terms, a United States without welfare, food stamps, and other national spon-sored and funded poverty programs did not then offer such incentives for the poor elsewhere as exist in the 1980s. Why go to the United States to starve? As the end of the Depression meshed with the outbreak of World War II, our immigration policy continued virtually unnoticed and unchallenged.

True, there were efforts to mitigate its severity on behalf of anti-Fascist refugees, notably — after Hitler's anti-Semitic policies became evident — Jews. Various organizations were formed to provide succor, particularly for distinguished European intellectuals, whose arrival and contributions to American culture and science constituted Hitler's one good deed toward the United States. But they constituted a mere handful of those in jeopardy, and an objective analyst can only feel a sense of shame at the callousness of the American people, from Franklin D. Roosevelt on down. In psychological terms, the Depression made the United States autistic. In economic terms, it became aut-archic.

Perhaps the point was made most vividly by an American scholar who as a child escaped from Austria after the Nazi takeover. His working-class Jewish relatives, originally from Austrian Poland, applied in 1938 for visas to the United States. They were informed that under the operation of the appropriate quota, their numbers would come up in 1954. In 1943 they were gassed in Auschwitz.

Probably the most macabre incident in this genre occurred in 1940 when a ship loaded with Jews escaped from Vichy France was turned away by Mexico and put into Norfolk, Virginia, for coal and, hopefully, asylum for the passengers. The State Department ordered the ship to return to France, Jewish organizations mobilized, and only after the intervention of Eleanor Roosevelt were the refugees given temporary asylum and the death sentence reprieved. However, in general, Assistant Secretary of State Breckenridge Long, whose diaries limn the mind of a paranoidal anti-Semite, kept the gates securely barred. The spirit of Vice President Calvin Coolidge, who in 1921 noted that "biological laws show us that Nordics deteriorize when mixed with other races," had triumphed in the land.

Internally World War II saw little of the xenophobia that characterized World War I, with one appalling exception – the treatment of the Japanese minority. In 1942, at a time of hysteria and rumors of sabotage by Japanese and Japanese-Americans (immigrant Japanese were still ineligible for citizenship), about 115,000, both foreign and native-born citizens, members of this group living on the West Coast were "relocated" in prison camps in the interior.

In Hawaii, by contrast, where the Japanese minority was very substantial, no special action was taken, although the islands were put under ethnically impartial martial law. With a handful of exceptions, the Japanese, both Issei (Japanese-born) and Nisei (native citizens), reacted with amazing patriotism. The Nisei in particular volunteered for the Army and fought valiantly in Italy. Indeed, the 442nd Regimental Combat Team (Mainland) and 100th Infantry Battalion (Hawaii) were among the most decorated units of the European War.

In Korematsu v. United States (1945) the Supreme Court sustained the legality of this treatment as an act of military necessity. However, as the early rumors of sabotage and espionage were refuted, largely by the Roberts Commission investigating the Pearl Harbor attack, the American people, in a somewhat shamefaced way, welcomed the Japanese into the greater society. Indeed, paradoxically, the relocation served to diffuse the continental Japanese throughout the nation (ninety percent had lived on the West Coast, notably California, before the war).

By 1980, it might be noted, Hawaii has become a Japanese-American political duchy. Both Senators, the Governor, and one of the two Representatives are Nisei. The 1942 expulsion and incarceration was a fearful ordeal for 115,000 people essentially accused (but never tried) for the crime of possessing "enemy chromosomes." Fortunately it was wholly atypical of the state of civil liberties in World War II America.

At the end of World War II the country again faced the refugee problem and again refused seriously to consider the existential anguish of displaced persons (DPs) wandering around Europe. Without suggesting for a moment that we should have taken them all sight unseen – there were fair-sized groups of Ukranian, Estonian, Croatian, and other Fascists who probably merited even Communist-style justice – we could at least have demonstrated national consciousness of the nature of the problem. Instead, some special arrangements were made, the first (predictably) exempting war brides, later expanded to fiancees of servicemen, from quota provisions. As far as DPs were concerned,

President Truman managed to admit some 40,000 in December 1945, by special administrative improvisation. It was not until 1948 that Congress opened the gates to an additional 200,000, but the quota principle remained intact by "mortgaging" future quotas to admit this influx. And the measure was rigged against Jews. As President Truman noted when he signed it with "very great reluctance," the statute was "flagrantly discriminatory."

Profoundly unhappy with this eccentric measure (30 percent of those admitted had to qualify as "farmers"!), the liberals went back to the legislative drawing board and in 1950 managed to enact a far more generous Displaced Persons Act which removed most of the bizarre provisions of its predecessor. The restrictions managed to retain the mortgage provision as a symbol of continued dedication to quotas (this was disposed of later), but another 400,000 DPs were admitted. It might be noted as a historical aside that the predicted post-War depression, which had provided the restrictionists with a horrendous argument about increasing domestic unemployment, never occurred. Therefore much of the labor movement's earlier support for barriers dissipated and the restrictionist coalition was severely undermined.

Immigration and nationality legislation in the 1950s and early 1960s can be summarized rapidly. As the Cold War chill set in, there were numerous alarms and excursions about subversive immigrants that crystallized in the McCarran-Walter Act of 1952. This added little in the way of positive policy, but a good deal to the repressive arsenal — expatriation, denaturalization, deportation. On the other side, DPs began to get a warmer reception as they took flight from Communist regimes. A Refugee Relief Act passed almost without dissent in 1953, and in the wake of the tragic Hungarian Revolution of 1956 President Dwight Eisenhower employed an existing device designed for individuals (a "parole") to admit 40,000 Hungarian Freedom-Fighters. Utilizing both administrative and legislative means, the Kennedy Administration authorized the entry of over half a million anti-Castro Cubans.

THE DEMISE OF NATIVIST LAW

By the mid-1960s, it was clear that the concept of "national origins" was a bad idea whose time had passed. As noted, during World War II the barred zone had been penetrated to the extent of making our Chinese, Filipino, and Indian allies honorary Caucasians. As the decolonization process accelerated in the post-war period, the position of the United States as the model democracy and bastion of the free world was patently compromised by relics of our once pervasive racism. In 1954 the Supreme Court took a major step by overruling the body of precedent that legitimated racial segregation in American law; the Constitution was finally "color blind." It only remained to bring our nationality legislation into accord with the increasingly egalitarian American ethos.

Restrictionism died, in T.S. Eliot's phrase, "not with a bang, but a whimper." Indeed, after recording this chronicle one has virtually a sense of physical shock at the anticlimax. The Hart-Celler Act of 1965 was part of the flood of reforms passed in the Johnson presidency, measures damned up for many years by the conservative coalition of Southern Democrats and Republicans that was temporarily blitzed in the 1964 election. The initial vote on the new measure was 318-95 in the House, and 78-16 in the Senate; the final version as tailored in Conference Committee passed the Senate on an unrecorded voice vote, and by 320-69 in the House. President Johnson signed it at the base of the Statue of Liberty.

The 1965 statute eliminated the Asia-Pacific barred zone, phased out over a three-year period the national origins quota system, set an overall limit of 170,000 immigrants from the Eastern Hemisphere, and — for the first time — a limit (120,000) on Western Hemisphere admissions. No more than 20,000 could come from any Eastern Hemisphere nation in a given year. These were the broad strokes, but there were enough small ones to provide immigration lawyers with full employment for generations. For example, percentage categories were established. Twenty percent of the intake was set aside for unmarried adult children of American citizens, 20 percent for immediate relatives of aliens admitted to permanent residence, 24 percent for brothers and sisters of citizens, 10 percent for persons with needed skills, 6 percent for political refugees.

In theory, this left but 20 percent to the open field, but these were combined with all unused slots in the preferred categories and visas were to be passed out on a first-come, first-served basis. There have been a number of amendments since, most designed to clarify, or create further need for clarification of, specific provisos. The only one of substance applied in 1976 the 20,000 per country maximum to the Western Hemisphere. Naturally enough, a statute of this complexity has given birth to an immense body of administrative law and interpretation, the details of which should be ascertained from the Immigration and Naturalization Service.

To conclude, there is a general consensus that the 1965 law as amended has provided the United States with an equitable immigration system in concord with our democratic ideals. Now, however, the focus of concern in the whole area has shifted from the legal aspects of nationality to the increasingly serious problem of "illegals" — illegal immigrants, mainly Mexican, whose number is estimated at perhaps five million. While it is unjust to accuse, say, Mexico or various West Indian states of deliberately exporting their unemployed to the United States, the latter have aroused great concern, particularly in the trade union movement. Many illegals live in virtual serfdom, whether as agricultural workers or housemaids, because any efforts on their part to obtain decent conditions or employment, a statutory minimum wage, social security, or public assistance will lead to their arrest and deportation.

The Immigration and Naturalization Service, which has been evicting about half a million illegals a year and in fiscal year 1976 to 1977 blocked over a million Mexicans attempting illegal entry, finds the task uniquely frustrating. No American in his right mind wants an East German-style border zone, complete with barbed wire, mind fields and automatic machine guns, along the Mexican border. However, without such monstrosities, it is virtually unpoliceable. Latest efforts, therefore, have approached the problem for the other end by attempting to penalize Americans who hire illegals thus paralleling the early laws penalizing shipmasters who brought in undesirable aliens. An act of 1974, for instance, made it criminal for a farm labor contractor "knowingly" to hire an illegal alien (farm labor contractors were already required to register with the government), but a first-year law student knows the difficulties in proving "scienter," i.e., that a criminal act was knowingly undertaken.

Various states have tried to tighten the provision by throwing the whole burden of proof on the employer, that is, assuming him guilty unless he has conclusive proof to the contrary. These enactments in turn have generated litigation on the right of a state to intrude in federal jurisdiction over aliens and other complex matters. Thus the law is thoroughly unclear and unsettled. The Carter Administration's effort to combine an amnesty for illegals long resident in the United States with more stringent federal regulation of employers is currently wandering around in the Congressional labyrinth.

Yet, as a terminal note, it is important to realize that disputes over current national policy have few racial overtones. No one seriously objects to the 20,000 Mexicans or Jamaicans who can legally immigrate. On the contrary, the objections are founded on concern for the quality of American life, and the closely related thrust for zero population growth. This reinforces the central theme of this analysis. The history of our immigration and nationality policy is in microcosm the history of the United States.

BIBLIOGRAPHY

The data here utilized have been drawn from possibly 300 or 400 original and secondary sources, including the Journals of the Continental Congress, the Congressional Record (in its varying titles), House and Senate Committee Reports, Territorial Papers of the United States; Historical Statistics of the United States: Colonial Times to 1970, 2 vols., Department of Commerce, Bureau of the Census, 1975; my greatest debt is to my 30 years of research incorporated, inter alia, below.

The Early Development of United States Citizenship. Ithaca: Cornell University Press, 1949.

"Prestatutory Denaturalization," Cornell Law Quarterly 25 (1949): 120.

"Loss of American Nationality: The Years of Confusion." Western Political Quarterly 4 (1951): 268.

"The Loss of American Nationality: The Development of Statutory Expatriation," University of Pennsylvania Law Review 99 (1950): 25.

"Statutory Denaturalization," University of Pittsburgh Law Review 13 (1952): 276.
The Quest for the Dream: The Development of Civil Rights and Human Relations in Modern America. New York: Macmillan, 1963.
"The Expatriation Cases." In Supreme Court Review -- 1963, 325 edited by Kurland. Chicago: University of Chicago Press, 1964.
Shadow and Substance. New York: Macmillan, 1964.
Courts and Rights. 2nd ed. New York: Random House, 1966.
Sentenced to Life. New York: Macmillan, 1974.

Other valuable works on various aspects of the chronicle include:

Abbott, Edith. Historical Aspects of the Immigration Process. Chicago: University of Chicago Press, 1926.
Berlin, Ira. Slaves without Masters: The Free Negro in the Antebellum South. New York: Pantheon, 1974.
Chase, Allan. The Legacy of Malthus: The Social Costs of the New Scientific Realism. New York: Knopf, 1976.
Divine, Robert A. American Immigration Policy, 1924-1952. New Haven: Yale University Press, 1957.
Graham, Howard J. Everyman's Constitution. Madison: State Historical Society of Wisconsin, 1968.
Handlin, Oscar. The Uprooted. Boston: Little, Brown, 1951.
Handlin, Oscar. Race and Nationality in American Life. Boston: Little, Brown, 1957.
Handlin, Oscar. Immigration as a Factor in American Life. New York: Prentice-Hall, 1959.
Higham, John. Strangers in the Land. New Brunswick: Rutgers University Press, 1955.
Keller, Moton. Affairs of State. Cambridge: Harvard University Press, 1977.
Morgan, Edmund S., American Slavery – American Freedom. New York: Norton, 1975.
Preston, William, Jr. Aliens and Dissenters. Cambridge: Harvard University Press, 1963.
Smith, Abbot E. Colonists in Bondage. Chapel Hill: North Carolina University Press, 1947.
Smith, James. Freedom's Fetters. Ithaca: Cornell University Press, 1956.
Solomon, Barbara M. Ancestors and Immigrants. Cambridge: Harvard University Press, 1956.
Wells, Robert. The Population of the British Colonies in America before 1776. Princeton, N.J.: Princeton University Press, 1975.
Williams, Robin M. American Society. New York: A.A. Knopf, 1954.

3 The "Human Resource" Problem in Europe: Migrant Labor in the Federal Republic of Germany

Ursula Mehrlaender

THE LABOR MARKET AND MIGRANT WORKERS: GERMANY

Between 1952 and 1955, the unemployment rate in the Federal Republic of Germany fell from 9.5 percent to 5.6 percent, while the number of job vacancies rose from about 120,000 to 200,000.(1)

Because of the increasing demand for labor, German firms were forced to look abroad for unemployed or underemployed workers. At the same time, the rapid upswing in German production had a magnetic effect on citizens of other countries in which economic development was progressing more slowly.

Consequently, in-migration of individual foreign workers from such countries into the Federal Republic of Germany increased. By the end of July 1955, about 80,000 foreign nationals already were employed in the FRG. In the light of this trend, Italy, having embarked upon economic negotiations with Germany, urged the conclusion of an agreement on the recruitment and dispatch of surplus Italian labor to Germany. The Federal Republic accepted this proposal because of the continued marked shortage of labor, mainly in agriculture and partly also in the building industry.(2)

The conclusion of the agreement on recruitment was preceded, however, by consultations among relevant German agencies, including the Federal Government, representatives of the Federal Employment Agency, the employers, and the trade unions. The employers were interested primarily in reaching a decision in principle to encourage

Publisher's note: The type employed in this book made utilization of diacritical marks unfeasible. Consequently, the German umlaut has been rendered as "ae," "oe," or "ue," respectively, in accordance with traditional practice, while French accents have been omitted, and so have diacritical marks in the case of Turkish, Czech, and other names.

recruitment of foreign workers. In contrast, the trade unions foresaw the danger that (nonunion) labor might be utilized to keep wages down, and, for that reason, demanded that foreign workers should be accorded the same rights with regard to wages and social benefits as their German counterparts. The unions reached agreement on this point with the Federal Government and the employers' representatives.(3)

Following these developments, the recruitment agreement between the government of the Federal Republic of Germany and the government of the Republic of Italy was concluded on December 20, 1955. This agreement with Italy has to be viewed, however, in the light of Articles 48 and 49 of the treaty establishing the European Economic Community, and of Regulation No. 38/64 EEC and/or directives 64/240 EEC and 64/221 EEC. These are the regulations concerning freedom of movement of workers from the member states. Citizens of the member countries of the European Community enjoy the right, in principle, to reside in any other member state. They require a labor permit for working purposes, but they have a legal claim to receive such permission. These EEC regulations were taken into account in a revision of the recruitment agreement on February 24, 1965.(4)

Between 1955 and 1960, the unemployment rate in the Federal Republic of Germany fell from 5.6 percent to 1.3 percent. At the same time, there was a marked increase in the number of job vacancies. During this period, the employment of foreign workers in the Federal Republic tripled. At the end of July 1960, about 280,000 foreign citizens were employed in the Federal Republic of Germany, of which roughly 44 percent were Italian.

Greeks, Spaniards, Yugoslavs, and Turks, however, also were working in the Federal Republic by this time. This development led to agreements between the Federal Republic of Germany and Spain (1960), Greece (1960), Turkey (1961) and Portugal (1964). The employment of Tunisians in the Federal Republic of Germany has been regulated contractually since 1965. In March of 1966, an earlier (May 1963) agreement with Morocco, on the temporary employment of Moroccan nationals in Germany, was revised and extended in scope. The final agreement of this kind on the recruitment of foreign workers was concluded in 1968 between the Federal Republic of Germany and Yugoslavia.(5)

Encouraged by the development of the economy and spurred by these various recruitment agreements, the number of foreign workers employed in the Federal Republic of Germany rose from about 280,000 (1960) to 1.2 million (1965), i.e., to 5.5 percent of the total labor force. The unemployment rate, in the same period, had fallen to 0.7 percent while the number of job vacancies had risen to 650,000.(6) However, due to the recession of 1966 and 1967, the total number of foreign citizens working in the FRG declined to about 900,000 by January of 1968. New recruitment ceased almost entirely. The number of unemployed rose from 160,000 in 1966 to 460,000 in 1967, while the number of openings available fell by 240,000 (to 300,000).(7) Subsequent years, however, witnessed an economic upswing, so that employers increased their demand for labor. Thus, the employment of foreign citizens rose continuously from early 1968 to the fall of 1973. At the end of September 1973, 2.6 million foreign workers, some 12 percent of the overall labor force, were employed in the Federal Republic of Germany. The number of unemployed fell to 150,000 in 1970, but then rose once more to 270,000 by 1973. The number of job vacancies rose to 800,000 in 1970, but fell again to 570,000 by 1973.(8)

Until 1973, the Bonn government had left employment of foreign citizens almost entirely to regulation by market forces. The recession beginning at the end of 1973, exacerbated by the oil crisis with its accompanying mass unemployment, caused the FRG to abandon the policy of entrusting the recruitment of foreign workers to the requirements of industry. A decision to halt recruitment came into force at the end of November 1973, and this approach has been maintained to the present. The continued unfavorable situation of the labor market is the most obvious reason for the current policy. The number of unemployed (Germans and foreign citizens) rose to 1.2 million by December 1975, and the unemployment rate reached 5.3 percent, while the number of openings available dropped to 170,000.(9)

The end of recruitment meant that, despite the various international agreements on this topic, no more foreign workers were being recruited for positions in the Federal Republic of Germany. This policy exempted citizens of member states of the European Community, such as Italians. The number of foreign nationals employed fell from 2.59 million in September 1973, to 2.12 million in March 1975, a decline of 18.3 percent. It must be pointed out, however, that not all jobless foreign workers necessarily return to their countries of origin; many remain in Germany. By the end of December 1975, 145,000 foreign citizens in Germany were out of work, an unemployment rate of 6.3 percent. It should be added, however, that the 2.1 million figure for foreign workers (men and women) in 1975 does not include their nonemployed wives and children. Since 1975, the number of such dependents actually increased. Thus, at the end of September 1974, a total of about 4.1 million foreign citizens were living in the Federal Republic of Germany. Turks, with about 1 million, constituted the largest single national entity; Yugoslavs were second, with 700,000.(10)

THE LABOR MARKET AND MIGRANT WORKERS:
OTHER WEST EUROPEAN COUNTRIES

This study focuses on the FRG and limits comparisons to France, the Benelux countries, Switzerland, and Austria. Britain, because of its Commonwealth links, constitutes a special case. With respect to the history of employment of foreign workers, the situation in the other host countries of Western Europe is similar to that of the Federal Republic of Germany.

Economic upswing in the 1960s and demographic contraction in all the host countries precipitated the demand for foreign labor. Employment of foreign citizens increased as the economy developed up to 1966/1967. With a recession hitting Western Europe at that stage, the number of foreign workers either declined absolutely or increased at a much smaller rate. The renewed improvement in the economic situation since 1968 again caused a marked rise in the in-migration of foreign workers.

Like the Federal Republic of Germany, the other West European host governments concluded recruitment agreements with the various countries of the Mediterranean Basin. France and the Benelux states, like the Federal Republic of Germany, of course, are members of the European Community, and for citizens of the member states the principle of freedom of movement applies. However, by approximately 1973, these host countries in Western Europe – like the Federal Republic of Germany – significantly cut back, or stopped entirely, the recruitment of foreign labor. The reasons given for this move were a renewed unfavorable turn in economic development, together with high unemployment rates, in host countries; and the social problems posed by the high level of employment of foreign citizens. This means that, in general, only the nationals of European Community member states are able still to migrate within the Community. Consequently, since 1973, the number of foreign workers in these countries has been declining.

All West European host governments, like the Federal Republic of Germany, take the line that theirs are not (permanent) immigration countries. They regard the entry of foreign workers as temporary and believe that most of them will return to the countries of origin. Despite this position, the host countries have not attempted seriously to curtail the in-migration of the family members of these workers. (An exception in this regard is Switzerland). The result is that recent years have witnessed particularly heavy in-migration of families (spouse and/or children) of foreign workers.(11) The problems raised by this phenomenon and the reaction of the host countries are discussed subsequently in this chapter.

The following statistics (p. 81) are offered for purposes of comparison.

THE COUNTRIES OF ORIGIN

As is evident, most of the foreign workers employed in Western Europe originate from the Mediterranean countries. This study omits discussion of the situation in the North African states of Algeria, Morocco, and Tunisia, since most of the migrant labor from these areas is employed in one country, France, the former colonial power. Consequently, analysis is confined to Turkey, Greece, Yugoslavia, Spain, and Portugal as countries of origin. Italy, as a member state of the European Community, will be dealt with in greater detail subsequently.

The situation during the early 1960s, in the five countries of origin mentioned, may be characterized as follows. There was a high degree of unemployment; in the agricultural sector there was substantial under-

Table 3.1.

Legend: (a) Total Foreign Population (b) Total Foreign Workers (c) Annual In-migration (all in thousands)

Year	Belgium (a)	(b)	(c)	Netherlands (a)	(b)	(c)	Luxembourg (a)	(b)	(c)	France (a)	(b)	(c)	Switzerland (a)	(b)	(c)	Austria (a)	(b)	(c)
1960				107.0									580.0					
1961	450.0																11.6	
1965												160.0						
1967												280.0						
1968				180.0			62.8										62.5	
1970									2.5			220.0						
1973	775.0			280.0	150.0							275.0						
1974	805.4	520.0				In-migration halt						Recruitment ended	1,060.0				226.4	
1975													1,010.0				185.2	
1976										4,200.0	1,900.0		960.0					

Origin of For. Pop. (in order of size)

Origin	Netherlands (c)	Luxembourg (a)	France (b)	Switzerland (a)	Austria (a)
Italians — 1st		23.4	564.0	Over 50% of total	
Spaniards — 2nd		2.1	580.0	" 11% " "	
Portuguese — 3rd		5.7	850.0		
Greeks — 4th					
Yugoslavs — 5th			some		1st
Turks — 6th			some		2nd
Algerians ⎫ 7th			870.0		
Moroccans ⎬			304.0		
Tunisians ⎭			some		
Moluccans	Additional to "Foreign Workers"				
Surinamer	"			⎫	
Antilles	"			⎬ 20% " "	
Germans	"				
French	"			⎭	
Austrians	"				

Sources: See notes 12–21.

employment; per capita incomes were low; and balance of payment deficits were the rule.

Under these circumstances, the countries of origin initially regarded the out-migration of workers altogether favorably; the exportation of labor led to a reduction of the labor surplus. From the remittances sent home by their citizens, these countries obtained important foreign exchange. Finally, employment abroad was expected to improve the training of the workers concerned, ultimately creating a larger reservoir of skilled labor in the countries of origin.

In line with this positive assessment of migration, the countries of origin initially permitted individual out-migration by their citizens and then went further, attempting to promote large scale out-migration by concluding bilateral agreements with prospective host countries on recruitment of workers. However, the individual recruitment agreements between the countries of origin and the Federal Republic of Germany, for example, do not say much more than that both parties see advantages in migration and wish to promote it. The Federal Employment Agency then established German (recruitment) Commissions in the countries of origin. An advantage of the recruitment agreements was that migrating workers entered the Federal Republic of Germany with one-year employment contracts; they could not be dismissed during the first year of their residence. Moreover, their German employers had to provide accommodation. The employers also paid travel costs from the country of origin to the Federal Republic of Germany. Movement to Germany took place by means of collective transport organized by the German Commissions, which also checked out the proposed candidates' health and vocational suitability and implemented the formalities connected with employment contracts, residence permits, and work permits. This method of operation furthered a significant increase in out-migration from the countries of origin.

Apart from these recruitment agreements, most countries of origin also have concluded agreements with the host countries on matters concerning social security for their citizens. This means that the foreign workers are put on an equal rights footing with indigenous workers within existing social security systems. This holds also for health insurance, old age pensions, and so forth.

In summary, it can be stated that through the conclusion of recruitment agreements and subsequent agreements on social security, the countries of origin have achieved equality for their migrating citizens with indigenous workers, in terms of labor and social security conditions. On the other hand, they must be regarded as the weaker party in these agreements. This is the case because, in accordance with the agreements, the migration of their citizens is dependent on the labor requirements of the host countries. The host countries' own labor market conditions take priority over the agreements, and the admission of foreign workers is determined accordingly. This is illustrated very well by the current situation in which the Federal Republic of Germany was able unilaterally to stop recruitment in line with the relevant provisions of the recruitment agreements. The same applies to France and the Benelux countries. It is evident that this is likely to give rise to friction between the governments concerned.

The difficulties between host countries and states of origin that have been generated by the cessation of recruitment surely would have been greater if there had not been, at the same time, a reassessment of the whole migration question on the part of the countries of origin.

The governments of these countries have come to pay increasing attention to the negative aspects of migration. The out-migration of labor brought difficulties for their own economic development; the foreign exchange remittances of their citizens did not achieve the expected volume; and the skills of their workers abroad did not improve as much as was hoped.

The out-migration of workers to other countries did help to reduce the labor surplus, but it was mostly the young and qualified workers who moved to Western Europe. Nor was it just the unemployed who left, but also workers already well employed in their home countries. Difficulties arose in replacing these workers. Therefore, in the early 1970s, most of the countries began attempting to curb out-migration. Yugoslavia, in particular, took this course from 1973 onward, and initiated measures to encourage the repatriation of qualified workers. In Greece, the reserves of unemployed were almost depleted from 1972 on, and bottlenecks began to appear on the labor market. Some out-migration of Greeks continued, but since Germany's cessation of recruitment, the Greek net migration has declined toward zero. From 1970 to 1974, Portugal also tried to reduce out-migration.(22)

In general, there has been less foreign exchange inflow than expected because citizens of the countries of origin stayed abroad longer than expected. With increasing length of residence, these workers brought their families out to join them, thus leading to fewer remittances home. In addition, most migrant workers tend to leave their savings deposited in the banks of the host country, rather than transferring them to the countries of origin. Although some of the latter are attempting to offer incentives to make their citizens change this pattern, they have not been very successful so far. Consequently, migration no longer appears so beneficial from the point of view of foreign exchange gains and improvement on the balance of payments.

On the whole, the majority of foreign workers have not received significant vocational training in the West European host countries. Such a project, to be implemented seriously, would have entailed offering a whole program of vocational courses and education specifically designed for foreign citizens. After participating in such courses and passing the requisite examination, foreign workers would have attained fully skilled status, with the appropriate diploma entitling them, in principle, to fill the relevant openings in any firm. Of course, there were some vocational training courses for foreign workers in the Federal Republic of Germany, but, with respect to the amount of courses offered and to the number of participants, this benefitted only few foreign workers. For this reason, it may be said that vocational advancement opportunities in the host countries were available for foreign workers only on a limited scale.(23) In most cases, upon arrival in the host countries, these migrants took on openings essentially as unskilled workers. A certain number received on-the-job training in such limited areas as the operation and maintenance of a particular machine, productivity enhancement in that particular function, etc. After such elementary training, lasting perhaps one or two weeks, they advanced in status from unskilled to semiskilled workers.(24) However, it must be noted that generally they did not receive theoretical training and they did not have to pass an examination or receive diplomas. These "promotions" were valid only within the firm in which they happened to be working. In short, this type of elementary technical training does not amount to systematic qualification of the majority of foreign workers and should not be regarded as a substitute for proper vocational training or education. Therefore, the out-migration policy of the countries of origin can be justified no longer by the argument that it enhances the skills and qualifications of their labor force.

In addition, it has become plain since the early 1970s, that there are few means of inducing migrant workers to return home. Despite repeated assurances, on the part of countries of origin and host governments alike, that migration of labor would be merely temporary, no measures were provided in the various recruitment agreements to facilitate eventual organized repatriation. This omission is now showing negative effects. At the same time, the notion of a purely temporary stay of foreign workers serves the host countries as a pretext for not implementing better social measures for foreign citizens. The countries of origin, therefore, have reached the conclusion that labor migration benefits the host countries more than it does them. In part, they have begun even to view it as menacing their own economic development. As a result, the governments of countries of origin now are calling for such measures as transfer of capital and skills from the host countries. They are demanding, furthermore, that the host countries introduce and promote measures for the repatriation and the reintegration of migrant workers in the social and economic environment of their native lands. The question is, however, just how much pressure the countries of origin will be able to exert.

In the host countries some approaches have been made toward fulfilling these demands on a very small scale. Turkey, Greece, and Spain are applying for full membership in the European Community. If they achieve this objective, it would strengthen their position vis-a-vis the West European host countries (with the exception of the non-European Community members, Switzerland and Austria).

FRICTION BETWEEN COUNTRIES OF ORIGIN AND HOST GOVERNMENTS

Turkey, the country with the highest population growth rate among the countries of origin,(25) continues to be interested in exportation of

labor. This has given rise to conflict with West European host governments, which have decided to stop in-migration of foreign workers. It
should be noted at this point that, so far, Germany has taken in 80
percent of Turkish migrant labor. Given the current labor market
situation with about one million unemployed, the government of the
FRG – supported by public opinion – is not prepared to resume
recruitment of foreign labor.

At this point, reference should be made to the Agreement of
Ankara. This was concluded between Turkey and the (then six)
European Community member states in 1963. It provided for the
gradual introduction of freedom of movement within the Community
for Turks between December of 1976 and 1986. So far, the host
countries of the European Community have not been prepared to fulfill
this provision of the Agreement. Meanwhile, three new members have
joined the Community – Ireland, Britain, and Denmark. This is bound to
delay still further the introduction of freedom of movement for Turkish
workers within the Community. It can be assumed even that the
Agreement of Ankara will have to be renegotiated.(26) Friction is likely
to be generated. There is understandable disappointment on the Turkish
side at the way in which the issue is being handled.

The host countries evidently are welcoming the additional delay in
implementing the Agreement. They fear that, with the introduction of
freedom of movement, a stream of perhaps one million Turks would
flow into Western Europe, and, judging by past experience, it would
have to be assumed that most of them would end up in the Federal
Republic of Germany. It is unlikely that an additional million Turkish
workers would find employment in the FRG. The inflow of so large a
number of Turks, remaining out of work in the Federal Republic, almost
certainly would give rise to a great many serious social and political
problems. Such a development might impair German-Turkish relations
even more significantly than any renegotiation of the Agreement of
Ankara.

In its migration policy, the Italian government has tried to promote
the welfare of Italian workers abroad, with an emphasis upon general
principles of human rights. On the other hand, Italy has attempted also
to seek a reasonable balance between its own interests and those of the
host countries of western Europe.(27)

In accordance with the articles in the Treaty Establishing the
European Economic Community, the policy of the Italian government
has pursued two aims: the application of provisions granting freedom of
movement to workers within the Community, and the establishing of
priority for workers from European Community member states over
migrants from nonmember states, the so-called "third" countries.
Workers from nonmember states should be allowed to enter only if none
were available from European Community member countries.   In
addition, special access privileges to the European labor market were
sought for Italian workers. In this way, Italy sought to dispose of its
labor surplus within the Community.(28)

From the mid-1960s onward, despite freedom of movement, there was less out-migration of Italians to West European host countries than the Italian government had estimated. This led to friction with the other member states of the European Community. The Italian government suspected that the employers in the host countries were interested more in hiring workers from nonmember states than in employing Italians. It attributed this trend to the principle of equal treatment of Italian and indigenous German workers, as a result of which Italian workers are more expensive to employ than is labor from other countries of origin. Thus, despite (or because of) regulations meant to protect its citizens, Italy perceived de facto discrimination against Italian workers. In fact, the Italian government formally voiced this charge in a memorandum to the European Community in 1971. The Commission thereupon called on the other member states to present their views. A group of European Community experts was also charged with this problem.

In regard to the Federal Republic of Germany, the suspicion is unfounded that foreign workers from other countries of origin are preferred because they receive lower wages and social security contributions. Bilateral agreements rule out such practices. Italy is correct, however, in believing that the introduction of freedom of movement has brought disadvantages for Italian workers. In accordance with the previously mentioned recruitment agreement between Italy and the Federal Republic of Germany, German Commissions of the Federal Employment Agency continued to work in Verona and Naples in the 1960s. However, from 1964 onward, most Italians were entering individually rather than through the Commissions, which deprived them of the guaranteed one-year employment contract, as well as the provision of housing and the payment of travel expenses by the employers. Consequently, these Italians found themselves worse off then other foreign workers.

The only apparent possibility of resolving this conflict is to go back to "organized" or "assisted" recruitment through German commissions in Italy. Although this would curb freedom of movement for individuals, it would bring Italian workers advantages in the form of better employment conditions in the Federal Republic of Germany.

Initially, Switzerland regarded the influx of Italian workers with favor. In the economic upswing of the 1960s, more labor was required. Italy tried to secure equal rights for its citizens, as compared to Swiss workers, with regard to pay, social security insurance, and so forth. Rome desired easing of entry to Switzerland for families of workers, as well as lifting of restrictions on the acquisition of the more advantageous legal status of "resident" by Italians.(29) Switzerland reacted to these Italian proposals slowly, if at all. A social security insurance agreement with Italy was not concluded until 1962. An agreement regulating the living and working conditions of Italians in Switzerland was concluded only in 1964, after years of discussions. It met some of the Italian demands mentioned above. However, shortly thereafter, Switzerland reintroduced unilateral restrictions on immigration which rendered the 1964 agreement ineffective.(30)

With Switzerland's adoption of a policy of "gradual reduction" in employment of foreign citizens in 1970, increased tension has built up between the two governments. The pressures Italy has been able to exert are proving to be of marginal significance. In addition, various campaigns by Swiss political groups "against overalienation" have made life difficult for Italian workers in Switzerland. The economic recession also is forcing Italian workers to leave Switzerland again, despite similar economic problems in Italy.

SOCIAL PROBLEMS OF MIGRANT LABOR

Social problems experienced by foreign workers and their families are likely to cause conflict with the host population. In the case of the Federal Republic of Germany, we conducted a survey of this problem area in 1971.(31)

Nearly all foreign workers have difficulty adjusting to life in Germany. It is caused by lack of knowledge of German, poor accommodation, loneliness, homesickness, and change of food and climate. Since most foreign citizens have undergone no preparatory training in coping with such problems, they are affected considerably. More than one-half of the migrants interviewed stated that these difficulties continued to afflict them for a long time after entry into Germany. However, they cannot be held responsible for this. On the contrary, this phenomenon reflects a lack of assistance. Ongoing difficulties, in addition to those mentioned, include problems related to work and prejudices by some Germans against foreign workers. An orientation program for foreign citizens during the first few months of their stay in Germany would be very helpful. Moreover, this author's 1971 survey showed that 30 percent of foreign workers had no one with whom they could consult in case of need, and 40 percent could discuss their problems only with their next of kin. It is obvious that more guidance and assistance for foreign workers is required in order to diminish these difficulties of adjustment.(32)

The majority of foreign workers did not have the same occupation in their countries of origin as in Germany. Only about 30 percent of those who were working in their native land are employed in the same division of industry in Germany. Some do not even fall within the same job classification in the Federal Republic of Germany as in the country of origin. Some foreign citizens – mostly women – do not have any experience in industry and their ideas about industrial work are unrealistic. One-fifth of the foreign workers said they felt disappointment during the first few weeks they worked for their new firm, apparently because of inadequate prior information and preparation for German working conditions. The causes for disappointment included difficulties with the German language and a poor relationship with colleagues and superiors. These disappointments tend to diminish with increasing length of stay in the Federal Republic of Germany. However, it must be added that more than 50 percent of the foreign workers interviewed had left the first firm in which they began to work in Germany.(33)

About one-fourth of the foreign workers stated that they were discriminated against by some Germans. These incidents with their colleagues and superiors occurred mainly at the place of work. This indicates that foreign citizens must be given sufficient time to be integrated into their firms; that they ought to receive better professional training, if necessary, on the job; and that their supervisors should be trained to work with persons from a different cultural environment.

The overwhelming majority of foreign workers now express satisfaction with the situation at the place of work — a feeling that is proportionate to the length of stay. Correlations can be found between length of stay, on the one hand, and knowledge of the German language, achievement of a better position (mostly promotion from unskilled to semiskilled status), and higher wages, on the other hand. Satisfaction at work is influenced positively by these factors. Conversely, those employed as unskilled workers reveal less contentment.(34)

In our survey of 1971, we found that 40 percent of foreign workers are employed as unskilled, while 40 percent are regarded as semiskilled (in the sense described earlier). Promotion from unskilled or semiskilled worker to higher status has been achieved only by few foreign workers in the Federal Republic of Germany.

Only 2 percent of the foreign citizens worked as supervisors, but about 20 percent can be viewed as skilled workers. Because they have not passed the same examination as German skilled workers, they are characterized as "skilled workers with respect to the firm in which they now work." As might be expected, the percentage of foreign women who were skilled workers in their firms was much lower (3 percent).(35)

Our survey indicated that the relations between foreign workers and their German colleagues generally were good, but this does not mean that there were no conflicts between them in the past. In 1971, however, only 11 percent of the foreign workers said that their relationship with their colleagues was bad or not good. As was mentioned earlier, the economic situation in the Federal Republic of Germany has changed since 1971. German and foreign workers are now competing intensely for jobs, and prejudices against foreigners have grown. Germans sometimes call for foreign citizens to be sent back because of unemployment of about 1 million Germans. Conflicts also occur in firms in which mass dismissals are announced. In a Cologne firm the German workers recently demanded that foreign workers should be dismissed first, but this demand was backed neither by the works council nor the trade union concerned.

Our survey indicated that membership in a trade union is both a cause and a sign of the integration of foreign citizens into German society. It can be shown that many foreign workers comprehend the function of trade unions only after a certain length of stay in Germany. Then, their willingness to become members of a trade union increases. In 1971 nearly 30 percent of foreign workers were members of a

German trade union. The percentage of men was higher (35 percent) than that of the women (21 percent). However, many foreign citizens stated that they were not familiar with trade unions, and had not been asked to join. For this reason, they considered that membership was not to their advantage. Only one-third of foreign workers thought the trade unions sufficiently responsive to their interests. Twelve percent disagreed with this view. More than half of those interviewed did not respond to this question.(36)

Until the early 1970s, the German trade unions did not record their foreign members separately; however, reliable statistics are available now. In December 1977, 32 percent of foreign workers were members of a trade union in the Federal Republic of Germany. There are differences among the nationalities. Only 26 percent of Yugoslavs and 31 percent of Italians, but 38 percent of Portuguese, 41 percent of Greeks, 43 percent of Spaniards and 46 percent of Turks are members of a German trade union. These proportions have to be compared with the percentage of German workers who are members of a trade union (around 43 percent).(37) The degree of labor organization, therefore, is slightly lower among foreign workers than among German workers.

Since the beginning of the employment of foreign citizens in the Federal Republic of Germany, foreign workers have been permitted to participate in elections for works councils. Usually they could vote for but not be elected to works councils. (Only if the employer and the German workers in the enterprise concerned agreed, could they become representatives on the works councils.) However, the Work Constitution Act of November 10, 1971, gave foreign workers the right to be elected to works councils.(38) In 1972, 3,824 foreign workers were elected to works councils, and in 1975 their number rose to 4,985 (the figures for 1978 are not available yet).(39) With regard to nationality, about 1,589 Turks, 970 Italians, 685 Greeks, 620 Yugoslavs, 335 Spaniards, and 137 Portuguese were members of works councils in 1975. Although the absolute figures seem impressive, the representation of foreign workers in works councils was much lower than their proportion of the labor force. With a total of 191,015 members in works councils (foreign citizens and Germans),(40) the share of foreign workers was only 2.5 percent, while their proportion in the labor force as a whole amounted to 9.7 percent in 1975.

This underrepresentation of foreign workers in the works councils and their general ignorance of the functions of the trade unions already have led to tensions. Since most foreign citizens do not see their interests represented adequately by the German trade unions, the Turks, for example, have formed large worker associations of their own. It is foreseeable that other national groups will form similar associations. Since their main objective is the representation of foreign workers in the labor field, future conflicts with German trade unions seem likely.

Ignorance of the German language limits the chances of foreign workers to further their vocational training and education. The knowledge of German is important also for social contact between foreign citizens and Germans. Data from a large survey in 1971 of foreign workers in Germany(41) indicated that only about 10 percent of recruited workers spoke any German at the time of entry. Eventually, most of them do acquire some basic German, but on the whole, they remain functionally illiterate in the language. Interest in attending language courses is minimal; availability of such courses is uneven. In short, the language program has failed for several reasons. In the first place, traditional teaching methods have proved inadequate, because of an emphasis on grammar and sentence structure which are not comprehensible to foreign workers with a minimal formal education. Attending a language course after working hours was an added burden upon foreign citizens who would prefer to use this portion of the day for overtime work. Second, the frequent utilization of a collective form of housing (grouping together members of a single nationality) has minimized the necessity of learning German (which, moreover, is needed rarely on the job, since many enterprises prefer employing workers of one ethnic group only). These practices have led to the creation of language enclaves. Furthermore, the de facto segregation of foreign workers does not encourage those with families to venture outside the immediate circle of kin and friends. Finally, the cultural and political activities of their own governments have laid further stress upon the national identity of each respective group of foreign workers, discouraging assimilation in the host country.

In addition to the official courses in German conducted by the various university extension field offices, there have been efforts by various voluntary agencies. The most successful of these programs was a televised German instruction program under the title of "Guten Tag," and a new series, "Viel Glueck in Deutschland." This program of the "Sesame Street" type was developed by the Goethe Institute on behalf of the Ministry of Labor and Social Affairs. Since 1972 most of the efforts in teaching German to foreign citizens have been coordinated centrally, on the federal level. Suggestions that the employer or the state should underwrite the cost of language training, which would take place during working hours, have been rejected by the unions.(42) The reason given is that the unions wish to achieve equal treatment for foreign workers, while this measure would constitute a privilege for foreign citizens which could lead to conflict with their German colleagues.

Because of acute housing shortages in the industrial areas, employers importing workers had to provide housing for them. Our survey indicated that in 1971 about one-fifth of the foreign workers lived in housing provided by their employer. Turks and Yugoslavs were more likely to be found in such accommodations than other groups. Among Turks who had been in Germany for less than a year, 43 percent were living in collective employer-supplied housing. Such accommodations tend to be marginal. More than two persons generally occupy a room, and men and women, even married couples, often are housed separately. These hostels, or dormitories, suffer from an overdose of house rules, against which complaints are often directed.(43) This type of accom-modation retards the foreign workers' adaptation to life in Germany and encourages the development of constrained forms of social life. Thus it hampers integration.(44)

It is not surprising, therefore, that the longer they stay, the harder foreign workers try to move out of these company accommodations. Actually, they are compelled to do so if they change employers. This combination of place of work and accommodation frequently has been criticized, since it increases the foreign workers' dependency on the employers. Among foreign citizens who had been employed in Germany from one to three years, there was increased tendency to move from hostel to private rooms. After more than three years, foreign workers generally desired an apartment of their own. It may be assumed that this is related to the wish to have their families join them. Most of the foreign workers had difficulties obtaining rooms or apartments; these problems, for the most part, traced back to the prejudices of the German population toward foreign workers, as well as to the shortage of low-priced private rooms or apartments.(45)

Foreign citizens tend to concentrate in certain districts of large cities. These are mostly industrial or mixed areas in which quality of housing is low and in urgent need of renovation. Such "foreign quarters" exist, for example, in the Berlin districts of Kreuzberg and Wedding. Developments there have prompted the authorities to prevent more foreign workers from moving in, so as to prevent the formation of ethnic ghettos. A study in Frankfurt am Main demonstrated that segregation of foreigners was due mainly to the private housing market. Most of their housing was either old and in too poor a condition for German families, or it consisted of one-room apartments, with rents that were too high for Germans, but which foreigners had to accept because of their greater difficulty in finding accommodations.(46)

While the development of local concentrations of certain population groups can have advantages, under the conditions prevailing in the FRG the disadvantages predominate. The integration of foreign workers in German society is made particularly difficult by differences in accom-modation standards and isolation from the German population. The slum character of many districts inhabited by foreign citizens also impedes community planning. The problems encountered by foreign workers seeking housing enable owners to rent out even low-quality accommodation at high profits. The incentive to renovate and modern-ize is thus minimized.

THE PROBLEM OF DEPENDENTS

In the 1960s, family separation among the recruited workers was quite common. The reason for coming to Germany was to earn and save money; thus foreign workers usually came without dependents (since, without the presence of family members, the head of household in the host country would be able to accumulate more savings). Also, residence and work permit regulations meant that (apart from the Italians, who fall under the European Community freedom of movement agreement) foreign workers often would have to wait for three years before bringing in their families. In addition, regulations require foreign workers to demonstrate that adequate housing is available for their families. Entry of dependents is restricted to the spouse and unmarried children under 21 years of age. Children under 16 require no residence permit. At a previous stage, foreign citizens usually had been able to bring their families after one year's stay, if housing was available.(47)

However, by now, it has become obvious that family reunification has occurred on a large scale, restrictions notwithstanding. In our opinion, this phenomenon is only one indicator that a de facto immigration situation exists in the Federal Republic of Germany.(48) Other signs are:

- The length of stay of foreign workers has increased considerably. In 1968, about 25 percent of Italians, Spaniards, and Greeks had worked more than seven years in Germany; 9 percent of the Yugoslavs and 4 percent of Turks had lived in Germany for more than seven years. (These figures cover men only.) Data for 1972 are available only for men and women together. In 1972, 33 percent of Italians, 36 percent of Spaniards, 23 percent of Greeks, 7 percent of Yugoslavs, and 11 percent of Turks had been working in Germany for more than seven years. Data available for 1976 indicate that the length of stay of foreign workers had increased still further. More than 50 percent of Italians, Spaniards, and Greeks, 35 percent of Yugoslavs, and 25 percent of Turks had been living in Germany for more than six years.(49)
- Both the data from our 1971 survey and the statistics of the Bundesanstalt fuer Arbeit, Nuremberg, indicate that family unification increases with length of stay in Germany.(50) In 1974, the number of new arrivals was small and was exceeded by the number of departing workers, but during that year about 320,000 dependents arrived in Germany. The number of foreign citizens at the end of September 1975 amounted to 4.1 million (including about 1 million children and adolescents).
- In 1972, 20 percent of the foreign workers stated that they would prefer to live permanently in the Federal Republic. About 30 percent did not know how long they would like to stay in Germany. It can be demonstrated, however, that the proportion wishing to stay permanently rises with increasing length of stay. In 1972, 25 percent of foreign citizens living in Germany for seven or eight years wished to settle permanently, 40 percent of those living there for nine or ten years, and 75 percent of those living there for twelve to fifteen years.(51)
- Quite a number of children of foreign workers have been born already in Germany. Our 1976 survey of 400 Italian youngsters in the state of Nordrhein-Westfalen indicated that 30 percent had

come to Germany aged less than 5 years, and about 60 percent arrived less than 10 years of age.(52) It may be assumed that only a few foreign youngsters will return to their parents' country of origin, in which they did not grow up and the language of which they do not speak very well. Our survey shows that less than 50 percent of the Italian youngsters interviewed wish to return to Italy, and that about 25 percent would like to obtain German citizenship.(53)

The continuing influx of dependents is causing strain on social facilities, especially in the heavily industrial areas of Germany. To address the issue, new regulations were introduced, imposing a limit (of 12 percent of the total population) on aliens in any Kreis administrative district. The difficulties in enforcing such regulations would have proved considerable. The regulation "absorptive capacity" of a city or area was more likely to be an intuitive guess than a thorough assessment of the capacity of housing, schools, recreational facilities and the like. Yet residence permits, under these regulations, could not be granted to foreign workers for an area which had been classified as overburdened.(54) These regulations did not apply to citizens of member states of the European Community. The regulations described came into force in April 1975. However, they were cancelled, and the reason given by the German government was that, according to an agreement between the European Community and Turkey (Assoziationsrat), such regulations could not be applied to Turkish workers living in Germany for more than five years. At that time there were similar bilateral agreements between Germany and Spain, and Germany and Greece. Consequently, the regulations mentioned would have applied from 1977 onward to Yugoslavs and Portuguese only. For this reason, the German government declared it would be better to cancel these regulations altogether.(55) In our opinion, however, this decision was made because the regulations did not achieve the goal desired by the government, i.e., family influx into the "overburdened" areas in fact was not stopped. In 1975 the Federal Government set up an interministerial committee to work out a coherent in-migration and aliens policy and to offer guidelines on integration of foreign workers. The report of the Committee was never published officially, since the various ministries were unable to come to an agreement on many issues. However, the press was able to obtain copies of the report and to publish it early in 1976.(56) Disagreements among the ministries centered particularly on the issue of dependents rejoining workers already living in the off limits areas. Not surprisingly, the representatives of the Ministry of Labor and Social Affairs appeared especially hard-line, opposing the unencumbered admission into Germany of dependents of foreign workers. Of course the Ministry would have to take care of all the social needs arising as a result of in-migration of families, but other groups in Germany, including churches, welfare associations, trade unions, and political parties, oppose limiting the entry of such families on humanitarian grounds. Another question is whether the Federal Republic of

Germany would be able to implement this measure in the face of opposition by the countries of origin of foreign labor. In the past, these countries have been able to exert some degree of pressure upon the enactment of German government measures in the social sphere.

In 1972 there were about 1 million children of foreign workers in Germany. About 37 percent of them were between 6 and 16 years old, i.e., of compulsory school age.(57) Mandatory schooling for children of aliens was introduced in 1964, after the number of such children had become substantial.

Normally, schools are administered by the individual German states (Laender); there is, however, a Standing Conference of Ministers of Education, which has powers of recommendation only. A recommendation dating from 1971 calls for the integration of foreign children into the school grades corresponding to their respective ages. A provision for instruction in their various mother tongues is also recommended "to maintain the students' links with the language and culture of their home countries."

There are built-in disadvantages in the way children of foreign workers are being educated at present. Their insufficient command of German is a barrier to their successful progress through the various grades. At home, children may not find much encouragement for their German schooling. Our study found that one-fifth of all foreign parents evaded sending their children to school.(58) The "para-schools," where instruction is provided in the mother tongue during regular class time, made students miss some subjects taught in German. Moreover, supplementary training in the mother tongue after school hours, and by their own fellow nationals, tended to discourage the integration of children into the new German society.(59) Thus, mostly for reasons of uncertainty concerning where they belong and what they should learn, children of foreign workers become doubly disadvantaged. Functionally "illiterate in two languages," they pose a problem for the future, in whatever country they might find themselves.(60)

Several political factors are responsible for the present educational concept and the resulting problems posed for foreign children. First, the Greek, Turkish, and Spanish governments are opposed to the integration of the children of foreign workers in the German school system. These countries of origin are determined that the children must not lose their cultural links with the home country. Underlying this idea is the expectation that the parents will return one day to their country, together with their children. Some countries of origin even demand national schools in Germany for the children of their citizens. This would make impossible the integration of these children in German society and thus would enforce their eventual repatriation.

Some of the demands of the countries of origin, with regard to the schooling of such foreign children, have been met in the Federal Republic of Germany. These include instruction in the mother tongue for foreign children in German schools. However, the demand for national schools, i.e., schools for only one particular group of foreign citizens, has been rejected in most instances.

This educational concept reflects the Federal Republic's migration policy, which presumes that only "temporary integration" of the foreign children is required. Like the countries of origin themselves, the Bonn government believes that the majority of foreign workers will return with their families to their countries of origin. The educational approach derives from the nonrecognition of the de facto immigration situation prevailing in Germany and, thus, so do the foreign children's problems detailed above. On the other hand, this educational concept does meet the demands of the countries of origin so that in the past deeper conflicts between the governments concerned have been avoided.

RECOMMENDATIONS

In conclusion, it may be said that conflicts between countries of origin and host governments have resulted mainly from the fact that the migration of workers has not brought the expected gains for the countries of origin which wanted to reduce their labor surplus and to benefit from an influx of foreign exchange through the remittances of their citizens, as well as to obtain advanced technical training for their workers. The following suggestions are put forward to ease tensions that have arisen:

1. Investment of more capital by the host countries in the countries of origin, to create employment opportunities in the latter. In this way, their labor surplus could be reduced.
2. Introduction of "assisted" out-migration for Italians, i.e., out-migration channeled through commissions of the host countries. These commissions would be notified of vacant jobs in the host countries which could be filled by Italians.
3. Initiation of freedom of movement for those Turks already living in host countries belonging to the European Community. This would enhance considerably the legal status of these Turkish workers and their families. Freedom of movement should not imply, however, that Turks should enter the host countries individually. Commissions of the host countries should be set up in Turkey which would fill vacant jobs in the EC.
4. Provision for repatriation (organized jointly by host governments and countries of origin) for those foreign workers who wish to return to their homeland, and support for their reintegration in the countries of origin.
5. Articulated realization by host governments and countries of origin that a great many foreign workers and their families will remain for very long periods, or even permanently, in the host countries of Western Europe. The host governments should provide opportunities for the full integration into society of these foreign citizens, particularly the second

generation. In the case of the Federal Republic of Germany, that would mean a turning away from the present migration policy and recognition of a de facto immigration situation. In the view of this study, the measures applied hitherto are not really suitable to eliminate the social problems of the migrant workers. These measures are of a stopgap nature only, for they are based on the assumption of a merely "temporary integration" of these foreign citizens.

NOTES

(1) Ursula Mehrlaender, Beschaeftigung auslaendischer Arbeitnehmer in der Bundesrepublik Deutschland unter spezieller Beruecksichtigung von Nordrhein-Westfalen, 2nd ed. (Opladen: Westdeutscher Verlag, 1972), p. 90.

(2) H. Weicken, Anwerbung and Vermittlung italienischer, spanischer und griechischer Arbeitskraefte im Rahmen bilateraler Anwerbevereinbarung, in Auslaendische Arbeitskraefte in Deutschland, ed. Hessisches Institut fuer Betriebswirtschaft e.V. (Duesseldorf: 1961), pp. 13-14.

(3) R. Lohrmann and K. Manfrass, eds., Auslaenderbeschaeftigung und internationale Politik (Munich, Vienna: Oldenburg, 1974), p. 112.

(4) Ursula Mehrlaender, Soziale Aspekte der Auslaenderbeschaeftigung (Bon-Bad Godesberg, Neue Gesellschaft, 1974), pp. 11-13.

(5) Ursula Mehrlaender, Soziale Aspekte, p. 11.

(6) U. Mehrlaender Beschaeftigung, p. 90.

(7) Statistisches Jahrbuch fuer die Bundesrepublik Deutschland 1970, Bonn, p. 125.

(8) Statistisches Jahrbuch fuer die Bundesrepublik Deutschland, 1975, Bonn, p. 156.

(9) Amtliche Nachrichten der Bundesanstalt fuer Arbeit, no. 2 (ANBA: Nueremberg, 1976), pp. 162, 172, 190.

(10) "Zahl der Auslaender bei rund 4.1 Millionen," in Sozialpolitische Rundschau, Presse- und Informationsamt der Bundesregierung, (Bonn: 1975).

(11) Daniel Kubat with collaboration of Ernst Gehmacher and Ursula Mehrlaender, eds., The Politics of Migration Policies (New York: Center for International Studies (in press)). The German version

of this book is Auslaenderpolitik im Konflikt, ed.   by E. Gehmacher, D. Kubat, and U. Mehrlaender, (Bonn: Verlag Neue Gesellschaft, 1978).

(12) G. Tapinos, L'immigration etrangere en France (Paris:
Presses Universitaire de France, 1975), p. 126.

(13) La nouvelle politique de l'immigration (Paris: Secretariat
d'Etat aux Travailleurs Immigres, 1977), p. 22.

(14) G. Dooghe, De bevolking in Belgie - demografisch oversicht
(Brussels: 1976), p. 135.

(15) G. Beyer, "Countries of In-Migration: Northwestern Europe,
The Benelux-countries," in: Kubat, The Politics of Migration
Policies.

(16) G. Als, "Les migrations du bassin mediterraneen vers le
Luxembourg," in L'emigrazione del bassino mediterraneo verso
l'Europa industrializzata, ed. Franco Angeli (Milano, 1976), pp.
221-238.

(17) Statistische Jahrbuecher der Schweiz, (Bern, various years).

(18) Ursula Mehrlaender, "Probleme der Auslaenderbeschaeftigung in der Bundesrepublik Deutschland," in "Oesterreich und in
der Schweiz" (Bonn-Bad Godesberg, 1974) (mimeo.), pp. 27-29.

(19) H.-J. Hoffmann-Nowotny and M. Killias, "Countries of In-
Migration: The Northwestern Europe, Switzerland," in Kubat,
The Politics of Migration.

(20) Bundesministerium fuer soziale Verwaltung and Haupt-
verband der Oesterreichischen Sozialversicherungstraeger (Vienna: various years).

(21) E. Gehmacher, "Countries of In-Migration: Northwestern
Europe, Austria," in Kubat, The Politics of Migration.

(22) I. Baucic, "Countries of Out-Migration: Exportation of Labor
to Northwestern Europe, Yugoslavia," in Kubat, The Politics of
Migration. Also sections by Th. P. Lianos and M.B. Rocha in the same
volume.

(23) Ursula Mehrlaender, Soziale Aspekte, p. 81.

(24) Ursula Mehrlaender, Beschaeftigung, p. 30.

(25) The population growth rate amounts to 1 million per year.

(26) S. Alias and D. Kubat "Countries of Out-Migration: Exportation of Labor to Northwestern Europe, Turkey," in Kubat, The Politics of Migration. (The senior author of this chapter wishes to remain anonymous for the time being.)

(27) F. Cerase, "Countries of Out-Migration: Exportation of Labor to Northwestern Europe, Italy," in Kubat, The Politics of Migration.

(28) V. Briani, Il lavoro italiano in Europa, Teri e oggi, (Rome: Ministero Affari Esteri, 1972).

(29) The Swiss have three categories of foreign workers with differing legal status: residents, year-residents, and seasonal workers.

(30) F. Cerase, "Countries of Out-Migration."

(31) This survey included Italians, Spaniards, Greeks, Turks, and Yugoslavs. Ursula Mehrlaender, Soziale Aspekte.

(32) Ibid., pp. 71-73.

(33) Ibid., p. 71.

(34) Ibid., pp. 104-113.

(35) Ibid., p. 80.

(36) Ibid., pp. 155, 156, 178.

(37) My calculation is based on information from the Deutscher Gewerkschaftsbund, Duesseldorf, and on the figures of German workers in the Statistisches Jahrbuch der Bundesrepublik Deutschland, 1977, p. 97.

(38) E. Piehl, "Gewerkschaften und auslaendische Arbeitnehmer," in Gewerkschaftsspiegel, 1 (1972): 19 ff.

(39) Information obtained from the Deutscher Gewerkschaftsbund, Duesseldorf, 1978.

(40) W. Schneider, "Betriebstratswahlen 1975 — eine zusammenfassende Darstellung," in Gewerkschaftliche Monatshefte 10 (1975): 602.

(41) Ursula Mehrlaender, Soziale Aspekte, pp. 100-103.

(42) Ursula Mehrlaender, "Countries of In-Migration: Northwestern Europe, Germany," in Kubat, The Politics of Migration.

(43) M. Borris, Auslaendische Arbeiter in einer Groszstadt (Frankfort am Main: Europaeische Verlagsanstalt, 1973), p. 137.

(44) A. Schildmeier, Integration und Wohnen (Hamburg: Hammon, 1975), p. 33.

(45) Ursula Mehrlaender, Soziale Aspekte, p. 193.

(46) A. Schildmeier, Integration, pp. 37-39; M. Borris, Auslaendische, pp. 130, 131.

(47) Ursula Mehrlaender, Soziale Aspekte, p. 181.

(48) Social scientists who share my opinion on a de facto immigration situation are, for example: K. Kaiser, "Statistische Uebersicht zur Auslaenderbeschaeftigung," in Gastarbeiter - Mitbuerger, published by von R. Leudesdorff und M. Zilleben, (Gelnhausen: Burckhardthaus-Verlag, 1971), p. 31; H.-J. Siewert, "Auslaendische Arbeiter — eine industrielle Reservearmee," in Der Buerger im Staat, published by der Landeszentrale fuer politische Bildung, Baden-Wuerttemberg, 23, 2 (1973), 111; U. Boos-Nuenning, "Berufsfindung und Berufsausbildung auslaendischer Jugendlicher," "Berichte und Materialien der Forschungsgruppe," ALFA, no. 11, Neusz (1978): p. 100.

(49) Bundesanstalt fuer Arbeit, "Ergebnisse der Repraesentativ-Untersuchung vom Herbst 1968," (Nuernberg, 1969), p. 29; Bundesanstalt fuer Arbeit, "Repraesentativ-Untersuchung '72," Ibid., p. 34; Auslaender im Bundesgebiet, in: Wirtschaft und Statistik 1 (1976): p. 4.

(50) Ursula Mehrlaender, Soziale Aspekte, pp. 200-217; Bundesanstalt fuer Arbeit, "Repraesentativ-Untersuchung '72" Ibid., p. 20.

(51) Ibid., p. 36.

(52) "Eheschliessungen, Geburten und Sterbefaelle von Auslaendern 1975," in: Wirtschaft und Statistik 3 (1977): 154-158.

(53) Ursula Mehrlaender, Einfluszfaktoren auf das Bildungsverhalten auslaendischer Jugendlicher (Bonn: Verlag Neue Gesellschaft, 1978). The Italian adolescents interviewed were aged from 15 to 20 years.

(54) J. Langkau and Ursula Mehrlaender, Raumordnungspolitische Steuerung der Auslaenderbeschaeftigung (Bonn-Bad Godesberg: Bundesministerium fuer Raumordnung, Bauwesen und Staedtebau, 1976), pp. 30-44.

(55) Ursula Mehrlaender, "Bundesrepublik Deutschland," in Aus-laenderpolitik im Konflikt, op. cit., p. 123.

(56) epd - Dokumentation, Entwurf von Thesen zur Auslaender-politik eines Ausschusses der Bundesregierung vom 23. Oktober 1976, Frankfurt a.M.: epd - Dokumentation, no. 5 (1976): pp. 4-10.

(57) Bundesanstalt fuer Arbeit, "Repraesentativ-Untersuchung 72 ueber die Beschaeftigung auslaendischer Arbeitnehmer im Bun-desgebiet und ihre Familien – und Wohnungsverhaeltnisse," (Nueremberg, 1973), p. 23.

(58) Ursula Mehrlaender, Soziale Aspekte, pp. 209, 210.

(59) U. Mehrlaender, "Countries of In-Migration: Northwestern Europe, Germany," in Kubat, The Politics of Migration.

(60) W. Grossmann, "Sozialisationsbedingungen und Bildung-schancen auslaendischer Arbeiterkinder," in Gettos in unseren Schulen?, ed. H. Feidel-Mertz and W. Grossmann (Frankfurt: Gewerkschaft Erziehung und Wissenschaft, 1974), no 137, pp. 11-25.

4 Scottish Nationalism and Devolution (Stage One, up to 1978): Regionalism and the Political Party System
H.M. Drucker

BACKGROUND

Until World War I, Scotland was a Liberal bastion. The Liberal Party polled particularly well in rural Scotland. The Conservative and Unionist Party (the "Union" referred to is between Ireland and England) held on to many safe seats, particularly in the cities. The larger number of Irish immigrants who might have voted against the Unionist Party did not have the vote in parliamentary elections until after the War.

After the War the situation changed dramatically and rapidly froze into the shape it was to retain until the Scottish National Party (SNP) broke it up again in the 1960s. The major beneficiary of the change which occurred at the end of World War I was the Labor Party. Helped by the enfranchisement of the large number of unskilled male laborers, it achieved an immediate breakthrough in the Scottish cities in 1922, the first postwar election in normal conditions. The formerly Liberal rural vote went to the Conservatives. With the exception of Edinburgh — which has remained predominately Conservative — Scotland's cities became Labor and have remained true to that party.

Gradually, over the period between 1922 and the emergence of the National Party as an electoral force in by-elections in 1967 and 1968, the Labor Party strengthened its hand. Labor has held a majority of Scottish seats at every post-World War II General Election except 2. In 1951 the two major parties had 35 seats each (the Liberals had one), and in 1955 the Conservatives had 36 seats to Labor's 34. (The Liberals clung to 'their sole seat.) In Scotland, even more than in England, the parties held on to their fortresses and made only the occasional foray into the opponent's camp. Partly as a result, the machines of the two parties atrophied. Both parties had relatively weaker party organizations in Scotland than in England. But since both were weaker it hardly made any difference to the total result.

There was no political science of Scottish politics in this period because there was nothing to study. Scots voted as Englishmen. They swung in General Elections in the same direction and to the same extent as Englishmen. The first sign of change came in the 1959 General Election. At that election Scotland moved in the direction of the Labor Party (as did the North-West of England) while the rest of Britain moved further into the Conservative camp. Mr. Macmillan, the Conservative Prime Minister, had campaigned in the 1959 General Election on the slogan "You never had it so good." In Scotland it wasn't true. The affluence which had become so evident in the south was not seen north of the border. Scotland continued to lose a high number of its educated middle-class youths to England and to other countries. Labor, the party of the working class, benefited.

Scottish politics in the period between World War I and the 1966 General Election was almost entirely characterized by a division along class lines. Scotland was a classically single cleavage society. This is no longer the case. Scottish society has been changing rapidly since 1961 and Scottish politics has been changing even more rapidly. Unusual for a Western country, the party system of Scotland has changed importantly without any large influx of new voters. There were three major parties in Scotland by the mid-seventies. Labor was the largest party; it won 36 percent of the popular vote and 41 seats at the October 1974 General Election. The SNP was second with 30 percent of the votes and 11 seats at that election. The Conservative Party had been displaced from second place. With 24 percent of the vote it managed to hold on to 16 parliamentary seats. The Liberal Party had three seats which it obtained with 8.3 percent of the vote. (It won 20.2 percent in England.)

The SNP is not only a newcomer, but it has a different sort of social base from the other parties, and a novel view of the main issue in politics. The SNP seeks to gain independence for Scotland. Its Constitution plainly states its aim:

> Self-government for Scotland – that is, the restoration of Scottish National Sovereignty by the establishment of a democratic Scottish Parliament within the Commonwealth, freely elected by the Scottish people, whose authority will be limited only by such agreements as may be freely entered into by it with other nations or states or international organisations for the purpose of furthering international co-operation and world peace.(1)

This aim is anathema to the British parties.

At the same time as Scottish politics has been undergoing rapid change, the economy of Scotland – and with it Scottish society – has been changing also. There are 5,205,100 people in Scotland. It is larger in population than Denmark, Finland, Norway, Ireland, and Iceland (in that order). More than half live in one local government area (Strathclyde Region) around the city of Glasglow. The overwhelming majority of Scots live in the central industrial belt which includes Strathclyde and stretches east to Edinburgh. This belt was one of the great forging houses of the industrial revolution and was among the world leaders in such basic heavy industries as coal mining, iron and steel manufacture, shipbuilding and locomotive building, almost to the eve of World War I. Since then the old industries have been gradually declining (in Scotland as elsewhere) and the central belt has been left with the sores of rapid industrial growth of the early capitalism with few of the softening benefits of later periods to compensate.

Scotland has all of the objective evidence of a highly divided class society. Most Scots are poor and Scotland is an unhealthy place in which to live. Scots have the worst teeth in the world; 44 percent of Scottish adults – half of the Scots over 16 – lack any of their own teeth.(2) In 1975 90 percent of Scots schoolchildren had some gum disease. Scotland also has the highest rate of heart attacks and deaths from coronary disease in the world. Mortality from heart disease is two-and-a-half times that of the South of England. Since 1972 Scotland has led the world in lung cancer; deaths from this source are now about 7 per thousand per annum (England – 5; Sweden – 1). More Scots than any other Britons smoke, and the Scots who do smoke more cigarettes.(3) In 1972, 1,500 prenatal deaths, which were connected with smoking by the mother, occurred in Scotland. Notoriously, Scots drink too much. Alcoholics are about 4 times more numerous in Scotland than in England or Wales. The problem is increasing; in 1957 840 people were admitted to hospitals in Scotland for alcoholism and cholic psychosis and in 1974 the number was 5,417.(4) Glasgow schoolchildren at age eleven are shorter and lighter than in any other British city.

But the most illustrative measure of Scotland's poverty is her housing. In 1976, 33.6 percent of Scots owned their own homes; 12.2 percent rented from private owners. The rest – 54.2 percent rented from public authorities.(5) All this public housing has been built since World War I to rehouse people who were living in slums. It has all been laid down to meet official specifications, and thus lacks charm. "A desert wi' windaes" is how one Scottish poet described the large estates of public housing.(6) No country in the Western world has a higher proportion of its population living in publicly owned housing – and several Eastern European countries (Bulgaria, Yugoslavia, Hungary, and Czechoslovakia) have higher proportions of owner-occupancy. Official figures show that 8.1 percent of the present housing stock is below tolerable standard. No less than 75 percent of all the overcrowded homes in the United Kingdom are in Glasgow; as are 93 percent of the homes lacking hot water or lavatory.(7)

Confirmation of the poverty of most Scots has come recently from the Royal Commission on the Distribution of Wealth and Income (known after its chairman as the Diamond Commission).(8) The Commission's 1973 Report showed that two-thirds of the Scots owned no wealth at all (i.e., none that the Inland Revenue thought sufficient to report.) Only half of Englishmen were in that position. On the other hand, the wealthiest 1 percent of Scots owned 32 percent of Scotland's wealth; in

England, the wealthiest 1 percent held 28 percent. In Scotland, the wealthiest 5 percent owned two-thirds of the wealth; in England the same proportion of the wealthiest owned but half of the wealth. Moreover, the trend in wealth distribution since 1950 has been toward greater inequality. This is the reverse of the position in England. In Scotland the position of the bottom 80 percent of Scots has been declining. After a period of decreasing inequality from 1939 to 1956 (when this part of the population reached its maximum of 20 percent of the wealth), the balance of advantage has been moving in favor of the wealthiest 20 percent since 1956. The 80 percent poorest owned 15 percent of the wealth in 1973. Whereas in softer climates the wealthy have learned the disadvantages of ostentatious display, this had not happened in Scotland. The most obvious and tangible display of wealth in Scotland is land. No official land register exists, but a recent private estimate by John McEwan is that 16.5 million of Scotland's 19 million acres are in private hands.(9) The 100 biggest landowners include the Duke of Buccleuch who owns 277,000 acres (the largest amount) and Lord Ailsa whose 21,000 acres only barely suffice to gain him inclusion in the 100 largest owners.

The starkness of the division between the many poor and the few wealthy has been more than sufficient to keep alive the political struggle between Labor and Conservative parties. The overall poverty of Scotland has also been made a political issue by the SNP. That party claims that an independent Scotland could be a wealthy country because it would have control over the oil resources underneath the North Sea, east and north of Scotland. "Rich Scots or Poor British" is how one SNP slogan put it. The two main British parties have sought to neutralize the charm of the SNP in many ways. They are ill at ease with the way the SNP has succeeded in forcing the cleavage between those Scots who think of themselves as Scots and those who do not primarily identify themselves in this way into competition with the old class divisions. Their reaction to the SNP advance has taken the form of shifting more public expenditure to Scotland, of devolving more central government functions to the Scottish Office in Edinburgh, and, more importantly, of promising to devolve to Scotland political control over the country's home affairs.

DEVOLUTION

All three of the major parties operating in Scotland became committed to devolution. None of them really believed in it when they were converted to it. Of the smaller parties in Scotland, the Liberals have been committed to devolution since their governments of the early twentieth century failed to bring it about. The small Scottish Labor Party (SLP) was formed in 1975 to press for a more vigorous form of devolution than the government was then offering. The Communist Party also backs devolution.

"Devolution" is an unfamiliar name for a delightful nineteenth century idea.(10) The concept means an unraveling of power. Some of the legislative, executive, and administrative authority of the central United Kingdom government is to be devolved to an elected Scottish (and, as it happens, a Welsh) Assembly. The proposal first surfaced in British politics at the end of the nineteenth century when the Liberal Party, anxious both to keep the Irish within the United Kingdom and to preserve the advantage their party gained at Westminster from its Irish seats and votes of its allies in the Irish parties, proposed "Home Rule All Around." The idea was to set up a series of Assemblies – one each for Ireland, Scotland, Wales, and England – which would have authority in domestic matters while retaining the imperial functions and powers of the Westminster Parliament. The position would have been very roughly similar to that of the Canadian Federation except that the Imperial Parliament would have created the National Assemblies by law, and could, therefore, have changed their powers or even abolished them by law.(11) The idea did not get very far. Few people really wanted it; the English did not see the need for it and the Irish wanted more. After World War I, Ireland broke free of British government (with the exception of Northern Ireland) and the issue lost urgency.

But the issue did not die overnight, nor was it ever entirely out of the political vocabulary of some Scots. The Labor Party which inherited much of the Liberals' former support in Scotland – and much of their ideology everywhere – formally embraced devolution. Resolutions in favor of devolution had been agreed to by the Labor Party in Scotland (which organizes an annual conference each spring and is called the Scottish Council of the Labor Party) on several occasions in the 1920s, the 1940s, and in 1951 and 1956.(12)

Then, in 1958, the party in Scotland agreed to a special conference on devolution; it was on the verge of renouncing its commitment. The Labor Party renounced (or rather its leadership tried to renounce) many of its cherished commitments at this time. It was a year later that Hugh Gaitskell tried, unsuccessfully, to get the party to devalue its commitment to "nationalize the means of production, distribution and exchange." The Labor Party in Scotland went through with the renunciation which the leadership desired. It was clear by 1958 that devolution was only a ritualistic commitment of the party. Nothing had been done about it during the Attlee governments of 1945 and 1950. Moreover, several large Scottish unions had already merged with their English brothers. (There is not now a single Scottish union affiliated to the Trade Union Congress.) The unions increasingly saw the United Kingdom, not Scotland, as their field of activity. They had come to accept that the run-down older industries of Scotland – particularly the coal and railways industries – required British subsidies. It seemed better to renounce devolution and make an honest job of living off the English. The Special Conference passed a resolution and the crucial paragraph read:

> We declare our belief in the principle of the maximum possible self-government for Scotland, consistent with the right to remain in the United Kingdom Parliament and continue full representation there. We reject the idea of being separated from the United Kingdom.(13)

The right to remain in the United Kingdom Parliament, with full representation there, was understood to mean "no devolution." (At present Scotland has 71 of the 635 British MPs. On a strictly proportional population basis, Scotland should have 57 MPs. The Labor Party is the main beneficiary of the excess.)

The Conservative Party had never been in favor of devolution. There its position remained until the rise of the SNP. The SNP was formed in 1934 from a union of the National Party of Scotland (itself formed in 1928) and the Scottish Party. In its early years, the party had a somewhat crankish and literary reputation. Senior members of the party organized a raid on the Houses of Parliament in which Scotland's ancient "Stone of Scone" was liberated and returned to Scotland. The party also contained a number of well-known Scottish poets such as Hugh McDairmid. But in the early 1960s, the SNP underwent a change of heart and direction. More organizationally minded men succeeded in ousting the literary members and set about creating a political machine. They changed a crankish party into a thoroughly conventional, if not dull, electoral machine.(14) McDairmid was kicked out. In 1962, as part of this change, the SNP agreed to back devolution as a first step to independence.

It was at about that time that the party began to perform credibly in by-elections. The SNP had fielded 5 candidates in the previous (i.e., the 1959) General Election, and won a mere 0.8 percent of the vote. It did not contest the May 1960 by-election in Edinburgh North, the April 1961 by-election in Paisley, nor the November 1961 by-election in East Fife. Indeed, the party had not contested a by-election since October 1948 when it fought Stirling and Falkirk Burghs. In the fourth by-election of the 1959 Parliament, it did however contest the seat at Glasgow, Bridgeton. It won a handsome 18.7 percent of the vote. Most of its votes were won from the Conservative opponent in this safe Labor seat. Heartened, it offered challenge at the next by-election in West Lothian in June 1962 where its current chairman, William Wolfe (an accountant and active supporter of the Boy Scout movement), came in second to Labor in a very high poll (71.1 percent). Wolfe won 23.3 percent of the vote to Tam Dalyell's (Labor) 50.9 percent. This result heartened the SNP and it went on to contest each subsequent by-election. The success in West Lothian had an even more important result. Individual membership in the party began to grow rapidly. The party's full-time organizer then found it possible to establish branches at the rate of 2 per month after West Lothian. In 1962, the party had only 2 recognized branches (a branch needs 20 members to be recognized). In 1969, 113 branches achieved recognition and in the first 4 months of 1967, 63 new branches were recognized.(15)

None of this was recognized at the time by the British parties. In the 1964 General Election, the SNP was able to contest 15 seats and gain 2.4 percent of the vote. It was still possible to ignore the SNP. In 1966, when Labor gained a large parliamentary majority helped by winning 46 of the 71 Scottish seats, the SNP also gained. In that election, the SNP could afford 23 candidates and it won 5.0 percent of the vote. After that the party really began to force the British parties to take notice. In the first parliamentary by-election of the 1966 Parliament, the Welsh National Party (Plaid Cymru) had won Carmarthen in July 1966. The first by-election of the Parliament in Scotland occurred in Glasgow, Pollock. The seat was fought on March 9, 1967. The SNP came in third with 28.2 percent of the vote. The intervention of the National Party helped Conservatives to win the seat from Labor. In November 1967 the Nationalists won the psychological breakthrough toward which they had been building. They captured the previously safe Labor seat of Hamilton with 46 percent of the poll.

Both the Labor and the Conservative Parties panicked. It is important to note that the panic gripped the Westminster headquarters of the parties before it made itself felt in Scotland. Indeed, it is not too much to say that neither of the British parties had a particularly healthy Scottish party when the Nationalists broke through. Each party's central organization had to wake up its Scottish section. The Conservatives acted first. Mr. Heath, the Conservative Leader, announced to a Conference of his Scottish Party in Perth in May 1968 that they were a Scottish Party committed to Scotland and, therefore, they would henceforth back devolution. Thus the formal commitment was made.

But Mr. Heath did not specify what form of devolution his party was committed to; nor did he win over his party's heart. To fill the first gap, he appointed a commission under the chairmanship of his predecessor, Sir Alec Douglas Home. The Conservative Party never did give its heart to devolution, but its formal commitment to the principle has done much to weaken the antidevolutionists. When the Labor government forced its Scotland Bill (embodying its proposals for devolution) through the House of Commons in 1978 and 1979, the Conservative opposition to the Bill was hampered by its inability to attack the principle of the proposal. The most effective and imaginative antidevolutionist amendments to the Bill came, not from the Conservative front bench, but from Labor back-benchers. Though the Conservative party remains formally committed to the principle of devolution, it is inching away from that commitment. It was committed by its Scottish Association to work for a "no" result in the referendum on devolution which the Labor government has called as a final test of whether the legislation is to be put into effect.

The Labor Party was slower to act than the Conservative party. Not until the National Party had won large numbers of seats in the municipal elections of 1967 and 1968 did it move. In April 1969, Harold Wilson committed his government to setting up a <u>Royal Commission on the Constitution</u> under the chairmanship of an English economist and antidevolutionist, Lord Crowther. Perhaps Wilson hoped that Crowther would report against the principle of devolution.

Both the parties' commissions on devolution reported in favor of a degree of devolution. The Home Commission reported early in 1970, recommending the creation of an assembly in Edinburgh. This assembly, which the Home Committee wanted to be called "The Scottish Convention," would be directly elected. It would perform the tasks presently performed by the Scottish Grand Committee (taking the Committee stage of Scottish legislation as that legislation was being enacted by the House of Commons), and the tasks performed by the Standing Committees on Scottish Affairs. Home also wanted his Convention to "provide a focus for the discussion in public of Scottish affairs." The main points in the Home Committee report were written into the Manifesto on which the Conservative Party stood in the 1970 General Election. Once elected the party did nothing.

It may have been comforted by the relatively poor showing that the National Party made in Scotland at the 1970 General Election. (It won only one seat with fewer votes per candidate than in 1966.) Indeed, the 1970 General Election saw a temporary, but marked return to two-party voting throughout the United Kingdom. The Labor Party, which was out of power, was not in a position to do anything. The Royal Commission that it had appointed was to report in 1973. By that time, support for the National Party, fueled by the discovery of large amounts of oil and gas in the North Sea, north and east of Scotland, had begun to recover. In the four by-elections in Scotland during the 1970 Parliament, the National Party never won less than 18.9 percent of the vote. In Stirling and Falkirk in September 1971 it lost with 34.6 percent of the vote; in March 1973 it won 30.2 percent of the vote and only narrowly failed to capture the previously safe Labor seat of Dundee East. Immediately after this encouraging result the National Party launched their successful "It's Scotland's Oil" campaign, an attempt to convince Scots that their future would be brighter in an independent Scotland.

The oil campaign resulted in large numbers of additional individual members joining the party. In November the party faced two by-elections, one in Edinburgh North and the other in Glasgow Govan. The party faced these tests of opinion in good heart as the Royal Commission on the Constitution had reported favorably on devolution. In the by-elections, the SNP performed credibly in Edinburgh North (18.9 percent) but won Govan (41.9 percent). Its candidate in Govan, Margo MacDonald, was an immediate success with the press and broadcasters.

When the Royal Commission finally reported, it was headed by Lord Kilbrandon, a prodevolution Scottish judge who took over from Crowther on the latter's death. It is not possible to say how much influence this accident of death had on the devolution argument, but it is perfectly obvious from the minutes of evidence that prodevolution spokesmen were given a much less hectoring reception by the Commission when Kilbrandon was in the Chair than under his predecessor. Kilbrandon said that there was a strong demand for a measure of devolution from the Scottish (and Welsh) people and proposed to grant the desired Assemblies. The Commission had considered the arguments in favor of separatism and federalism and rejected them.(16) They rejected separatism on economic grounds and federalism on the grounds that there was no demand for it. They had found considerable support for devolution and thought that a scheme of devolution which was both administratively workable and consistent with the continued existence of the United Kingdom could be created.

For Scotland they proposed that an Assembly of members directly elected by proportional representation be established. This Assembly should be given legislative and executive control over the following subjects: local government; town and country planning; new towns; housing; building control; water supply and sewerage; other environmental services; ancient monuments and historic buildings; roads, road passenger transport; harbors; education (probably excluding universities); youth and community services; sport and recreation; arts and culture; social work services; health; miscellaneous regulatory functions; agriculture, fisheries, and food; forestry; Crown estates; police; fire services; criminal policy and administration; prisons; administration of justice; legal matters; Highlands and islands development; and sea transport. An independent board would determine the correct grant for Westminster to give the new Assembly for the discharge of these functions.(17) Kilbrandon's report was greeted with glee by Scottish devolutionists of all parties, but largely ignored in Westminster. Devolution, even with the backing of the Nationalist victory in Govan, was not a major preoccupation during the first 1974 General Election. But the Nationalists won seven seats at that election with 21.9 percent of the Scottish vote. Labor realized that it would have to hold another General Election soon and that it could easily lose a number of seats in Scotland (the party had won 40 seats with 36.6 percent of the vote) unless it stopped the advance of the Nationalists. To this end the Prime Minister committed the government to produce a White Paper and a bill for devolution in the debate following the Queen's Speech (which outlines the government's policies for the coming year) on March 12, 1974.(18) It is interesting to note that the Labor Party, like the Conservative Party, has been true to the word of its leader; it has produced a White Paper and a bill, and that bill (a modification of Kilbrandon's proposals) is being enacted.

The creation of a devolved Assembly for Scotland is a considerable compliment to the National Party. The Assembly has been conceded in order to head off the National Party. At its lowest, the Assembly is a concession which Labor and Conservatives hope will satisfy the nationalist aspirations of the Scottish people for a time; at a higher estimate, the Assembly is an attempt by the British parties to legitimize the continued sovereignty of the British state within Scotland. It is hoped that the new Assembly will satisfy the national feeling of the Scots and reconcile them to remaining within the United Kingdom.

It is important to note that the decision to take the step of creating the Assembly was taken at the center of British politics. It was not taken as the result of a direct demand by the Scottish people for more control over their own affairs but by their willingness to vote for the SNP, a party committed to devolution as a step to independence. Support for the National party is not, however, the same thing as support for devolution. And, while it is the case that opinion poll after poll has shown a considerable majority of Scots in favor of devolution, it is also the case that these same polls show that devolution is not a high priority for Scots.(19) Like Englishmen, they are primarily interested in the economic questions – inflation and unemployment.

Support for devolution had been consistent at about 60 percent of the electorate ever since the October 1974 election. This was what Kilbrandon discovered. However, even on the eve of the October 1974 election, only about 10 percent thought to mention devolution to ORC pollsters when asked for their priorities. This is consistent with the most recent systematic poll (that of MORI) taken on the eve of the Garscadden by-election in March 1978. At this more recent poll, devolution was the eighth most frequently mentioned item.(20) There is another way of looking at the way the SNP has successfully translated popular feeling into law. The Kilbrandon Commission recommended devolution for Scotland and Wales. These are the two parts of the United Kingdom which have active separatist political parties. The argument Kilbrandon used for devolution was popular pressure; but if popular pressure had been the moving force, Kilbrandon would have made quite different recommendations. The evidence collected by the Commission on which it based its recommendations showed that support for greater regional autonomy was actually greater in some parts of England than in Wales:

	Total	Scotland	Wales	Yorkshire	N. West	S. East
Percentage for more devolution:	61	73	57	60	69	57

There was broad majority support for devolution.(21) More to the point, support for devolution grows the further one travels from London; and the Yorkshire and North West Regions are further from London than most of Wales.

ECONOMIC AND SOCIAL FACTORS

This chapter has sought to explain the success of the move to devolution as a response by the British parties to the electoral success of the National Party. This explanation leads to another question: Why has the National Party risen? Is this simply the expression in Scotland of the dissatisfaction with the two major parties which also finds expression in England and Wales? Or is it specifically Scottish? Why have such large numbers of Scottish voters moved from their previous electoral allegiances? Have there been any social changes which have undercut the allegiances of the past?

It is not possible to produce a definitive answer to these questions. But some changes are beyond dispute, and one is that the Scottish economy and Scottish society were undergoing rapid and painful changes in the 1960s and early 1970s which have altered the occupations and housing structure considerably.(22) The main force of the change has been a sharp reduction in employment in the old mining and manufacturing industries and a replacement of those jobs with others in public service and white collar professions. Within that change there were other, less dramatic but no less important, changes. The proportion of new investment which came from business owned outside Scotland rose dramatically. The proportion of jobs available to skilled manual tradesmen – usually males – declined; the proportion of jobs for women increased. Moreover, many of the new jobs were located on green field sites away from old city centers; new towns of publicly owned – but very comfortable and attractive – housing were built in these new growth centers. These new towns attracted a large number of commuters from the large cities. People with jobs in the growing sectors which happened to be located in the old cities often lived in the new towns. All these changes occurred rapidly in the period between 1960 and 1975. Scotland had not participated in the similar change in occupational structure which had occurred in England during the 1950s, and hurried to catch up in the 1960s. It was precisely at this time that the National Party made its breakthrough in Scottish politics; and that breakthrough was most noticeable in the new towns.

The 1950s had been the most depressing decade in recent Scottish history. Scotland's performance in growth, output, productivity, and employment fell behind England and Wales. The economic changes which occurred in England – especially in the English midlands and the South-East – did not touch Scotland. In 1961 the Scottish Council (Development and Industry) set up a committee to report on the position of the Scottish economy. That report (known after its chairman as the Toothill Report) showed that the new science-based industries, which had been the foundation of economic growth in England, had contributed only an additional 50,000 jobs – about 2 percent of total employment – to Scotland between 1951 and 1958.(23) Indeed, only 95,000 new jobs had been created in all industries in Scotland in that period. The growth rate of the Scottish economy had been cut in half between 1954 and 1959 and was substantially below that of England and Scotland's European competitors.

This report became something of a milestone in Scottish public debate. Both Labor and Scottish National parties latched on to it. Labor used it to argue that central government must direct more resources to Scotland. At the same time, the specific form of this direction remained vague. The National Party used Toothill to convince people that the British (or the English, as the SNP would call it) government was serving only the interests of England and that, therefore, independence was needed.(24) These are the basic categories of the public debate between these two parties up to the present day.

But Toothill was well timed. It was published in 1961. From that point the Scottish economy embarked upon a decade of change which had several related features: the old heavy industries, formerly the centerpiece of the Scottish economy, declined rapidly; the output lost by these industries was to a considerable extent made up by their replacement by new lighter industries; the newer industries were largely foreign owned; employing fewer skilled men and a higher proportion of unskilled workers and women than the old industries (they employed fewer workers than the industries which were shedding labor); because the new jobs were unskilled and often women's work, they were less well paid than the jobs which were being lost; and there was also a considerable rise in the number of jobs in the professions and the service industries generally.(25)

The basic outline of the change in the structure of employment is given in table 4.1. The changes shown here were noticed immediately. Thirteen years after the Toothill Report, the Scottish Council (Development and Industry) published another report (called "Nicol" after its chairman). Nicol noted the drop in the old industries and the rise in the new. In their figures, employment in coal and mining had dropped by 56 percent; agriculture by 46 percent; retail distribution by 15 percent; rail transport by 52 percent; shipbuilding and marine engineering by 29 percent; textiles by 26 percent; and railway stock manufacture by 74 percent in the 10 years from 1961 to 1971. On the other hand, Nicol noted the rise in employment in the new industries. Food and drink had 12 percent more employees in 1971 than in 1961; electronics had grown by 159 percent; motor vehicles by 302 percent; insurance by 43 percent; education by 45 percent; medical and dental by 34 percent; and local government service by 22 percent.(26) What Nicol did not point out (it was a document designed to encourage cheer) is that the decline in the industries he mentioned had lost 46,000 more jobs than the gain in the new industries. For Scotland's 8 major productive sectors, the drain was about 20,000 jobs yearly. Seven of 8 jobs lost had been held by men.

The fact that the new jobs were much more likely to involve process work than skilled labor, were more often held by women, and were often part-time jobs and were badly paid, kicked out the middle rung in the working-class ladder. There was a small and declining skilled manual labor sector. In 1961 one-fourth of the work force was skilled; in 1971 one-fifth. The drop was as large as the total drop since 1921. This has tended to entrench the position of the poorer sections of Scottish society even more than in the past. In the first instance, that entrenchment may help the Labor Party. But Labor's traditional voting strength and its largest number of activities and leaders have traditionally come from skilled manual laborers. This group has shrunk considerably.

At the same time, there has been a considerable rise in employment in professional and other service industries — the traditional centers of middle-class employment. As Table 4.1 shows, the number of people employed in education increased from 93,700 in 1961 to 165,000 in 1976. Similarly, employees in medicine increased from 87,000 to

Table 4.1. Employment by Industry in Great Britain and Scotland
for May 1961 and June 1976
(in thousands)

	May 1961		June 1976	
	Scotland	Gt. Britain	Scotland	Gt. Britain
Total:	2,155	22,490	2,071	22,047
Agriculture, forestry and fishing	98	598	49	381
Mining and quarrying	89.3	737	35	345
(coal sector)	83.1	668	28	297
Manufacturing Industries	760.2		607	7,098
Food, drink, and tobacco	98.9	812	91	691
Chemicals and allied industries	37.7	533	28	420
Metal manufacture	58.3	637	39	469
Engineering and electrical goods	167.6	2,133	158	1,796
Shipbuilding and marine engineering	65.9	252	42	175
Vehicles	37.2	894	32	733
Metal goods not otherwise specified	28.1	563	27	519
Textiles	106.6	843	57	480
Leather, leather goods and fur	4.3	63	3	40
Clothing and footwear	30.7	573	31	364
Bricks, pottery, glass, cement, etc.	23.4	347	17	258
Timber, furniture	24.8	290	20	259
Paper, printing, and publishing	58.2	615	44	536
Other manufacturing ind.	18.6	307	16	321
Construction	177.3	1,510	171	1,269
Gas, electricity and water	30.4	382	29	343
Transport and communication	174.5	1,657	137	1,453
Distributive trades	288.4	2,829	237	2,670
Insurance, banking and finance	40.3	560	76	1,087
Professional and scientific	218.1	2,059	352	3,559
Educational services	93.7	931	165	1,834
Medical and dental services	87.9	775	142	1,250
Miscellaneous services	168.8	2,007	227	2,252
Public admin. and defense	109.0	1,277	150	1,580

Sources: Scottish Statistical Office, Digest of Scottish Statistics, no. 19, April 1962 (HMSO) pp. 24-26, and Department of Employment Gazette, "Annual Census of Employment: June 1976," December 1977, pp. 1351-1354. The figures have been rounded and are not entirely comparable in any case. See N.K. Burton, and D.I. MacKay, British Employment Statistics: A Guide to Sources and Methods (Oxford: 1977) p. 115.

142,000. The change in the relative importance of some of the old industries and the new ones is dramatic. In 1961 employment in mining and education was of the same order; in 1976 there were four times as many people employed in education as in mining. In 1961 there had been two-and-a-half times as many people employed in Scotland in the textile industry as in insurance; by 1976 there were nearly twice as many in insurance as in textiles. While there had been a drop in the number of skilled working-class jobs, there was a considerable increase in the number of middle-class jobs.

One of the distinguishing features of Scotland among the British nations has been the relative weakness and lack of self-confidence of the middle class. Employers and managers, professional workers, and white collar employees declined between 1921 and 1961. Many would-be members of this class emigrated; not a few to England.(27) Scotland is a net exporter of university graduates. Since 1961 there has been a considerable expansion in numbers in all professional groups in Scotland. In 1921 Scotland had 100,000 employers and managers; in 1971 it had 200,000. Emigration came to a halt during the 1960s. Many of the parts of this group which expanded fastest were in public employment — nurses, teachers, and administrators. Moreover, since entry into this group is by educational qualification, and all the universities and other forms of tertiary education are state owned and controlled, these groups owe their success and their position to the growth in the power of the state. In England many people in these professions joined the Labor Party. In Scotland this did not happen.

Clearly there have been important changes in Scottish society in the past 15 years. But these changes are not all in one direction. Some people are better off as the result of the changes; others are worse off. How have the changes affected political allegiances?

PROSPECTS

It is difficult to believe that the rise of the SNP and the fast changes in Scottish society simply coincided. But it is equally important not to imply that the change in Scottish society caused the change in Scots' voting patterns. It is possible, however, to build up a rough outline profile of SNP voters from survey evidence now available. The best information is contained in the British Election Study (BES) after the October 1974 General Election. In that election the parties' votes were: Labor 36 percent; SNP 30 percent; Conservative 24 percent; Liberal 8.3 percent. One result of this study is that support for the SNP was found to be more evenly spread across occupations than support for the other major parties. (See Table 4.2.)

It is noticeable, however, that support for the Labor Party is substantially stronger than for the SNP among "Other manual" workers, and higher than for the SNP among "Skilled manual" and "Other nonmanual" workers. Since these are the poorest paid sections of society, it can be surmised that the SNP does not do particularly well among the poorest voters.

Confirmation of this pattern comes from the BES's correlation between voting intention and housing tenure (table 4.3).

Fifty-one percent of the BES sample (54.2 percent of Scots) lived in houses they had rented from a local council. Labor's strength in this group is manifest. Conversely, the Conservative's strenth – about 33.6 percent of Scots who own their own homes – is also clear. The National Party is more evenly represented among all categories of occupants than the other major parties. But its only lead is in mortgaged property. Again, the SNP does not do well among the poorest or the richest sections of Scottish society.

One feature of Scottish voting which distinguishes Scotland from England is the strength of the Labor Party among Scotland's Catholics (16 percent of Scots are Catholics). The SNP has not been able to break through this strength. The BES study showed that 69 percent of the Catholics supported Labor. Later studies have confirmed this figure.(28) The parties draw equally from among Protestant voters.(29) Most Scottish Catholics lived in the Strathclyde region around Glasgow and many are descended from Irish immigrants. They are more working class and more unionized than Protestant voters.

The SNP is often accused by the other large parties of lacking policies on social issues. "Still No Policies" is one adumbration of SNP. There is some sign that the electorate shares this view. The SNP does not have a definite social profile. Many voters – of all parties – think that it doesn't do as well in economic policies as the British parties. On the other hand, it scores highly on its ability to speak for Scotland. On economic issues, Conservative and Labor voters favored their own parties. On prices, 16 percent of SNP voters preferred the Conservative Party, 6 percent favored the Liberal Party, and 26 percent favored the Labor Party. Thirty-two percent were "Don't knows." Only 18 percent of SNP voters favored their own party's ability to do something about wage controls.(30) Concerning Scottish government, however, the position was different.

Another hint about the social basis of SNP's support is contained in the age distribution of Scottish voters. The BES survey discovered, and many subsequent polls have confirmed, that the SNP is the most popular of the 3 major parties among voters who are less than 35 years old. It was in third place, however, behind both Labor and Conservative in every group over the age of 45.

Another hint to SNP's social composition is found in the fact that its best performance in local elections has been in the new towns. It has been continuously in control of Cumbernauld and Kilsyth District Council since it was set up in 1974, and before that (since 1968) it controlled Cumbernauld. Cumbernauld has 43,000 residents. The SNP also did well in the other new towns – East Kilbride (73,500 residents) and Irvine (50,000 residents), in particular. This success has not gone unnoticed by the British parties. The government had a plan to build an additional new town at Stonehouse. Like Cumbernauld and East Kilbride, this new town would have taken people mainly from Glasgow. The proposal to build on this site was dropped in 1976, ostensibly

Table 4.2.   Voting Patterns, October 1974
General Election by Occupation
Percentage Voting For

	Con.	Lib.	Lab.	SNP	(Did not Vote)
Higher managerial	37	11	11	37	3
Lower managerial	35	10	16	29	9
Skilled nonmanual	36	5	26	27	7
Other nonmanual	24	10	30	26	10
Skilled manual	12	3	39	33	12
Other manual	11	4	52	20	14
By Trade Union Contacts					
Respondent in a TU	11	6	46	26	11
Someone else in household in a TU	16	5	36	32	11
Neither	31	8	26	22	13

Source: W. Miller, "Nationalists Cut Across Class Division,"
Scotsman, October 15, 1975, center page.

Table 4.3.   Voting Patterns by House Tenure
Percentage Voting for:

	Con.	Lib.	Lab.	SNP	DnV.
Owned - no mortgage	49	7	14	19	11
Mortgaged	28	12	17	33	10
Rented privately	27	9	23	24	16
Rented from Council	11	5	49	24	12

Sources: W. Miller, "Nationalists Cut Across Class Division,"
Scotsman, October 15, 1975, center page; see also Market and
Opinion Research, Weekend World: Scottish Survey (London,
1978), p. 5.

because the town was not needed. Certainly it was dropped at a time when building new towns looked like a sure way to build political bases for the SNP.

It is very tempting to suggest that our evidence shows that the new Scotland votes for the SNP and the old Scotland remain true to past allegiances. The high SNP support in the new towns and its success among the young makes this an attractive explanation. However, it would be more to the point to look at the change from the other end first. Labor's voters are most clearly distinguished from the rest by social indicators. They are over 45, members of trade unions, council house dwellers, and many of them are Catholics. The Conservative Party's voters also fall into a fairly clear social stereotype. They, too, are over 35, own their homes, usually have a mortgage, and do not belong to a trade union. Conservative voters are also likely to be managerial or skilled nonmanual workers.

Table 4.4. Percentage Preferring Party's Stand On Scottish Government

	Con.	Lib.	Lab.	SNP.	DnV.
Among Con. voters	47	6	2	11	34
Among Lib. voters	18	41	4	9	33
Among Lab. voters	1	1	51	22	25
Among SNP voters	6	4	7	67	15
All voters	15	7	21	30	27

Source: W. Miller, "Nationalists Cut Across Class Division," Scotsman, October 15, 1975, center page.

SNP voters do not fall into such easily delineated categories. The party makes a virtue of this. It says that it speaks for all Scots, regardless of class. The older parties, of course, pooh-pooh this claim. But I think it should be taken seriously. The SNP voters are people for whom the old battle lines have little meaning. They come from a variety of areas in Scotland. They are spread out geographically and this spread helps to account for poor return of 11 seats for 30 percent of the vote. They have an impressive number of second places. They are the new Scotland, not in the sense that they are a distinct new group seeking to gain advantage over the old Scotland; but in the sense that the old – mostly class – lines of division do not retain their loyalty. If the new Scotland is postindustrial, may we suggest that the new SNP voters are postclass.

We should also suggest that it is not clear that the SNP will be able to retain this loosely compiled support. The old questions of class politics are still real enough in Scotland. The SNP will have to be for higher council house rents or lower council house rents. They will have to acquiesce in the perpetuation of the separate state-supported Catholic school system or attack it; they will have to support comprehensive state schooling or the encouragement of the private schools section. Once the Assembly is in operation, it will be necessary for the SNP to make up its mind on these issues and speak for one side or the other. Whichever way they go, it will cost them some support. Then the very indefiniteness of their class position, until now an advantage in so far as it has allowed this new party to attract support from across the class spectrum, may become a positive disadvantage. They will need a solid basis of support to resort to in times of trouble.

This can be expressed another way. The Scottish branches of the Conservative and Labor Parties have been failures. They have not been able to get out of their ghettos to attract new support. Each of them found the old fight against the old enemy too comfortable for their own good. When the society changed rapidly and a new group of voters with new interests appeared who were unwilling to identify themselves with either ghetto, the Conservative and Labor Parties were not nimble enough to attract them. We have already seen how these parties fumbled the devolution issue. The nationalism which exists in most Scots was strong enough, once they had broken the conditions of class, for the National Party to attract these voters to its banner.

There are signs that the need to compete against the new energetic enemy has had a tonic effect on the Conservative and Labor organizations. No better emblem of this change could be found than the 1978 by-election in Hamilton. This was the second by-election in recent memory there. In November 1967 the SNP had captured Hamilton against a rundown depressed Labor opposition. Hamilton was a steel and coal town. Its Labor Party was dominated by the Miners Union and it has profited by new industries and was the perfect symbol of the new Scotland replacing the old. The SNP fought a magnificent campaign in 1967, bringing in bus loads of workers from all over Scotland, particularly from nearby new towns. Labor recaptured the seat in the subsequent General Election and had held it with decreasing majorities when, in March 1978, the sitting MP died. The SNP candidate was their best-known figure and Senior Vice-President, Margo MacDonald. Labor held the seat with an increased majority against all expectations when the by-election was declared. This time it was Labor who could bring in workers from all over the central belt of Scotland. The Conservative Party, too, managed to fight bravely for this seat on which they have lost their deposit more than once. This kind of vigor and energy was unimaginable when the first by-election in Hamilton was fought.

But neither Labor nor Conservative has changed social policies. If anything, each has retreated further into its safe base as the SNP has won over the middle ground. If the problem for the SNP is to win over a safe base, then the problem for the Labor and Conservative Parties is to go beyond their base. Or to put it another way, if politics in Scotland is still like a war in which each side does its best to build up its fortress while making the occasional sally at the enemy, the future for the SNP is bleak. If, on the other hand, movement and mass armies have arrived, the future for the old parties is bleak.

NOTES

(1) Constitution and Rules of the Scottish National Party, para. 2.

(2) See R. Cunningham, Scotland: Facts and Comparisons, (Edinburgh, 1977).

(3) See "Smoking: Scotland's Lethal Scourge," Scotsman, December 28, 1977, centerpage; and N. Ascherson, "Wha's Like Us?," Scotsman, August 6, 1977, centerpage.

(4) Cunningham, Scotland, chap. 10.

(5) Ibid., chap. 8.

(6) Billy Connolly – of Garscadden in particular.

(7) Cunningham, Scotland, chap. 8.

(8) Royal Commission on the Distribution of Income and Wealth Report #1 (Command 6171) HMSO, July 1975, Chap. 5, especially pp. 122-3; and Report #3 January 1976 (Command 6383), p. 124 (on incomes). See also the summary of this evidence by Michael Fry, "No Fair Shares in the Wealth of a Nation," Scotsman, October 5, 1976, p. 11.

(9) See John McEwan, Who Owns Scotland? (Edinburgh, 1977).

(10) See the lucid account in A.H. Birch, Political Integration and Disintegration in the United Kingdom (London, 1977) chap. 4, 5, and 6; and H.J. Hanham, Scottish Nationalism (London, 1969).

(11) See the provocative account by J.P. Mackintosh, "Federalism: Central/Regional Government Relations," in Paper No. 1, ed. J.N. Wolfe (Center of Canadian Studies, University of Edinburgh), pp. 1-15.

(12) See the more detailed account of both Labor and Conservative Party vacillations in H.M. Drucker, Breakaway: The Scottish Labor Party (Edinburgh, 1978), chap. 1 and 2.

(13) Cited in Drucker, Breakaway, p. 11.

(14) A useful short history and analysis of the SNP can be found in R. Mullin, "The Scottish National Party" in Multi-Party Politics in the United Kingdom, ed. H.M. Drucker (London, 1979).

(15) Mullin, "Scottish National Party." A table of post-1975 Scottish By-Elections can be found in The Scottish Government Yearbook 1979, ed. H.M. Drucker (Edinburgh: University of Edinburgh, 1978).

(16) Royal Commission on the Constitution 1969-1973, vol. 1 (London, 1973), chap. 12 and 13.

(17) Ibid., chap. 17 and 18.

(18) See the hostile but fair account of T. Dalyell, Devolution: The End of Britain (London, 1977), p. 99.

(19) See the summary of Scottish political opinion polls in Scottish Government Yearbook 1979, ed. H.M. Drucker. (Edinburgh: University of Edinburgh, 1978), appendices.

(20) Market and Opinion Research, Weekend World: Scottish Survey (London, 1978) p. 5.

(21) See J.P. Mackintosh, "The Report of the Royal Commission on the Constitution," Political Quarterly 45, no. 1., January-March 1974; 117.

(22) I am very grateful to Gordon Brown of Glasgow College of Technology for allowing me to see the unpublished text of his book on Scottish society in the 1960s and 1970s. The ideas he expresses in the book helped me write this section. I alone, however, accept responsibility for it.

(23) Report of the Committee of Inquiry into the Scottish Economy, Scottish Council (Development and Industry), 1961.

(24) See Mullin, "Scottish National Party."

(25) This is a summary of Brown's argument.

(26) A Future for Scotland, Scottish Council (Development and Industry) 1973, p. 29.

(27) The peak emigration abroad (26,800) was reached in 1967. Registrar General Scotland, Annual Report 1976, Part 2, "Population and Vital Statistics," HMSO 1977, p. 16.

(28) Ibid.; See also MORI.

(29) Miller, "Nationalists," and MORI, Ibid. – 36 percent Conservatives; 33 percent Labor; 29 percent SNP; 3 percent Liberal; and 2 percent SLP.

(30) W. Miller, "Catch 22 for Labour," Scotsman, October 16, 1975, centerpage. Again, confirmed by MORI, p. 6. Perhaps the interviewees took the poll less than seriously. Fifteen percent of MORI's SNP interviewees agreed to the proposition: "The SNP will promise anything to get votes."

5 Flemish and Walloon Nationalism: Devolution of a Previously Unitary State *

Jean Ellen Kane

The observation has been made countless times: Belgium is but a geographical expression. The statement has become a cliche, and a tired one. Yet its validity, rarely disputed in the past except by a few ardent bilingual and bicultural individuals in Brussels or abroad, is unassailable today. After decades of Flemish and Walloon nationalist rivalry, Belgium is on the verge of casting off the political trappings of unity and adopting the governmental structure of a regional federation.

Federation is hardly a novel solution to Belgium's ethnic and linguistic difficulties. Indeed, it was first proposed by Flemish nationalists near the end of the nineteenth century when a Fleming's right to use his own language in his official dealings with the government was just beginning to gain legal recognition. The reforms adopted during this period were based on the half-hearted acknowledgment that Flemish culture ought to prevail in Flanders and that the use of the Dutch language should be accorded equality with that of French in the

Publisher's note: The type employed in this book made utilization of diacritical marks unfeasible. Consequently, the German umlaut has been rendered as "ae," "oe," or "ue," respectively, in accordance with traditional practice, while French accents have been omitted, and so have diacritical marks in the case of Turkish, Czech, and other names.

*The author wishes to express her appreciation to Uri Ra'anan, Professor of International Politics at the Fletcher School of Law and Diplomacy, under whose guidance and with whose encouragement this paper was prepared. Special thanks are due also to Andre Navez and Ivan Couttenier, both of the American Embassy in Brussels, and to M. Vergauwen, of the Central Administration of the Belgian Armed Services, for their time and help in tracking down elusive bits of information.

northern half of the country. This meant that local government services, including education, were to be offered in both national languages. In the ensuing decades, a profound change occurred in the principles which underlie the cultural and linguistic regime in Belgium. Present theories insist that the maintenance of the Flemish culture – and that of the Walloons to the south – requires identifying each cultural group exclusively with a precise set of territorial boundaries. The capital, Brussels, an overwhelmingly French-speaking city surrounded by Flanders, alone is to retain its bilingual character.

While upon first impression the plan appears fairly straightforward, the process of drawing the frontiers of each region has been fraught with political controversy. Bits of territory have been traded back and forth across the linguistic border, often in exchange for language concessions in other parts of the country. Almost inevitably, as Flanders and Wallonia have approached linguistic exclusivity, the problems of Brussels and its spreading periphery have been intensified and remain the focus of the difficulties today.

This chapter traces the development of Flemish and Walloon nationalism and focuses on the rise of the language parties which gave political expression to ethnic concerns. By analyzing their sources of electoral support, it suggests reasons for the upsurge in nationalist sentiment in Belgium. It assesses the role that the language parties have played in the devolutionary process of the past several years.

THE HISTORICAL ORIGINS OF THE LANGUAGE DIVISION

The origins of the ethnic and linguistic division in Belgium can be traced back to the third century AD when invading Franks overran and absorbed the Celtic and Gallic peoples living in the region now known as Flanders. Although Frankish settlements were made outside this area, their numbers were assimilated into the Gallic culture which prevailed south of a line running roughly from the modern cities of Maastrict in the Netherlands to Boulogne in France.(1) North of this line to the banks of the Rhine River, the Germanic culture of the Franks flourished and their language developed into what is today modern Dutch. South of the division, the evolving French language remained dominant.

During the Middle Ages, French acquired prestige as the language of nobility throughout Europe. This was no less true among members of the upper class in Flanders, although Dutch never lost its position as the predominant language spoken by the mass of the population. Indeed, in a gesture laden heavily with symbolism, the Burgundian and Hapsburg rulers of the region always took their oaths upon their Joyeuse Entrees in Dutch as well as in their native tongues.(2) When Philip II of Spain reigned over the Low Countries in the sixteenth century, the Dutch oath was supplanted by one in French,(3) and that language was decreed the only official one for communications on a national level. Philip did require, however, that local government administrators conduct their official business in the vernacular.

Throughout the eighteenth century French remained unchallenged as the language of both the Walloon and Flemish nobilities. The language of Paris and the court of Vienna was intensely admired by ethnic Flemings who strove to imitate French styles and insisted that their children be educated solely in the French language and culture. The antiauthoritarian and anticlerical ideas current in France during the latter part of the century found numerous followers among the members of the francophone Flemish elite and further separated them from the conservative and traditionally Catholic Flemish masses. These French speakers were among the leaders of the independence movement and later formed the nucleus of the Liberal Party in Flanders.

As happened to the English language during the period of Norman rule,(4) Dutch was used only by the illiterate peasantry and urban poor. Within the space of a few generations, it had become fragmented into a plethora of distinct local dialects, and little effort was made to preserve a standard literary form of the language. While regional dialects of Walloon and Picard developed among illiterate French-speaking inhabitants of the rural south, this phenomenon did not have as devastating an impact upon the unity of the French language in Belgium because a universal pattern was consistently spoken – and written – by members of the aristocracy.

A concerted policy of Gallicization was launched during the period from 1792 until 1815 when France ruled Belgium,(5) and it was favorably received even in the Flemish provinces. French was declared the only official language throughout Belgium. Its use in the judicial system and local government administration resulted in a renewed emphasis upon French instruction in the educational system in Flanders. New schools were established in which the language of instruction was exclusively French. By the time French presence was withdrawn after Napoleon's defeat, the French language had attained unquestioned predominance among Flemish intellectuals and most government officials in Flanders.

When William I of the Netherlands decreed that Dutch was to be used in Flanders and French in Wallonia, his policy was accorded a mixed reception, especially among French-speaking Flemings. His edict that the language of instruction in primary and secondary schools in Flanders be changed to Dutch was met with only a modicum of dismay, and government officials generally acquiesced quietly in his decision to use Dutch in local business. The core of opposition to William's policy was found among the Flemish lawyers, who objected to being required to use Dutch in the courts. Virtually the entire generation then practicing before the bar had been trained exclusively in French and its members were quick to point out that their education prevented their following William's directive.(6) They were further enraged, as were their Walloon counterparts, by the Dutch monarch's insistence that high central government posts be reserved for Dutch and bilingual speakers, a requirement that most ethnically Flemish lawyers could not fulfill. In consequence, these positions were frequently given to Dutchmen instead of to Belgians.

It is then hardly surprising that when Belgium's independence was won in 1830, French was declared to be the only official language of the newly created state. The leaders of the revolution were entirely an educated group of men. Almost all were unilingually French speaking, and they wished symbolically to emphasize the separation of Belgium from Dutch rule. They explained that Dutch was not chosen for this reason and for the practical consideration that an official Dutch language would have been difficult to extract from the maze of mutually incomprehensible dialects. However, a stigma of cultural inferiority was undoubtedly attached to speakers of Dutch despite its no longer being an essentially illiterate tongue. "French in the parlor; Flemish in the kitchen"(7) was a common aphorism that made the prejudice readily apparent.

THE RISE OF FLEMISH NATIONALISM

The first signs of "linguistic patriotism"(8) among the Flemings were seen during the period of Dutch rule when political union led to closer intellectual ties between the Dutch and Dutch-speaking Belgians. Many of the early efforts were directed solely at enhancing the cultural appeal of the Dutch language. Jan-Frans Willems, a poet lauded as the father of the Flemish movement, wrote of the splendors of the Flemish tongue and, in correspondance with the renowned German philologist Jacob Grimm, he devised a system of orthography widely used in Flanders.(9) Jan David, a priest and professor of history and Flemish literature at the Catholic University of Louvain, prepared a Flemish grammar, organized the Met Tijd en Vlyt (With Time and Diligence) Flemish students movement, and wrote an eleven-volume history of Flanders. Their efforts reawakened an interest in Flemish culture and speeded the process of unifying the fragmented Dutch language in Belgium.

The Flemish cultural and literary revival rapidly became infused with the romantic spirit of the times. A crouching lion with out-stretched claws and a red tongue was borrowed from the coat of arms of the Count of Flanders and became the symbol of the Flemish movement. His virtues were celebrated in a song adopted as the official hymn of the movement.(10) The exploits of Flemish warriors, especially those in the Battle of Golden Spurs fought against the French King Philip the Handsome in 1302, were recounted in epic poems and historical novels. Among the most famous was De Leeuw van Vlaan-deren (The Lion of Flanders), published in 1839 by Hendrik Con-science.(11) In the preface to his work, he wrote a clear manifesto of the Flemish nationalist position:

There are twice as many Flemings as there are Walloons. We pay twice as much in taxes as they do. And they want to make Wallons out of us, to sacrifice us, our old race, our language, our splended history, and all that we have inherited from our forefathers.(12)

The discontent among the Flemish romantics led to the appointment of a commission in 1856 to investigate the causes of the Flemish agitation. The catalog of grievances published by the commission included the charge that the Belgian government had committed lese-langue in denying the Dutch language its rightful place in Belgian life. It enumerated a long list of specific circumstances in which the use of Dutch was demanded. These included its use in schools in Flanders, in communications between the central government and the Flemish provinces, and in the court system. These demands were adopted as the platform of the Flemish movement and were later used as a standard to measure its progress until after World War I.(13)

In 1864, the language used in the Netherlands was adopted as the official form of written Dutch in Belgium, and this change, together with the Liberals' loss of their parliamentary majority in 1870, helped ensure that efforts to introduce Dutch into official usage would be met with significant success.(14) The use of Dutch in all local judicial proceedings in Flanders was required in 1873, and five years later this directive was broadened to include all local government business. In both of these cases, Dutch was intended to supplement, not supersede, the use of French. Offering Dutch as an academic course in all state secondary schools was made obligatory throughout Flanders in 1850, but French continued to serve as the primary language of instruction. In 1883, a law was passed requiring primary education in Flanders to be taught in Dutch, although French language instruction was available to those who preferred it. Because the exclusive use of the French language was perceived as a means of fostering national unity and of facilitating a central administration, the language of nearly 60 percent of the population of Belgium was not declared an official language of the state until 1898. As a result, the Flemish movement remained focused upon the language itself rather than upon the social, political, and economic aspects of Flemish inferiority.

Throughout the later years of the nineteenth century, the efforts of the Flemish activists were often overlaid with heavy sentimentality. Alfons Willems, writing in 1895, frequently used phrases like "the language is the whole people" and lamented that "the language is more than an instrument; it is the soul of the people." "To outrage it," he continued, "is more than a misdeed, it is a sacrilege."(15) Although cultural and literary associations flourished, organized political activities were few, except for the Flemish antimilitarist league in Antwerp at the turn of the century.(16) French remained the primary language of the national courts, the civil service and diplomatic corps, of the government, of parliamentary debates, of almost all city councils, of the army, of the universities, and of large businesses.(17) More importantly, the knowledge of French continued to be viewed in Flanders as an essential prerequisite to upward social mobility. The anger and frustration among Flemish intellectuals at the pervasive French domination was perhaps most succinctly voiced in the often heard remark that "to be Belgian, we have to cease being Flemish."(18)

World War I served as a catalyst in bringing about a more radical and politically active Flemish movement.(19) The war inflicted a disproportionate number of casualties among the Flemings. Since Wallonia was more heavily industrialized than Flanders, the skilled Walloon workers were kept in the factories and mines, while their Flemish compatriots bore the burden of trench line defense. Not only did the Flemings make up by far the greatest bulk of the foot soldiers,(20) but the Belgian army's officer class was almost exclusively French-speaking. (It was, however, ethnically mixed. The language problem persisted despite the 1892 requirement that each officer take a course in the Dutch language before being permitted to graduate from the military academies and officers' schools. Because it illustrates well the difficulties in administering a bilingual state, an explanation of how the linguistic laws work in the Belgian Armed Forces is contained in Appendix B, at the end of this chapter.) Communications between the two language groups was difficult, quite often impossible, and antagonisms increased.

When the Germans invaded Belgium, they deliberately manipulated the ethnic-linguistic schism within the country and appealed to the close kinship between the Flemish and German peoples.(21) Some of them appeared genuinely persuaded that an eventual union of the ancient Germanic tribes along the northern Rhine was entirely possible.(22) They openly supported those Flemish nationalists who demanded a separate administration for Flanders, and many of the most ardent Flemish Activists, convinced that Germany was going to win the war, accepted German aid.(23) In February 1917, the Activists set up their own separatist government in Ghent called the Council of Flanders. At German insistence, they later moved it to Brussels where it could be more closely supervised by the German administrators. (Perhaps attempting to appeal to those Flemings who insisted on the inclusion of Brussels in Flanders, the Germans directed that the administration for Wallonia remain headquartered in Namur.) The Germans were careful to preserve the appearance of Flemish control, however, and even permitted the Council to issue a declaration of independence for Flanders that rang with nationalist sentiment.

> (T)he oppression under which the Flemish people have lived since 1830 has ceased. The state of Flanders is born. Flanders follows the current of world politics – the independence of nationalities. The Flemish people have finally been saved.(24)

Attempts by the Activists to recruit support from among the Flemings led to counter rallies condemning them,(25) and by the time the Armistice was signed, most of the Activists had fled clandestinely to Germany and the Netherlands. (With the disappearance of the remnants of the German Confederation's territorial outlines in the 1918 Versailles settlement, a new language group was added to the Belgian state. While Belgium's attempt to acquire Dutch Limburg and Zeeland Flanders – the regions around the Meuse and Schelt rivers, respectively –

and to recover the half of Luxembourg lost in 1839 ended in failure, it was permitted to annex an area east of Liege. The region included the town of Eupen and Malmedy whose German-speaking population then numbered close to 34,000.) They were tried in absentia as collaborators and traitors. Forty-five were condemned to death, while others received prison terms ranging from several months to life. The only one among those condemned to death who remained in Belgium was August Borms, a former secondary school teacher who had achieved prominence as an Activist despite his apparent lack of leadership and comparatively small following.(26) His sentence was almost immediately commuted to life imprisonment, but he dramatically played a martyr's role until pleas for amnesty led to his release in 1929.(27)

The Flemish nationalist movement was not effectively diffused, however, and in the election of 1919 several nationalist parties were represented. The Front Party, led by disgruntled Flemish former soldiers and encouraged by the exiled Activists, won five parliamentary seats. The Front's electoral support was strongest around Ghent, the site of the Party's headquarters and a center of Flemish cultural activity. Its university was the first in Flanders to use the Dutch language, and the Flemish intellectuals who had gathered there were at the vanguard of the nationalist movement.

Ghent also boasted a long tradition of political dissent. It was the birthplace of Belgian socialism and was the city from which the Catholic Party had launched its "social" crusade to recapture workers' votes. The Front's appeal in working-class districts of Ghent and Antwerp was most evident in the sections where migration from rural areas had been recent, as expanding industry's need for labor disrupted secure village ways. No abiding tradition of loyalty to the Socialist Party had yet developed among the uprooted farmers as evidenced by the Catholic Party's success in luring back their support.

The Front's subtle blending of religion and linguistic pride appealed also to the more radical workers and young intellectuals who were immediately aware that a small but dominant minority of French speakers controlled the major industries and barred Dutch speakers from positions of social and political prominence. By painting the 1920 pact with France as a deliberate attempt on the part of the French speakers to tighten their domination over Belgium, the Front Party gained the support of both these groups. They even drew world attention to their cause by writing to Woodrow Wilson, pleading that

> ...you may so far interest yourself in the pitiful case of the oppressed Flemings...as to cause an independent inquiry to be made into the Flemish question...to satisfy yourself that the new order of things in Europe is incompatible with a continuation of the wilful oppression of the race within the Kingdom of Belgium.(28)

Support for the Flemish nationalists spread to the countryside only after the movement became entangled with religious symbolism and mystical overtones. In a de facto alliance with local village priests,(29) a new slogan "Alles voor Vlaanderen, Vlaanderen voor Kristus" (All for Flanders, Flanders for Christ) was invented, and presented to the devoutly Catholic peasantry in the form of a cross. The West Flanders town of Diksmuide became a rallying point for Flemish nationalism, particularly when a tower was built in the town square displaying the symbolic letters $\stackrel{\wedge}{v\stackrel{\vee}{v}\kappa}$.

The Flemish nationalist parties continued to increase their strength throughout the interwar years. A slight decline in electoral support in 1932 led the Front Party to merge with several smaller factions to form the Vlaams Nationaal Verbond (Flemish National League). Just before the elections of May 1936, the VNV moderated its demands for the division of Belgium into two independent states to a position advocating strong separatism within the existing state. The election returns doubled the Flemish nationalist representation in Parliament, raising it to 16 members.(30)

The fascist ideology of the interwar years was not without appeal to small numbers of the Flemish nationalist leaders. Some drew their inspiration directly from Nazism, and one group, known as the Verdinasos, openly advocated the subjugation of the French-speaking provinces.(31) In 1937, the VNV allied with the Rexists, a fascist party of French-speaking Belgians led by Leon Degrelle. Together the two parties held mass rallies and campaigned vigorously against the left, especially after the strikes of 1937.

Inspired partly by a belief that German victory had become inevitable, cooperation with the Nazi occupation was widespread during the summer of 1940. Although the general willingness to acquiesce in the German administrative and economic measures lessened as the war wore on, collaboration by the VNV continued and became tainted with the ideological fervor of national socialism. At the Nazis' behest, the VNV played down its advocacy of federalism and, during the Russian campaign, it dutifully preached the twin themes of antibolshevism and solidarity among Germanic peoples.(32)

Despite incontrovertible evidence that collaboration pervaded the French-speaking community, and was especially prevalent in Rexist circles, the postwar punishment drive against incivisme appeared directed primarily against the Flemish nationalist movement. As cne Belgian commentator wrote,

> In the years which followed the liberation of Belgium in 1944, Flemish nationalism was destroyed from top to bottom...the repression was without pity, and even today it still has serious repercussions in the Flemish community. Generally speaking, all who had touched Flemish nationalism from near or far were hit by the repression, and the movement was literally decapitated, losing both its leaders and its faithful cadres.(33)

POST-WAR FLEMISH NATIONALISM

The Dutch language parties received no significant electoral support until the elections of 1954 and 1958. Even in those years, the newly unified party of Flemish nationalists, the Volksunie, won only one parliamentary seat from the province of Antwerp.(34) As during the interwar years, the nationalists drew their strength from an urban center long dominated by a French-speaking minority. The largest portion of Volksunie support came from those sections of Antwerp where port facilities were expanding and where the textile, chemical, automobile, and computer industries had built new plants and factories. Again support was strongest among the recent migrants to the city and among the younger university educated Flemings whose ambitions were repeatedly checked by the necessity of speaking French at the higher levels of every profession.

The low level of support for the Volksunie during these years belied the extent to which a crucial shift in moderate Flemish nationalist policy had been accepted. (More radical nationalists insisted on nothing short of full independence for a sovereign state of Flanders.) The change, which had occurred sometime before the war, was clearly reflected in the altered party slogan. "In Vlaanderen Vlaams" had been the cry of the early nationalists. It implied a campaign to introduce Dutch on an equal basis with French in the north of Belgium. Volksunie literature dropped the essential first word, and the expression "Vlaanderen Vlaams" led the party's drive for a unilingual Flemish culture throughout Flanders.(35)

For the first time in 1961, the party found support in every district in Flanders (Maps and a listing of the electoral subdistricts of Belgium [indicating the results of the 1977 elections]are found in Appendix A at the end of this chapter; the numbers that follow the district names in the text refer to their location on these maps), although the excesses of its rhetoric undoubtedly cost it the votes of many who might otherwise have agreed with its aim.(36) In keeping with the pattern established earlier, Volksunie support remained concentrated in urban and industrialized areas, especially in those with substantial numbers of French speakers. The Volksunie's appeal was less pronounced in rural and agricultural regions like Arendonk (#76) and Naderbrakel (#44). The single exception to the urban-rural division of Volksunie support was in the poultry and potato farming area of Nevele (#34), east of Ghent. A strong local party organization with encouragement from several prominent village officials, including a parish priest, explains the higher level of support. (The Volksunie had strong confessional ties which probably prevented its destruction during the postwar campaign against incivisme; in 1954 it simplified its name, the Christelijke Vlaamse Volksunie, to deemphasize its Church connections.)

Serious public debate of the Flemish nationalists' goals was overshadowed by distress at the activities of the Volksunie's militant wing. Hundreds of Flemings took to the streets armed with paint brushes and began to rectify French language street names and other official signs.(37) The Volksunie youth league was prone to more serious acts of violence. Street demonstrations against the use of French in Flemish cities often erupted into riots accompanied by sporadic episodes of looting and wanton destruction of property.

A PERMANENT LANGUAGE FRONTIER

Early in 1960, the Harmel Center, a prestigious social and political research organization, suggested that Belgium homogenize its provinces and electoral districts along linguistic lines. The idea was vehemently opposed by fervent unionists who feared that such a close identification of population and territory would give credence to the concepts of "Flanders" and "Wallonia" which, at that time, had no legal existence.(38) Previously there had been less concern with homogeneity. Language preference surveys were conducted as part of the ten yearly national censuses. According to the laws then in effect, if a linguistic minority numbered 30 percent, a bilingual administration was automatically provided. Conversely, if a linguistic minority failed to reach the required percentage, then the region reverted to unilingual local government services. Changes back and forth occasionally occurred, usually in the mixed communes along the border between Flanders and Wallonia.(39)

Although there were exceptions,(40) the communes surrounding Brussels tended to change only in the direction of bilingualism. After the 1961 elections, both members of the Volksunie and the Flemish members of the traditional parties denounced the spreading Brussels "oil stain" as gebiedscroofd (literally, "the stealing of territory"). They called for the permanent fixing of a language frontier and for the abolition of the linguistic census. Flemings had long argued that the language survey was an inaccurate reflection of the linguistic composition of the population and was instead a referendum on the language of government services. Those services included education, and a French language education was still regarded as the best pathway to success in Belgian and European life. The linguistic census, Flemings insisted, artificially inflated the numbers of French speakers in Flanders, especially along the border areas and in Brussels, and prevented the evolution of any true equality between the languages in Belgium.

There were other difficulties with the census. The languages spoken in many areas were hard to classify. The local patois in Brussels was clearly an amalgam of the two national languages and in Enghien, a Flemish town which grew up around a large chateau, a French vocabulary was superimposed on Dutch syntactical structure. More significantly, the surveys made no provisions for bilingual speakers until after World War II, and gave the false impression of mutually exclusive language groups.(41)

In May of 1961, the Social Christian-Socialist coalition of Theo Lefevre and Paul-Henri Spaak announced a compromise that divided Belgium into four linguistic regions: a Dutch language region in the north, a French language region in the south, a German language region in the east, and a bilingual French-Dutch region around the capital city of Brussels. The boundaries of all but the Brussels region were agreed in 1962 after a new language census was taken by Socialist Justice Minister Pierre Vermaylen. (Its results were kept secret as part of the accord.) At first it was planned to keep Comines (#119) and Mouscron (#120) in West Flanders and allow Liege to maintain control of the Fourons (St. Martens-Voeren). However, both Comines and Mouscron had French-speaking majorities and, under pressure from Walloon federalists, they were transferred in 1963 to the province of Hainaut. (The Parti Unite Wallon had organized a campaign for federalism in the elections of 1961. Its activities are discussed at length in the following section.) As a concession to the Flemings, the Fourons (#85) were simultaneously given to Limburg(42) and the French language was accorded a "protected" status. (This status was granted the minority language in a number of communes along the linguistic frontier; Appendix A, fig. 5.1. It guaranteed that an individual could use that language in his dealings with the local authorities and, if a sufficient number of families desired it, schooling for his children would be provided in the minority tongue.)

A similar compromise was reached for six communes along the border of the bilingual Brussels Capital region. The six were to remain part of the Dutch language region with all facilities being provided for French speakers. (These six communes — Wemmel, Kraainem, Wezembeek-Oppem, Drogenbos, Linkebeek, and Rhode-Saint-Genese — are shown in Appendix A, fig. 5.7.)

THE WALLOON RESPONSE

Dissatisfaction with the unitary structure of the Belgian state was not confined to the Flemish community. Strong sentiments of national identity among Walloons can be traced far back into Belgian history, but those feelings had traditionally received adequate expression in the very existence of the Belgian state, dominated as it was by French language and culture. The brief exception was the period of rule by William I, and that monarch's insistence on the use of Dutch contributed immeasurably to the unrest which culminated in the revolution of 1830. Ethnic and linguistic differences formed a continuous undercurrent in Belgian politics, and just prior to World War I, it was a Walloon who offered the King this celebrated advice:

> No, Sire, there is no such thing as a Belgian soul. The fusion of Flemings and Walloons is not to be desired and, if one were to desire it, one would have to admit that it is not possible.(43)

The question of royal succession, the settlement of the Congo crisis, and the controversy over religious and secular roles in education dominated political discussions in the decade and a half immediatley after the war. Walloon nationalism did not become politically organized as a force to counter the Volksunie during this period, except insofar as efforts to promote investment in the coal-mining sections of Liege were intermittently tinged with charges of ethnic discrimination against the region on the part of the government's economic planners. The results of the 1947 linguistic census severely jolted the complacency of the Walloon community, however. They revealed that 51 percent of the country spoke Dutch, 33 percent spoke French, 1 percent spoke German, and the remaining 15 percent, almost all of whom lived in Brussels, spoke both Dutch and French.(44) The figures became even more alarming to the Walloons when they were coupled with statistics for the birthrate – declining among Walloons and increasing among Flemings. (This is no longer true; birthrates for the two groups have been approximately the same since 1973.)

In the elections of 1961, two French language parties received significant support. The Bloc Francophone organized in the Brussels district to oppose the two-state federal plans advocated by the Volksunie. In that proposal, the status of predominantly French-speaking Brussels, located within Flanders, was clearly in jeopardy. The Bloc Francophone received virtually all its backing from the urban sections of the district, while support in the countryside surrounding the city was negligible.

The Parti Unite Walloon (PUW), which campaigned strenuously for federalism, drew its support from throughout the province of Liege, although its numerical strength was concentrated in the urban and industrial sectors around the party's headquarters. That Liege was the site of the first proposals of autonomy for the French language regions was consistent with its historic tradition of radical behavior on behalf of France and French culture. An independent ecclesiastical principality while the rest of Belgium was united under foreign rule, Liege became enamored of the ideas of the French revolution and the city was made a center for anti-Austrian and later anti-Dutch activism. The radicalism, independence, and political daring continued after 1830. The industrial sectors of the city gave birth to the Walloon socialist movement and the Social Christians never succeeded in regaining the workers' support. In 1945, a Walloon nationalist convention, meeting in Liege, voted for prompt separation from Flanders and immediate union with France.(45)

In the elections held four years later, the French language party in Liege attempted to increase its strength by fusing socialist and nationalist aspirations in the Parti Walloon Travailleur. Its strategy proved successful in those districts where industrial workers broke from their established loyalty to the Socialist Party, and the PWT received more votes in 1965 than the PUW had in 1961. It did not, however, even try to organize on a provincial level, and made no effort to appeal to those French speakers living in the eastern German language districts nor to those living in the declining inner city. (Under the d'Hondt system used in Belgium to apportion parliamentary seats, a smaller party organized at the provincial level can sometimes gain a seat from among those not won outright at the local level.)

In the province of Hainaut, the Front Wallon was the first linguistic party to gather significant support. Its strength was heaviest in the coal-mining regions of Jumet (#147) and Marchienne au Point (#146) near Charleroi, in the building industry and machinery shops of Soignies (#139), and in the steel mills of Chatelet (#144). In these urban areas, the network of social organizations and workers' clubs was used with great effect in marshaling votes for the Front. Discontent among the workers was widespread. The surface veins of coal and iron were fast becoming too depleted to be worked by obsolete mining equipment, and the economy of the region had slumped badly. Periodic general strikes further crippled production and added to the atmosphere of uncertainty and restlessness which pervaded the industrial quarters. Support for the Front in the less densely populated textile-manufacturing regions in the northwest was less pronounced perhaps because, although the industry there was also faltering, the decline occurred more gradually than in the mining districts. The Front's support in the rural southern regions of Hainaut was characteristically lower than in the urban areas. However, it offered testimony to both the Front's organizational efforts and to the appeal of nationalist sentiment in conservative districts. (Had the Front's overall support been somewhat higher, it might well have benefited from the provincial apportioning of parliamentary seats.) The strength of the French language party was not noticeably higher in Comines and Mouscron, nor was any attempt made to organize a Dutch linguistic party in those districts. (The one notable exception to the apparent contentment along the language frontier was in the Fourons. In the elections of 1965, over 57 percent of the population voted for a local party headed by the mayors of the six villages. The party's entire platform was indicated in its name, Parti Retour a Liege.)

The residents of Brussels were far less satisfied with what they perceived to be inequities in the 1963 linguistic laws. Two French language parties were organized in 1964 and were committed to protecting the interests of French speakers, particularly those in the unilingual Dutch communes outside the city. The smaller of the two new parties, the Union Francophone, received little support, but the Front Democratique des Bruxellois Francophones (FDF) did extremely well. Its umlauted slogan, "Brussel Vlaams, Jamais,"(46) adroitly designed to stir memories of Germanic domination, appealed to the shopkeepers and lower level professionals who initially formed the bulk of FDF support within Brussels. At first glance, support to the north and west of the city appeared lower, but it constituted a substantial portion of the French speakers living in those areas.

No French language parties were formed in 1965, or subsequently, among the Francophone minorities living in the major cities of Flanders. Their numbers were small and most found their interests adequately served by the firmly unionist Liberal Party. Even when that party divided along linguistic and regional lines after its defeat in the election of 1968, French speakers in Flanders continued to support it. (The Catholic Party had split into linguistic sections in 1936, after the

VNV won 16 parliamentary seats, most of them at the expense of the Catholics in Brussels and Flanders. The Socialists had similarly divided before the 1968 elections. Both parties ran virtually autonomous campaigns in each region. Instead of the landslide victory for which they had hoped, the Liberal Party lost one seat in those elections. Shortly thereafter, it divided into 3 sections, 1 for each of the major language regions and a third for Brussels.)

In October 1976, 6 out of 10 liberal members of the communal council in Ghent were Francophones. Two of these, Roger Pernot and Luc Beyer, had refused to join the Liberal Flemish Union. Beyer had sat for 12 years on the council and campaigned exclusively in French before Francophone audiences and in both national languages before other groups. He frequently expressed his "ferveur gantoise" and his "foi dans la culture francaise."(47)

THE VOLKSUNIE IN 1965

The strength of the Volksunie rose substantially throughout Flanders in the elections of 1965 and, for the first time, the correlation between urbanization and a high level of support for the nationalists did not hold consistently. To be sure, support was still lowest in the rural areas of eastern Brabant, particularly in Aarschot (#98), Diest (#93), and Landen (#95); and it was high in the textile, machinery, and shipbuilding sections of Temise (#56) and Sint Niklaas (#55). But it was not especially high in the older industrial subdistricts of Antwerp (#59) and Boom (#66), where the Socialist Party increased its support among the workers.

The populations in 2 regions where Volksunie strength was higher than average, the southeastern section of West Flanders and the region east of Antwerp, shared a common history of providing migrant labor for seasonal work and industry outside their own areas. During the 1880s and 1890s, when the importation of American wheat led to a decline in Flemish agriculture, nearly 50,000 workers(48) left East and West Flanders annually to work in the fields and textile mills in the French cities of Lille, Tourcoing, and Roubaix. Nearly as many went south to the mines of Hainaut and Liege. At one point, almost 30 percent of the work force in Wallonia was of Flemish blood.(49) Although most returned seasonally to Flanders, many were gradually assimilated into the French and Walloon cultures, for they had left as young men without the family ties that provide the social structure necessary to the maintenance of a minority's culture.(50) A similar phenomenon happened each year in the Kampellen region of Antwerp. Approximately 10,000 workers left that province to labor in the factories of the Netherlands.

Attachment to old ways and a fierce pride in their region characterized inhabitants of both areas. The tenacity with which the farmers clung to dialects and tradition in West Flanders had been especially legendary. Yet initially, support for the nationalist parties had not been strong despite declining agriculture and the vicarious contact with more prosperous, non-Flemish groups. Instead, the sharp increase coincided with dropping migration and the postwar influx of capital investment into each area.(51) The series of tax incentives designed by the government to attract foreign money into these regions worked well,(52) and the 1960s were a decade of rapid industrial expansion in both regions. Once again, the disruption and dislocation caused by the shift from farming to factories appears to be a fundamental cause of ethnicity and language attaining political expression.

The continued use of French in Flanders was the focus of repeated controversy during this period, particularly after a suit was brought in the European Court of Human Rights by French speakers against the unilingual educational policies of the Belgian government.(53) Ekeren (#60), Berchem (#84), and Beveren (#58) were among districts specifically cited in the suit, and the Volksunie was able to organize a significant demonstration of Flemish nationalism in these areas. Several communes around Brussels were also involved in the case, and the Volksunie gathered a high portion of Flemish votes in those districts. (Although it was not involved in the legal dispute over education, controversy over language and provincial designation raged in the Fourons. Nearly half the region's Dutch-speaking population supported the Volksunie.)

THE CONFRONTATION AT LOUVAIN

In 1966, the Volksunie began a concerted campaign to end the bilingual status of the Catholic University of Louvain. Latin had been the language of instruction at the world renowned university from its founding in 1495 until the nineteenth century. From that time until 1932, all students were instructed in French regardless of mother tongue. The language laws of 1932 gave Flemings an equal right to use their language at the university level, and the university was divided into a Dutch and a French section. By the early 1960s, each language section enrolled approximately 12,000 students.(54) Many faculty members and all major facilities were shared by the two sections.

After the language frontier was fixed, the French-speaking population of Louvain was left in an increasingly isolated position. While the right to use French within the University was assured, its use in the city of Louvain was not similarly sanctioned. Louvain was without question part of the region in which the official language of the government and all publicly run institutions was exclusively Dutch. However, included in the 1963 compromise on the limits of bilingual Brussels was a concession to the French-speaking professors at the University. Their children were allowed to attend local, publicly financed schools in which the language of instruction was French.

This concession touched off bitter resentment in the Flemish community on the grounds that it produced an alien elite in the midst of Flanders. Fear that some Flemish parents might desert their fellow linguists and enroll their children in the "caste schools" underlay much of the controversy.(55) Demonstrations, student strikes, and riots became commonplace in Louvain, but the bishops who governed the university were steadfast in their determination to preserve the bilingual unity of the school. In March 1968, after an especially violent dispute over the construction of an extension to a building used primarily for French language instruction, Bishop de Smedt of Bruges broke ranks with the other bishops and announced his belief that the French section of the University should move to Wallonia. Eight ministers from Vanden Boeynants Socialist-Liberal coalition government, which had come into office pledging a two-year truce on linguistic matters, resigned in sympathy with the bishop's position and the government fell.

In the elections which followed, a second French language party was formed to unite members of the three traditional parties who were dissatisfied with the manner in which the government was handling the Flemish nationalists' demands and demonstrations. The program of the Rassamblement Wallon (RW) stressed protection of Walloon linguistic interests and proposed economic decentralization on a regional basis within Belgium. The lists that the RW presented in the election were meticulously balanced among candidates of Social Christian, Socialist, and Liberal ideological persuasions to give the party greater appeal in specific districts and to promote cooperation with the traditional parties within parliament. The leadership of the RW and the Brussels-based FDF agreed formally to support each other's candidates and programs after the collapse of the Vanden Boeynant government.

The two parties achieved a stunning success in the 1968 elections, significantly increasing support for French language parties throughout Wallonia. The RW ran especially strongly in the depressed coal mining regions surrounding Namur and Charleroi. It also did well in the livestock, chicory, oats, and potato farming regions in the southern district of Brabant. Voters there expressed concern with the violence in Brussels and feared the southward spread of bilingualism. The region is overwhelmingly Francophone, however, and it is probable that bilingualism was closely identified with dreaded urban and industrial expansion. The strength of the FDF continued to climb in Brussels. The levels of support in such diverse subdistricts as working class St. Josse-ten-Noode (#110) and professional Uccle (#113) show clearly that its appeal had moved beyond the shopkeepers and small businessmen who had founded it.

The pattern of support for the Volksunie remained quite similar to that established in previous elections, although its strength increased considerably. Two areas in which support was strikingly higher were the coal mining region near Genk (#91) and along the sea coast in West Flanders. The mines in Genk had been worked steadily since ore was discovered in 1901. As had happened in Liege and Hainaut, the industry had become outmoded, causing a decline in production and generally depressed economic conditions in the surrounding towns. In Veurne (#6), Nieupoort (#5), Oostende (#4), and Blankenberg (in the Bruges sub-district — 1) the constant contact with a dominant French-speaking class, both residents and vacationers, had caused the area to become a focus of Flemish agitation. (In late summer of 1965, for example, officials in Oostende prepared 10,000 police to control unruly crowds in an expected protest march against the use of French in public buildings in the seaside resort town frequented by both Walloons and Flemings. While that particular demonstration failed to materialize, rioting did break out the following morning in front of the Cathedral of Saints Peter and Paul after the local paster had routinely preached a sermon in French to the visiting Walloons.)(56) The situation was further exacerbated by the French language press which constantly cited the area as an example of extreme Flemish irrationality. (Stories of a lifeguard's refusing to allow the parents of a lost Walloon child to speak French over the loudspeaker system on a beach at Oostende received widespread publicity.)(57) Truthful or not, the press accounts infuriated moderate Flemings and undoubtedly contributed to the support of the Volksunie.

CONSTITUTIONAL REFORM

Even more significant than the increased support for the linguistic parties in 1968 was the acknowledgment by the three traditional parties that some form of regional devolution had become inevitable in Belgium. Gaston Eyskens's Social Christian-Socialist coalition announced plans for a fundamental revision of the constitution. (It had taken 132 days to form the government. The coalition was reached only after two educational ministers, two cultural ministers, and three economic counselors, one each for Flanders, Wallonia, and Brussels, were appointed.) Parliament was divided into two language groups in which a member's linguistic affiliation was determined by the language region he represented. (Members representing the German language region were assigned to the French language group. This move precipitated the formation of a new language party, the Partei der Deutschsprachigen Belgien (PDB). Its program called for the political and economic decentralization of Belgium with the German language region enjoying a status similar to that of Flanders and Wallonia in controlling its own affairs. It also demanded an end to the protection guaranteed French speakers in Malmedy, St. Vith, and Eupen and desired compensation for the region's sufferings during the postwar period.)(58)

Only those members representing Brussels were permitted to choose their preferred language group. (Slightly over one-third chose to belong to the Dutch language group, a percentage in excess of the proportion of Dutch to French speakers in the district. The choice was a crucial one for many bilingual Brussels politicians. The population of the city was overwhelmingly French speaking, yet its bilingual designation clearly was going to require that Dutch speakers be somewhat over-represented in an eventual governing structure for Brussels.)(59) The members of the language groups, sitting as the newly created Cultural Councils, functioned almost as regional parliaments, with authority in cultural, educational, and linguistic matters.(60)

Unilingual policies without provisions for minority speakers, except in the "protected" areas, were applied as broadly as possible within each region.(61) Within the central administration, unilingual policies pertain only to those ministries divided along language lines. In the bilingual bureaucracies, a test of competence in both national languages is required.

(The hiring policies are carefully regulated to ensure that the bureaucracies approximately reflect the language division of the population. A 60/40 Dutch/French proportion has become the rule of thumb for government employees at the lower and middle-level positions. At the highest level, rough parity between the language groups is enforced, giving rise to complaints from Dutch speakers. Both the armed forces and the diplomatic corps, traditionally the reserves of Francophones, remain dominated by French-speakers, particularly at the higher levels.)(62)

These changes reinforced the linguistic and regional divisions within the traditional parties. The Social Christian party split into two entirely independent political organizations: the Parti Social Chretien (PSC) and the Christelijk Volkspartij (CVP). Each section has complete freedom in formulating party policies on regional and linguistic issues. Policies on nonlinguistic matters are supposed to be kept within the general philosophical principles advocated by the whole party, but regional differences have tended to make the "social" aspects of the party's ideology more pronounced in Wallonia while in Flanders the confessional ties have not entirely disappeared. The Socialist Party constitution permits less than total autonomy but it is headed by two presidents, one for the Parti Socialist Belge (PSB) and another for the Belgische Socialistische Partij (BSP). The Liberal Party, which alone stood for the unchanging unitary structure of the Belgian state in 1968, divided into three regional sections: the Parti de la Liberte et du Progres (PLP) in Wallonia (in 1977 its name was changed to Parti de la Reforme et de la Liberte Wallon (PRLW), the Partij voor Vrijheid en Vooruitgang (PVV) in Flanders, and a Brussels section simply called the Parti Liberal (PL). Each division draws up policies on all matters independently, but the programs are monitored and coordinated in a joint committee at the top of the party's hierarchical structure.(63)

The degree of regionalism reached during three years of negotiating a revised constitution was insufficient to curb the increasing strength of the language parties. In 1971, their support rose, especially in the Brussels region. In 1974, the RW ran in alliance with the Parti Liberal and both parties became part of Leo Tindemans's Social Christian-Liberal coalition. That government announced its intention to implement a detailed plan entitled "The Preparatory Phase of Regionalization."(64) The program envisioned the creation of several regional councils and ministerial committees which would exercise advisory power in matters of regional policy.(65) Disputes over the future course of regionalization, especially over the economic decentralization demanded by the RW, brought the coalition down before its term had expired. New elections were called for April 1977.

The elections recorded a significant decline in RW support, which cut its parliamentary representation in half, a loss of five seats. (The higher figures in the province of Luxembourg are entirely a result of a campaign alliance between the RW and the Socialist Party.) The FDF in Brussels was spared such a fate and its support continued unabated. The Volksunie lost some of its backing, reducing its parliamentary delegation to twenty seats, but its support among Flemings in Brussels remained strong. (See Appendix A, Fig. 5.4.) Indeed, except in the Brussels area, the Christian Socialists and the Liberals appeared to have checked the ever increasing trend of language party support.

TOWARDS A REGIONAL FEDERATION?

So much had the traditional parties' views on community relations changed, however, that their victories could scarcely be interpreted as a mandate to restore the unitary state. With the formation of his new coalition government, Leo Tindemans appears to have achieved a compromise which will foster genuine devolution in Belgium. What is most astounding about this latest compromise is that it was agreed to not only by the Socialists and the Social Christians, but also by the FDF and the Volksunie. For the first time, the Belgian government is a 4-part coalition, and each of the 2 language parties holds ministerial posts. This represents a considerable change in the policies long advocated by the language parties. The Volksunie had been especially adamant in insisting that Brussels have as little separate power as possible. The FDF traditionally maintained that, in addition to possessing the same measure of power as Flanders and Wallonia, the Brussels region should be expanded beyond the 19 boroughs which presently comprise it. Together the 4 parties control well over the two-thirds vote necessary to obtain parliamentary ratification of the reforms. Should some members of the language parties desert, the compromise could still be passed, providing that the discipline of the traditional parties remains intact. The devolutionary changes must, however, be reapproved by the parliament convened after the next general election before they can be put into effect.

The agreed-to program (the Egmont Pact) contains the essential features of a regionally federated state that most Belgians have come to accept as the inevitable solution to the problems of language and ethnicity which have plagued Belgium since its creation in 1830.

Flanders and Wallonia are each to have their own popularly elected regional councils with executive bodies responsible to them. These legislatures are to have ultimate authority in all matters of regional concern and their powers will be reinforced by the capacity to levy taxes. Brussels will also have its own parliament with powers like those planned for Wallonia and Flanders. Its 7-member executive body will

Table 5.1. Support (1977) for the Volksunie Among
Dutch-Speaking Residents of Brussels

#	DISTRICT	% Total Vote for Volksunie	% Dutch Speakers	% Dutch Speakers for Volksunie
106	Anderlect	9.4	22	42.7
107	Molenbeck St. Jean	6.5	21	31.0
108	Brussels	5.6	13	43.1
110	St. Josse-ten-Noode	5.2	15	34.7
111	Ixelles	6.4	15	42.7
112	St. Gilles	2.4	5	48.0
113	Uccle	4.0	17	23.5

Table 5.2. Support (1977) for the FDF among
French-Speaking Residents of Brussels

#	DISTRICT	% Total Vote for FDF	% French Speakers	% French Speaking for FDF
106	Anderlect	23.1	78	29.6
107	Molenbeek St. Jean	30.3	79	38.6
108	Brussels	31.0	87	35.6
110	St. Josse-ten-Noode	43.5	85	51.2
111	Ixelles	33.4	85	39.3
112	St. Gilles	36.8	95	38.7
113	Uccle	38.1	83	45.9

Source: The figures in these tables were calculated from the figures for the percentage of French speakers given in Appendix A. and the population statistics for
each borough listed in the Moniteur Belge, October 13, 1971.   The approximate
number of French speakers in each borough was determined and these figures were
added to give the proportion of French to Dutch speakers in each electoral district.
It was impossible to compute proportions for the districts of Vilvoorde (#101), Meise
(#102), Asse (#103), Lennik (#104), Halle (#105), and Schaerbeek (#109) because
complete borough figures on the percentage of French speakers were unavailable.
See appendix A, figs. 5.4. and 5.6.

Table 5.3. National Percentage Distribution of
Votes in Parliamentary Elections 1961-1977

Party	1961	1965	1968	1971	1974	1977
CVP/PSC-Christian Social	42	35	30	30	32	34
BSP/PSB-Socialist	37	28	28	27	27	27
PVV/PLP-Liberal	12	22	21	16	15	16
PCB/KPB Communist	3	5	3	3	3	3
VU-Volksunie	3	7	10	11	10	11
FDF/RW-Francophone	-	1	6	11	11	8
Other	3	3	1	1	1	1

Source: These figures have been computed from the raw voting totals
published by the Belgian Ministry for the Interior.   Data is
from the elections to the Chamber of Representatives only.
The numbers are accurate to the nearest whole percent; the
process of rounding has caused some totals to equal slightly
more or less than 100 percent.

have a minimum of 2 Dutch-speaking officials and will be responsible to
the Brussels legislature on all matters pertaining to the Brussels region.
(The province of Brabant will be abolished. Brussels, defined as the 19
bilingual boroughs, will be given provincial status, with the rest of the
province being divided along the language frontier between Flanders
and Wallonia.) The rights of French speakers in the 6 peripheral
boroughs ("with facilities") will be protected by placing these areas
under the jurisdiction of the central administration. In addition, the
rights of French-speaking minorities in 7 other boroughs and in 3 small
sections of boroughs will be increased by permitting them to choose
whether they want to be subject to the Brussels authority. Should they
choose this option, they would be able to take full advantage of the
bilingual facilities available in the city, vote in Brussels, and pay their
taxes there. The boroughs "with option" would remain part of Flanders.(66)
    The central administration and parliament would retain power in
those areas not specifically given to the regional authorities. These
would include responsibility for such matters as defense, foreign
affairs, international trade, commerce, and monetary policies. Although
details to the plan remain to be worked out, Tindemans clearly hopes

that ultimately most of the central government's responsibilities will be carried out within a European Community framework.(67)

Is the latest compromise for harmony between the language communities in Belgium one that will work? It appears to be a tenable scheme, at least insofar as it promotes the autonomy of Flanders and Wallonia in matters of education, culture, social welfare, and local economic planning. Decentralization and regional control can increase the participation of individuals in the process of formulating policies in those areas, and perhaps reduce the feelings of alienation inherent in a technological society. Language per se is no longer an issue in either region. Defining language and ethnicity in terms of territory finds its justification in the essentially homogeneous nature of the population. The unilingual policies may have negative consequences, however, if they tend to isolate members of the two cultures. Until the last ten years, the number of Belgians who were completely at home in both national languages rose annually. Although learning the second national language in school is encouraged, a decline in the number of persons with an "active" knowledge of the second language has already occurred, primarily because the opportunities to use it are fewer. In addition, the inflexible enforcement of linguistic laws, especially those concerning private enterprise, could have harmful economic consequences and result in a loss of foreign capital.(68)

Because sizable pockets of minorities are sprinkled along either side of the language frontier, complete unilingualism was impractical. In these areas, a personal definition of language and ethnicity has been applied and appears to have found acceptance. Herstappe, whose population of 110 is equally divided between Flemings and Walloons, has not held a communal election since 1970. Burgomaster Renard puts together a list of candidates so carefully balanced between language groups that it has never been contested.(69) There is evidence, too, that several of the "protected" border areas are gradually becoming more homogeneous. No separate Dutch-speaking list of candidates was proposed in the 1976 communal elections in Comines, once the site of violent linguistic disputes.(70) The Fourons are the outstanding exception to the calm along the language frontier. The 6 villages have become a symbol to both sides in the language controversy, with ardent Flemish nationalists refusing to relinquish control ("gebiedscroofd") and Walloons decrying Flemish domination. The Parti Retour a Liege continually receives over 50 percent of the popular vote, but it is unlikely that the Flemings will soon acquiesce in their desires, especially after the concession they made over Brussels in the Egmont Pact.

It is in the periphery of Brussels that the recent accords will face their most severe test. Although the area in which an individual can choose his linguistic affiliation has been broadened, it has not been extended to include the entire region of mixed population around the capital. Support for the language parties has spread among minorities even in Louvain and Nivelles. (The FDF has received support in Louvain since 1971; the Volksunie has found support in Nivelles since 1974.)

Especially in the boroughs bordering the bilingual region, it is doubtful that the newly drawn territorial limits will induce increased linguistic homogeneity. Because Brussels is the headquarters of the European Community and the North Atlantic Treaty Organization as well as a center for international business, the importance and predominance of French is likely to continue. It is seriously open to question whether those French speakers who live in the Dutch language region will long be content to have facilities in their own tongue denied to them and their children.

The situation in Brussels illustrates a fundamental difficulty in identifying only one language and ethnic group with each precise set of territorial limits. The fixing of linguistic boundaries and frontiers gives to the system a rigidity designed to halt the gradual shifts and movements of populations. Should it fail to stop such changes, that inflexibility ensures that specific areas are quite likely to become the subjects of future controversy.

POSTSCRIPT

During the early fall of 1978, support for the Egmont Pact within the Flemish Social Christian Party of Prime Minister Leo Tindemans crumbled over the issue of Brussels. The discontent was centered on the belief that in the proposed federation, French speakers would inevitably control two of the three regions (Wallonia and Brussels). The CVP refused to back the government in passing legislation necessary for the transitional phase of the reform and questioned instead the constitutionality of the entire compromise. The Tindemans government resigned, forcing general elections to be held in December. The results of those elections are still inconclusive, but the composition of the parliament appears little changed. The controversy over Brussels continues and the fate of the Egmont Pact is uncertain.

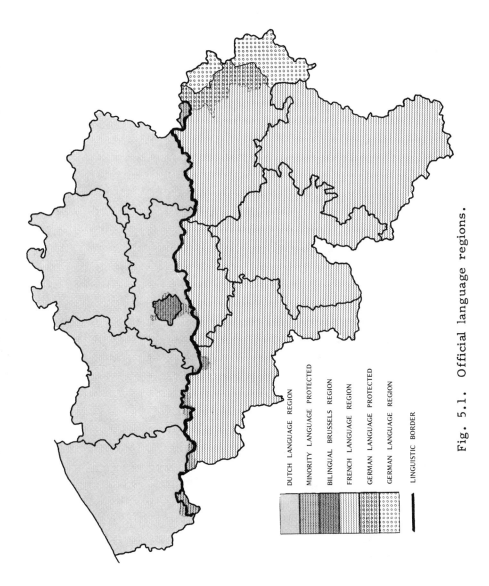

DUTCH LANGUAGE REGION

MINORITY LANGUAGE PROTECTED

BILINGUAL BRUSSELS REGION

FRENCH LANGUAGE REGION

GERMAN LANGUAGE PROTECTED

GERMAN LANGUAGE REGION

LINGUISTIC BORDER

Fig. 5.1. Official language regions.

145

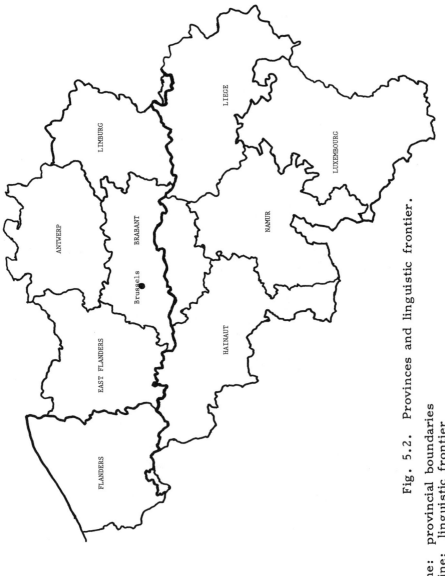

Fig. 5.2. Provinces and linguistic frontier.

Thin line: provincial boundaries
Thick line: linguistic frontier

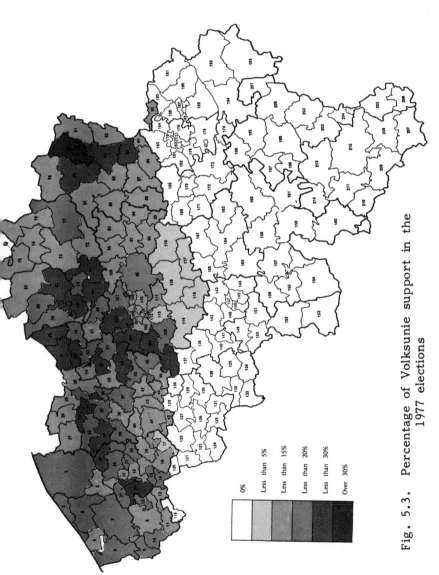

Fig. 5.3. Percentage of Volksunie support in the
1977 elections

Source: Adapted from map in Wilfried Dewatcher, Politieke Kaart Van Belgie: Atlas van de
parlementsverkiezingen van 31 Maart 1968 (Brussels: 1969).

Key to Fig. 5.3.
(Listing of Electoral Subdistricts)

1 Bruges	55 Sint Niklaas	109 Schaerbeek	162 Ciney
2 Torhout	56 Temise	110 St. Josse-ten-Noode	163 Andenne
3 Gistel	57 St. Gilles-Waas	111 Ixelles	164 Namur
4 Oostende	58 Beveren	112 St. Gilles	165 Fosses-La-Ville
5 Nieuwpoort	59 Antwerp	113 Uccle	166 Gembloux-Sur-Orneau
6 Veurne	60 Ekeren	114 Nivelles	167 Eghezee
7 Diksmuide	61 Brecht	115 Genappe	168 Hannut
8 Ieper	62 Zandhoven	116 Wavre	169 Waremme
9 Vleteren	63 Borgerhout	117 Perwez	170 Verlaine
10 Poperinge	64 Berchem	118 Jodoigne	171 Heron
11 Mesen	65 Kontich	119 Comines	172 Huy
12 Zonnebeke	66 Boom	120 Mouscron	173 Nadrin
13 Wervik	67 Puurs	121 Estaimpuis	174 Ferrieres
14 Menen	68 Mechelen	122 Celles	175 Aywaille
*15 Moorsele	69 Duffel	123 Tournai	176 Seraing
16 Kortrijk	70 Lier	124 Antoing	*177 Grevegnee
17 Avelgem	71 Heist-op-den-Berg	125 Peruwelz	178 Fleron
18 Harelbeke	72 Westerloo	126 Leuze	179 Herstal
19 Izegem	73 Herentals	127 Frasnes-Lez-Anvaing	180 Liege
20 Roesclare	74 Turnhout	128 Flobecq	181 Saint Nicolas
21 Hooglede	75 Hoogstraten	129 Ath	182 Grace-Hollogne
22 Lichtervelde	76 Arendonk	130 Chievres	183 Bassenge
23 Meulebeke	77 Mol	131 Beloeil	184 Dalhem
24 Oostrozebeke	78 Neerpelt	132 Boussu	185 Aubel
25 Tielt	79 Peer	133 Dour	186 Herve
26 Ruiselede	80 Bree	134 Frameries	187 Dison
27 Eeklo	81 Maaseik	135 Mons	188 Verviers
28 Kaprijke	82 Mechelen-aan-de-Maas	136 Lens	189 Spa
29 Assende	83 Bilzen	137 Enghien	190 Limburg
30 Lochristi	84 Riemst	138 Lessines	191 Eupen
31 Evergem	85 St. Martens-Voeren	139 Soignies	192 Malmedy
32 Waarschoot	86 Tongeren	140 Roeulx	193 Saint Vith
33 Zomergem	87 Borgloon	141 La Louviere	194 Stavelot
34 Nevele	88 Sint Truiden	142 Seneffe	195 Erezee
35 Ghent	89 Herck-de-Stad	*143 Gosselies	196 Durbuy
36 Destelbergen	90 Hasselt	144 Chatelet	197 Marche-en-Femme
37 Oosterzele	91 Genk	145 Charleroi	198 Nassogne
38 Nazareth	92 Beringen	*146 Marchienne-au-Point	199 La Roche-en-Ardenne
39 Deinze	93 Diest	*147 Jumet	200 Houffalize
40 Kruishoutem	94 Zoutleeuw	148 Fontaine-L'Eveque	201 Vielsalm
41 Oudenaarde	95 Landen	149 Binche	202 Bastogne
42 Ronse	96 Tienen	150 Merbes-Le-Chateau	203 Saint Ode
43 St. Maria-Horebeke	97 Glabbeek-Zuurbemde	151 Thuin	204 Fauvillers
44 Brakel	98 Aarschot	152 Beaumont	205 Arlon
45 Geraardsbergen	99 Louvain	153 Chimay	206 Messancy
46 Ninove	100 Haacht	154 Couvin	207 Virton
47 Zottegem	101 Vilvoorde	155 Philippeville	208 Etalle
48 Herzele	102 Meise	156 Walcourt	209 Florenville
49 Aalst	103 Asse	157 Florennes	210 Bouillon
50 Wetteren	104 Lennik	158 Dinant	211 Paliseul
51 Dendermonde	105 Halle	159 Beauraing	212 Neufchateau
52 Zele	106 Anderlecht	160 Gedinne	213 Saint Hubert
53 Hamme	107 Molenbeek-St. Jean	161 Rochefort	214 Wellin
54 Lokeren	108 Brussels		

*absorbed into surrounding subdistricts

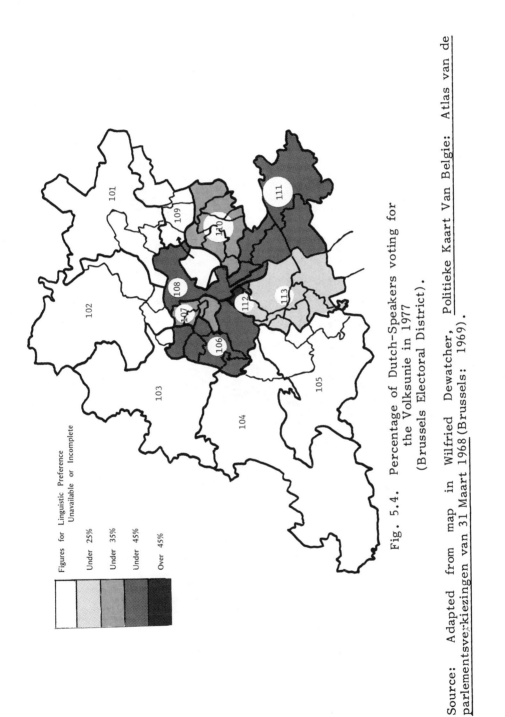

Figures for Linguistic Preference
Unavailable or Incomplete

Under 25%

Under 35%

Under 45%

Over 45%

Fig. 5.4. Percentage of Dutch-Speakers voting for
the Volksunie in 1977
(Brussels Electoral District).

Source: Adapted from map in Wilfried Dewatcher, Politieke Kaart Van Belgie: Atlas van de
parlementsverkiezingen van 31 Maart 1968 (Brussels: 1969).

149

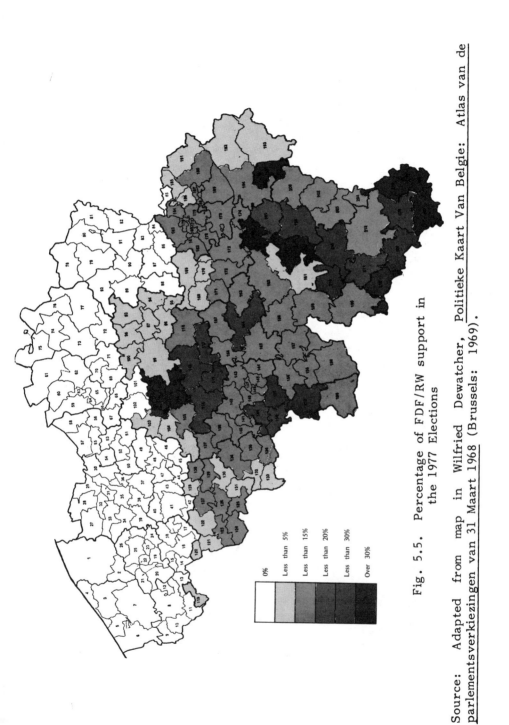

0%

Less than 5%

Less than 15%

Less than 20%

Less than 30%

Over 30%

Fig. 5.5.   Percentage of FDF/RW support in the 1977 Elections

Source: Adapted from map in Wilfried Dewatcher, Politieke Kaart Van Belgie: Atlas van de parlementsverkiezingen van 31 Maart 1968 (Brussels: 1969).

150

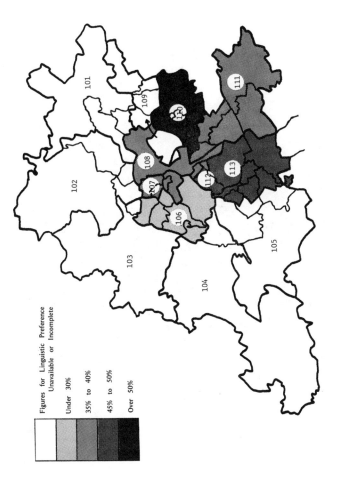

Fig. 5.6.   Percentage of French-Speakers voting for
the FDF in 1977
(Brussels Electoral District).

Source: Adapted from map in Wilfried Dewatcher, <u>Politieke</u>
<u>Kaart Van Belgie: Atlas van de Parlements-verkiezingen van 31</u>
<u>Maart 1968</u> (Brussels: 1969).

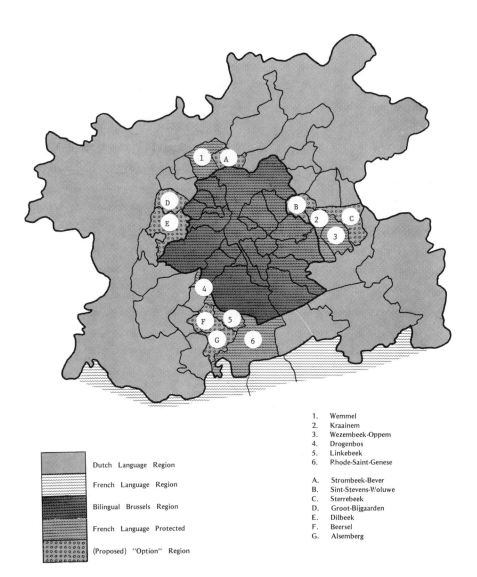

Dutch Language Region

French Language Region

Bilingual Brussels Region

French Language Protected

(Proposed) "Option" Region

1.   Wemmel
2.   Kraainem
3.   Wezembeek-Oppem
4.   Drogenbos
5.   Linkebeek
6.   Rhode-Saint-Genese

A.   Strombeek-Bever
B.   Sint-Stevens-Woluwe
C.   Sterrebeek
D.   Groot-Bijgaarden
E.   Dilbeek
F.   Beersel
G.   Alsemberg

Fig. 5.7.   Official linguistic status of Brussels
          and surrounding communes.

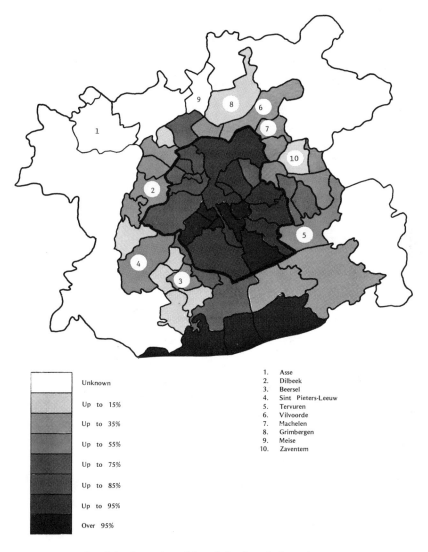

Unknown	1. Asse
	2. Dilbeek
Up to 15%	3. Beersel
	4. Sint Pieters-Leeuw
Up to 35%	5. Tervuren
	6. Vilvoorde
Up to 55%	7. Machelen
	8. Grimbergen
Up to 75%	9. Meise
	10. Zaventem
Up to 85%	
Up to 95%	
Over 95%	

Fig. 5.8.   Percentage of French-Speakers in Brussels
and surrounding communes.

Sources for Fig. 5.8.

    The geographical and political aspects of Fig. 5.8 are taken from "Les In-
stitions Politiques de la Belgique Regionalisee," Dossiers du CRISP, no. 6
(Brussels: 1973).   It was modified to include the communes of Braine l'Alleud,
Waterloo, and La Hulpe.
    The figures indicating the percentage of French speakers in the bilingual
Brussels region and in the communes with facilities were collected during a 1969
inquiry by the Institut Solvay at the Free University of Brussels and are cited in
Herve Hasquin, La Wallonie: Le Pays et les Hommes, vol. 2, p. 413.   The Solvay
figures were confirmed, and those in the outlying areas were compiled from an
analysis of identity cards, social contributions, driving licenses, television licenses, conscripts' linguistic options, civil registrations, education lists, and
parliamentary questions in a further study by Fernand Rigot, Bloc de la Liberte
Linguistique (Brussels: 1971).   The Solvay figures, available for only ten outlying
communes, were generally somewhat lower.   These figures, together with the
percentages obtained from analyzing the votes for French and Dutch lists in the
1971 national elections and the 1976 local elections, follow (table 5.4).   The latter
two groups of figures were printed in De Standaard, October 25, 1976.

Table 5.4.

Communes with Facilities*

	Solvay	1971	1976
Kraainem (2)	70	60	58
Wezembeek-Oppem (3)	65	61	60**
Linkebeek (5)	73	53	66
Rhode-Sainte-Genese (6)	60	53	41

Outlying Communes

	Rigot	Solvay	1971	1976
Asse	--	8	10	4
Dilbeek	45	24	25	15
Beersel	55	21	23	17
Sint Pieters-Leeuw	35	20	33	10
Tervuren	40	18	22	18
Vilvoorde	30	23	16	13
Machelen	25	14	10	5
Grimbergen	15	20	18	14
Meise	--	10	7	4
Zaventem	18	18	19	14

---

*No analysis was done for Wemmel and Drogenbos.

**This figure would have been 70 if the votes for the bilingual Socialist list were added.

APPENDIX B:
LANGUAGE AND THE BELGIAN ARMED FORCES

The detailed laws regulating the use of language in the Belgian armed forces are designed to balance the principles of linguistic equality with the requirements for efficient operation of the military chain of command. A year's military service is compulsory for all male citizens of Belgium,(1) and the basic law of 1938 (amended in 1955, 1961, 1963, and 1970) stressed the individual's right to use his native tongue while satisfying his military obligations. Accordingly, each new conscript is assigned to a unit on the basis of language. The language preference of each soldier is presumed to be that of the region in which he resides upon entering the armed services unless he makes a specific request to be assigned to another language grouping. (This privilege is usually reserved for residents of areas with "protected" languages.) Residents of Brussels declare their preference at the moment of induction. The program of basic training is then given to the recruit in his native tongue. All orders, communications, commands, and general administrative work are conducted exclusively in the language of the unit concerned. All future official communications between the administration of the armed forces and the individual soldier is done in the language of the borough in which he lives.

Commissioned and noncommissioned officers are required to have at least a working knowledge of both national languages. (Throughout the rest of his life, all official communications to an officer on active duty, in the reserves, or on indefinite leave are written both in Dutch and French. The language of the officer's legal residence is placed ahead of the other national language.) Language competency is established through a testing system(2) similar to that used in the civil service. A thorough working knowledge of one of the national languages and a working knowledge of the other is required for entrance to the Royal Military Academy and for promotion up through the ranks of the officers' corps. For promotion to all senior officers' ranks above that of captain, a thorough knowledge of both languages is now a prerequisite. (In addition, if an officer is called upon to take command of a German-speaking unit, he must demonstrate a working knowledge of that language.) Those officers promoted before this requirement went into effect in 1970 have been strongly urged to take the language tests and additional promotions have been held up until they pass. Because French speakers have historically dominated the officers' corps, they continue to be over represented in the higher ranks. Their numbers are expected to diminish in the years to come as they retire and are replaced by Dutch speakers. Current personnel policies of the armed forces envision rough parity between the language groups among senior officers, and a 60 percent Dutch/40 percent French split among junior officers, noncommissioned officers, and civilian personnel. The inability of the government to induce more early retirements among high-ranking French-speaking officers has been the cause of much impatience among younger Dutch-speaking officers and Flemish nationalists. The policy

Table 5.5. Language Preference of Enlisted
Personnel and Noncommissioned Officers

Service	Dutch	French	German
Army			
enlisted	17,436-62%	10,470-37%	104-.37%
noncommissioned	7,466-60%	5,060-40%	
Air Force			
enlisted	2,466-55%	2,041-45%	
noncommissioned	4,728-59%	3,316-41%	
Navy			
enlisted	951-73%	346-27%	
noncommissioned	1,033-74%	355-26%	
Medical			
enlisted	1,624-61%	1,170-42%	
noncommissioned	347-58%	266-42%	
TOTAL			
enlisted	22,477-61%	14,027-38%	104-.28%
noncommissioned	13,601-60%	8,997-40%	

Note: Figures were computed from the data provided in the "Rapport
sur l'application de la loi du 30 Juillet 1938, concernant l'usage des
langues a l'Armee (1976)." Administration Centrale (Brussels: 1976),
Annexes H and J-1.

of equality between language groups in the upper echelons has also been
severely criticized by these same groups.

Enlisted men assigned to take special courses of technical instruction as part of their training do so in their native language. However,
when they emerge from these courses, they are often assigned to units
which can no longer be kept unilingual because specialized functions are
not divided along language lines. These mixed units are composed of
unilingual subunits, with the language of communication between the
unit and the subunit legally required to be that of the subunit. Thus,
the individual soldier can continue to use only his native tongue because
his superiors are required to translate all communications into that
language. (Mixed specialized units in the Army include the parachutists,
commandos, and those assigned to logistical tasks. In addition, German-
speaking recruits are often assigned to non-specialized mixed units if
their numbers are insufficient to form their own unit. The Air Force's
mixed units include specialized squadrons, administrative units, and
logistical groupings. The Navy maintains a unilingual rule on ships but
mixes language groups in schools, shore command, research vessels, and
logistical support.)(3) The overall administration of a mixed language is

Table 5.6. Belgian Armed Forces*

(officers in 1975)

LANGUAGE	General	Colonel	Lt. Colonel	Major	Lower Ranks	TOTAL
Native Tongue: Dutch						
number	16	87	221	467	2,903	3,694
percentage	43	35	45	51	59	56
Native Tongue: French						
number	21	159	275	447	1,985	2,887
percentage	57	65	55	49	41	44
Native Tongue: Dutch and Thorough Knowledge: French						
number	15	59	139	225	311	749
percentage	41	24	28	25	6	11
Native Tongue: French Thorough Knowledge: Dutch						
number	11	60	103	88	164	426
percentage	30	24	21	10	3	6
Thorough Knowledge: Dutch						
number	27	147	324	555	3,167	4,120
percentage	73	60	65	60	63	63
Thorough Knowledge: French						
number	36	218	414	672	2,296	3,636
percentage	97	89	83	74	47	55

*Excluding   the   National   Guard   (Gendarmerie/Rijkswatch)

Table 5.7. Civilian Administrative Personnel (1975)

	Army		Air Force		Navy		Other		TOTAL	
	D	F	D	F	D	F	D	F	D	F
Level 1										
number	16	16			2		10	13	28	29
percentage	50	50			100		43	57	49	51
Level 2										
number	87	90	7	7	13	2	153	99	356	286
percentage	49	51	50	50	87	13	61	39	55	45
Level 3										
number	254	151	108	15	70	3	132	108	598	309
percentage	63	37	87	13	96	4	55	45	66	34
Level 4										
number	59	22	20	7	7	1	38	32	127	68
percentage	73	27	74	26	90	10	54	46	65	35
TOTAL										
number	416	279	135	29	92	6	324	252	1,109	692
percentage	60	40	82	18	94	6	56	44	62	38

conducted in the language of the majority of subunits, and all administrative personnel are required to have at least a working knowledge of both languages. All communications addressed to several units of differing languages are made in the language of the majority, while orders to all units are issued in both Dutch and French.

In order to ensure that the language regulations are fairly enforced within the armed forces, an inspection commission was established to investigate complaints of linguistic discrimination. The president, vice-president, and four members of the commission are chosen from among the parliamentary delegates who sit on the national defense committee. Three additional members are senior military officers, and the secretariat of the commission is located within the defense department. Yearly reports to parliament on the application of these laws is required.(4) The numbers of appeals to the commission has dropped virtually to none in the past several years.(5)

Table 5.8. Linguistic Division of the
Belgian Armed Forces[a]

	Dutch	French	Mixed
Units[b]			
Army	175/166	119/111	90
Air Force	25/24	18/18	79
Navy[c]	8/8	1/0	18
Medical	2/1	1/1	3
Battalions[d]			
Army	32/32	20/20	52
Air Force	4/4	2/2	18
Navy	0/0	0/0	8
Medical	3/2	1/1	6
Brigades[e]			
Army	2/2	1/1	6
Special Groupings			
Army	1/1	0/0	5

[a]Excluding the National Guard.

[b]The term includes companies, squadrons, batteries, and ships in which enlisted personnel receive their basic training. The total number of units in each language group is followed by the number of units commanded by an officer who has demonstrated a thorough knowledge of the language of the unit. The remaining commanders have only a working knowledge of the language concerned.

[c]Note that the Navy is the one service in which Dutch speakers have traditionally dominated. The reason is self-evident; the seacoast is entirely in Flanders. Since the Belgian Navy was begun under the aegis of the Royal British Navy during World War I, much of the vocabulary used by both Dutch and French sailors is, in fact, English.

[d]Or naval squadrons and medical corps.

[e]Figures include the mixed language paracommando unit.

Source: Figures are from "Rapport," annex S and p. 7.

Table 5.9.

Divisions	Total Number	Commanders' Language Status
Army	2	1-French; 1-Dutch with thorough knowledge of French
Air Force	3	1-French; 1-French with thorough knowledge of Dutch; 1-Dutch with thorough knowledge of French
Navy	3	2-French; 1-Dutch with thorough knowledge of French
Medical	2	2-French with thorough knowledge of Dutch

161

NOTES

Text

(1) The reasons that the language border took the precise path that it did was once a hotly debated topic among Belgian historians. So many possible explanations can weave together the few surviving evidences of a forest and remnants of a Roman wall that one Belgian scholar finally put an end to the controversy by persuasively arguing that the subject was not a legitimate one for historical inquiry. See Jean Stengers, "La Formation de la Frontiere Linguistique en Belgique," Collection Latomus, 41 (Brussels, 1959): 51-55. His conclusions are cited in Aristide R. Zolberg, "The Making of Flemings and Walloons: Belgium: 1830-1914," p. 182.

(2) Eugene K. Keefe, Area Handbook for Belgium, p. 156.

(3) Shepard B. Clough, "The Flemish Movement," in Belgium, ed. Jan-Albert Goris, p. 108.

(4) For an analysis of this phenomenon, see the discussion in Albert C. Baugh, A History of the English Language, pp. 127-187.

(5) See Clough, "Flemish Movement," p. 109.

(6) See Clough, "Flemish Movement," p. 109.

(7) Quoted in Val R. Lorwin, "Belgium: Religion, Class, and Language in National Politics," in Political Oppositions in Western Democracies, ed. Robert A. Dahl, p. 158.

(8) A phrase used by Lorwin, "Belgium," p. 159.

(9) For details on the activities of Willems's and others in the early Flemish nationalist movement, see the discussion in Clough, "Flemish Movement," pp. 110-114.

(10) Clough, "Flemish Movement," pp. 110-111.

(11) Conscience, much influenced by the literary style of Sir Walter Scott, ironically wrote all of his early works in French. M. de Vroede, The Flemish Movement in Belgium, p. 24.

(12) Quoted in Clough, "Flemish Movement," p. 111.

(13) Ibid., p. 112.

(14) The anticlerical Liberal Party received most of its backing from members of the industrial, commercial, and professional bourgeoisie; it

was predominantly French-speaking. The Catholic Party was supported by the more conservative elements throughout the country and its appeal among Dutch speakers was almost universal.

(15) Quoted in Lorwin, "Belgium," p. 159.

(16) Ibid., p. 160.

(17) See George Armstrong Kelly, "Belgium: New Nationalism in an Old World," pp. 348-349.

(18) Quoted in Lorwin, "Belgium," p. 160.

(19) A detailed account of Flemish activism during World War I which draws on contemporary sources is contained in Loode Wils, Flamenpolitik en Aktivisme.

(20) Estimates place their numbers at about 80 percent of the infantry soldiers; Clough, "Flemish Movement," p. 117; de Vroede, "Flemish Movement," p. 49; and M. van Haegendoren, The Flemish Movement in Belgium, p. 27.

(21) See Wils, Flamenpolitik, pp. 28-36.

(22) General von Bissing, the Governor General of Belgium, did not share this opinion. Although he favored the outright annexation of the country for strategic reasons, he did not, in his words, "nourish the thoughtless hope of seeing the Flemings make the domination of Belgium easy." Quoted in Clough, "Flemish Movement," pp. 115-116.

(23) See Margot Lyon, Belgium, p. 61. The term "Activist" was applied to those who cooperated with the Germans; "Passivists" were those Flemish nationalists who refused to collaborate.

(24) Quoted in Clough, "Flemish Movement," p. 117.

(25) Lyon, Belgium, p. 82.

(26) See the analysis of Borms' character in Wils, Flamenpolitik, pp. 94-101.

(27) In 1928, a by-election was held to replace a deceased member of parliament from Antwerp. The Flemish nationalists nominated the imprisoned, and therefore ineligible, Borms. He received twice as many votes as his victorious Liberal opponent. See de Vroede, "Flemish Movement," p. 54.

(28) Quoted in Emile Cammaerts, Albert of Belgium, p. 241.

(29) Unlike the parish priests in Flanders, the hierarchy of the Belgian Roman Catholic Church was heavily dominated by French speakers. Although it later softened its opposition to the increased use of Dutch in Flanders, it had once fiercely enunciated its hostility to the spread of that "Calvinist" tongue. Haegendoren, Flemish Movement, p. 25.

(30) See Emile Cammaerts, The Keystone of Europe: History of the Belgian Dynasty, 1830-1939, pp. 336-337.

(31) Lyon, Belgium, p. 71.

(32) See de Vroede, "Flemish Movement," pp. 60-62.

(33) Quoted in James A. Dunn, " 'Consociational Democracy' and Language Conflict: A Comparison of the Belgian and Swiss Experience," p. 10.

(34) See Belgium, Ministry for the Interior, Table of Parliamentary Composition by Party since 1929, (Brussels: 1974).

(35) M. de Vroede argues that the first recognition of the unilingual character of Flanders excluding Brussels can be found in the 1921 bill on the use of Dutch in public services. See de Vroede, "Flemish Movement," p. 51. While this legislation and other language bills, passed in the 1930s, contained the principle of unilingualism, the provisions added during the course of parliamentary debates stressed that Dutch be the primary language of Flanders, in effect reaffirming the bilingual character of the region.

(36) One party pamphlet, for example, complained that Flanders had been "intellectually and materially crippled. . .slaughtered. . .a case of mental genocide." Quoted in Lyon, Belgium, p. 156.

(37) Florimand Grammens, a little-known Flemish partisan, is credited with developing this technique of protest. He used it with great effect prior to the elections of 1936. See de Vroede, "Flemish Movement," p. 58.

(38) Herve Hasquin, La Wallonie: Le Pays et les Hommes, p. 341.

(39) See Maurice Henrard, L'Emploi des Langues dans l'Administration et dans les Enterprises Privees, p. 35. It should be noted that the overwhelming proportion of communes along the language frontier were sufficiently homogeneous and did not require a bilingual administration.

(40) In 1930, the French-speaking population of Sint Stevens-Woluwe failed to reach the required percentage, and the commune reverted to a unilingual Dutch administration. See de Vroede, "Flemish Movement," p. 70.

(41) For a detailed discussion of these problems, see Paul M.G. Levy, La Querrelle du Recensement, Zolberg, "Making of Flemings and Walloons," especially p. 183; and Hasquin, La Wallonie, pp. 341-342.

(42) A majority of the 4,000 inhabitants of the 6 villages in the Fourons (Voeren) hills were French speaking. Original dwellers in the area had spoken a dialect closer to low German than to Dutch. The extent of Frenchification during centuries of French language rule was probably unknown to many parliamentarians, and the pressure to achieve a compromise on the language frontier was intense. As demonstrators marched through the streets of Liege, confusion over the issue was evident in the Belgian Senate. On July 18, 1962, it voted 73 to 71 with 2 absentions against the transfer of the Fourons to Limburg and then voted 72 to 70 with 2 absentions against keeping the region in Liege. Three months later, the Lefevre-Spaak government decided that the Fourons would become part of Limburg. See Hasquin, La Wallonie, pp. 341-342.

(43) Quoted in Paul Harsin, Essaie sur l'Opinion Publique en Belgique de 1815 a 1830, (Charleroi), cited in Zolberg, La Wallonie, p. 179.

(44) Figures are from Keefe, Area Handbook, p. 26.

(45) de Vroede, "Flemish Movement," p. 62.

(46) Quoted in de Vroede, "Flemish Movement," p. 88.

(47) See "Les Derniers Francophones," Pourquoi Pas?, October 6, 1976.

(48) See the figures in Zolberg, "Making of Flemings and Walloons," p. 181.

(49) Haegendoren, Flemish Movement, p. 19.

(50) See the discussion on the differences between the French minority in Flanders and the Dutch minority in Wallonia in Zolberg, "Making of Flemings and Walloons," pp. 184-185.

(51) See Firmin Lentacker, La Frontiere Franco-Belge; Etudes Geographique des Effects d'une Frontiere Internationale sur la Vie de Relations.

(52) The Volksunie later claimed that the more direct governmental aid given the Kampellen region was offered only to balance that given the depressed coal mining region of Boringe. This was cited as evidence of discrimination against Flanders in national economic planning.   See Haegendoren, Flemish Movement, p. 19.

(53) See the European Court of Human Rights, "Relating to Certain Aspects of the Law on the Use of Languages in Education in Belgium," Vol. 1 and 2.

(54) See Keefe, Area Handbook, pp. 100-101. The university was governed by the Church but received 90 percent of its funds from the Belgian state.

(55) Lyon, Belgium, p. 131.

(56) See the New York Times, August 22-23, 1965.

(57) See Kelly, "Belgium," p. 349.

(58) See Parti des Belges de Langue Allemande, Programme du parti. The party ran most strongly around its headquarters in St. Vith, but received substantial backing in Malmedy and Eupen as well. It received less than five percent of the vote in the other subdistricts where the German language is protected.

(59) For a constitutional discussion of the parliamentary language groups, see Robert Senelle, The Belgian Constitution: Commentary, pp. 101-102; see also the law of July 3, 1971 in the Moniteur Belge, July 6, 1971; the French language text of the law is reproduced and analyzed in Paul de Stexhe, La Revision de la Constitution Belge, 1968-1971, pp. 222-226.

(60) For a discussion of the competence of the Cultural Councils, see the Moniteur Belge, July 21, 1971; Senelle, Belgian Constitution, pp. 179-180; and Pierre Louis Wigny, La Troisieme Revision de la Constitution, pp. 116-121.

(61) For details on the language laws concerning provincial and municipal administrations, the judicial system, and the educational system, see Senelle, Belgian Constitution, pp. 53-60.

(62) See Henrard, L'Emploi; Administration Centrale, "Rapport sur l'Application de la Loi du 30 Juillet 1938, Concernant l'Usage des Langues a l'Armee", and Les Codes Larcier, Edition 1975, pp. 494-496.

(63) See Statuts Nationaux, Parti de la Liberte et du Progres.

(64) Senelle, Belgian Constitution, p. 392; the plan was advanced in pursuance of article 107-D in the revised constitution.

(65) The jurisdiction of these bodies is defined in the Moniteur Belge, August 22, 1974.

(66) For more specific terms of these plans, see the "Declaration du Gouvernement" and the "Pacte Communautaire" in the Moniteur Belge, June 7, 1977.

(67) For his views on European integration, see the interview of Leo Tindemans by Andre Fontaine, Le Monde, March 9, 1977.

(68) See "Belgium Loses Allure for U.S. Manufacturers," Electronic News.

(69) La Libre Belgique, September 14, 1976.

(70) Ibid., September 17, 1976.

Appendix B

(1) Compulsory military service is regulated by the laws of April 30, 1962. Beginning at the end of 1974, a conscript's tour of duty was reduced to ten months if he was posted to West Germany. The Military Balance, 1974-1975 (London: 1974), p. 18.

(2) The exact testing requirements for each level, "working" and "thorough," are established by law to include both written and oral examinations. For details, see Les Codes Larcier: Edition 1975, pp. 494-6.

(3) See "Rapport," p. 6.

(4) Article 31bis, Les Codes Larcier, pp. 497-498.

(5) Robert Senelle, The Belgian Constitution: Commentary, p. 62.

BIBLIOGRAPHY

Primary Sources

Administrative Map of Belgium. Brussels: Institute Geographique Militaire, 1975.
Annuaire Administratif et Judiciaire de Belgique/Administratief en Gerechtelijk Jaarboek voor Belgie. Brussels: Etablissement Emile Bruylant, 1975.
Belgian Information and Documentation Institute. Belgium at the Heart of Europe. Brussels: 1975. (Maps by Willy Rousseau et Fils.)
Belgian Information and Documentation Institute. Belgium: Basic Statistics 1969-1973. Brussels: 1975.
Belgian Information and Documentation Institute. Belgium: Facts and Figures. Brussels: 1972.

Belgian Ministry for the Interior. Communal Elections of October 10, 1976.

Belgian Ministry for the Interior. Statistics for the Chamber of Deputies and the Senate. National Elections of 1961, 1965, 1971, 1974, and 1977.

Belgian Ministry of Foreign Affairs, External Trade, and Cooperation in Development. Basic Facts About Belgium. Memo from Belgium, no. 147. Brussels: 1972.

Les Codes Larcier. Brussels: Edition 1975.

Dembour, Jacques. Droit Administratif. The Hague: Martenus Nijhoff, 1972.

Descamps, Pierre P. (President of the Party of Freedom and Progress) Letter of October 12, 1976.

European Court of Human Rights. Case "Relating to Certain Aspects of the Law on the Use of Languages in Education in Belgium." Vol. 1 and 2. Strasbourg: The Council of Europe, 1967.

Front Democratique des Bruxellois Francophones. "Bruxelleis Maitre Chez Toi." FDF Contact. Verviers: Editions Maramount, 1977.

Institute Geographique Militaire. Administrative Map of Belgium. Brussels: 1975.

Le Moniteur Belge. 1948-1977.

Parti des Belges de Langue Allemande. Programme Du Parti. Saint Vith: Secretariat of the PDB, 1972.

Parti de la Liberte et du Progres. Statutes Nationaux. Doc. F/4144. Brussels: 1969.

"Rapport sur l'Application de la Loi du 30 Juillet 1938 Concernant l'Usage des Langues a l'Armee." Brussels: Administration Centrale, 1976.

Rigot, Fernand. Statistics on Numbers of French Speakers in the Brussels Region. Brussels: Bloc de la Liberte Linguistique, 1971.

Secondary Sources: Periodicals and Articles

"Belgium Loses Allure for U.S. Manufacturers." Electronic News, June 13, 1977.

"Belgium: Now a Third Language." The Economist, January 29, 1972.

La Cite. October 1976.

Cook, Don. "Belgian Premier Seen in Good Position to Lead Nation away from Linguistic Strife." Los Angeles Times, April 19, 1977.

Dunn, James A. " 'Consociational Democracy' and Language Conflict: A Comparison of the Belgian and Swiss Experience." Comparative Political Studies 5, no. 1 (April 1972).

Foreign Broadcast Information Service. Western Europe, January 1974 to May 1977.

Francis, Anne. "Language – Bridge or Barrier." Behind the Headlines 23, no. 4. Canadian Institute of International Affairs, 1964.

Kelly, George Armstrong. "Belgium: New Nationalism in an Old World." Comparative Politics 1, no. 5 (April 1969).

La Libre Belgique. 1976-1977.

Lorwin, Val R. "Belgium: Religion, Class, and Language in National Politics." In Political Oppositions in Western Democracies, edited by Robert A. Dahl. New Haven: Yale University Press, 1966.

"Louvain University: The Great Divide." The Bulletin, March 5, 1976.

New York Times. January 1960-June 1977.

"Party Congress: Reforming the Belgian State." The Bulletin, March 12, 1976.

Pourquoi Pas? October 6, 1976.

"Schaerbeek: After the Raid." The Bulletin, March 12, 1976.

"Schaerbeek: Counters Row Settles?" The Bulletin, March 5, 1976.

"Setting it Suburb by Suburb." The Economist, May 28, 1977.

"Socialist Party: A Deal for Three Regions." The Bulletin, June 11, 1976.

Le Soir. 1976-1977.

De Standard. 1976.

"The Tindemans Touch with Belgium's Dilemma." The Economist, April 23, 1977.

Zolberg, Aristide R. "The Making of Flemings and Walloons: Belgium 1830-1914." The Journal of Interdisciplinary History 5 (Autumn 1974).

Secondary Sources: Books

Baudhuin, Fernand. Histoire Economique de la Belgique 1945-1956. Brussels: Etablissement Emile Bruylant, 1958.

Baugh, Albert C. A History of the English Language. 2nd ed. New York: Appleton Century Crofts, 1963.

Bernard, Henri, La Resistance 1940-1945. Brussels: La Renaissance du livre, 1968.

Blanpain, Roger. Public Employee Unionism in Belgium. Ann Arbor, Michigan: Institute of Labor and Industrial Relations, University of Michigan-Wayne State University Press, 1971.

Cammaerts, Emile. Albert of Belgium. London: Peter Davies, Ltd., 1935.

Cammaerts, Emile. The Keystone of Europe: History of the Belgian Dynasty 1830-1939. London: Peter Davies, Ltd., 1939.

Craig, Gordon A. Europe Since 1815. 3rd ed. New York: Holt, Rinehart, and Winston, Inc., 1971.

Dewachter, Wilfried. Politieke Kaart van Belgie: Atlas van de Parlementsverkiezingen van Maart 1968. Brussels: Europees Kartografisch Instituut, 1970.

Gilissen, John. Le Regime Representatif en Belgique depuis 1790. Brussels: La Renaissance du Livre, 1958.

Goris, Jan-Albert, ed. Belgium. Los Angeles: University of California Press, 1945.

Groupe d'Etudes Sociographique de l'Institut de Sociologie Solvay. Les Elections Legislatives du 4 Juin 1950. Brussels: Les Editions de la Librairie Encyclopedique 1953.

Haegendoren, M. van. The Flemish Movement in Belgium. Antwerp: Flemish Cultural Council, 1965.

Hasquin, Herve. La Wallonie: Le Pays et les Hommes Histoire, Economies, Societe. Vol. 2 de 1830 a Nos Jours. Brussels: La Renaissance du Livre, 1976.

Henrard, Maurice. L'Emploi des Langues dans l'Administration et dans les Enterprises Privees. Brussels: Les Editions Administratives, Heule, 1964.

Les Institutions Politiques de la Belgique Regionalisee. Dossiers du CRISP, no. 6. Brussels: CRISP, 1974.

Keefe, Eugene K.; Giloane, William; Long, Anne K.; Moore, James M.; Shema, Jean Coutts, and Walpole, Neda A. Area Handbook for Belgium. Washington, D.C.; American University Foreign Area Studies, United States Government Printing Office, 1974.

Lentacker, Firmis. La Frontiere Franco-Belge: Etude Geographique des Effects d'une Frontiere Internationale sur la Vie de Relations. Brussels: 1974.

Levy, Paul M.G. La Querrelle du Recensement. Brussels: Institut Belge de Science Politique, 1960.

Lyon, Margot. Belgium. London: Thames and Hudson, 1971.

Molitor, Andre. L'Administration de la Belgique. Brussels: Centre de Recherche et d'Information Socio-Politique CRISP, 1974.

Paxton, John, ed. The Statesman's Yearbook: Statistical and Historical Annual of the States of the World. New York: St. Martin's Press, 1946-1976.

Reed, Thomas Harrison. Government and Politics of Belgium. New York: World Book Company, 1924.

Rowies, Luc. Les Partis Politiques en Belgique. Dossiers du CRISP, no. 7. Brussels: CRISP, 1975.

Salm, Ilse Carola. Flandern. Vienna: Erscheinungsort, 1973.

Senelle, Robert. The Belgian Constitution: Commentary. Memo from Belgium, no. 166. Brussels: Ministry of Foreign Affairs and External Trade, 1974.

Senelle, Robert. The Political, Economic, and Social Structure of Belgium. nos. 122-123-124. Brussels: Ministry of Foreign Affairs and External Trade, March, April, May 1970.

Senelle, Robert. La Revision de la Constitution, 1967-1971: Textes et Documents. nos. 279-280-281. Brussels: Ministry of Foreign Affairs, External Commerce, and Development Cooperation, 1972.

Senelle, Robert. The Revision of the Constitution, 1967-1970. Memo from Belgium. nos. 132-133. Brussels: Ministry of Foreign Affairs and External Trade, 1971.

Shepard, William R., ed. Shepard's Historical Atlas. New York: Harper and Row, Publishers, 1976.

Stexhe, Paul de. La Revision de la Constitution Belge, 1968-1971. Namur: Societe d'Etudes Morales, Sociales, et Juridique, 1972.

Van Impe, Hermann. Le Role de la Majorite Parlementaire dans la Vie Politique Belge. Brussels: Etablissement Emile Bruyland, 1966.

de Vroede, M. The Flemish Movement in Belgium. Brussels: Kultuurraad voor Vlaanderen and Instituut Voor Voorlichting, 1975.

Wigny, Pierre Louis. La Troisieme Revision de la Constitution. Brussels: Etablissement Emile Bruylant, 1972.

Wils, Lode. Flamenpolitik en Aktivisme: Vlanderen Tegenover Belgie in de Eerste Wereldoorlog. Louvain: Davidsfonds, 1974.

6 Cyprus, 1974 to 1978: Problems of Conflict Resolution in a Multiethnic Country *

Gavriel D. Ra'anan

The Cyprus case presents but one of many contemporary examples of the difficulties that arise when an attempt is made to link (self-perceived) antithetical Gemeinschaften (i.e. communities with long-standing traditions of animosity) in order to arrive at a synthesis – Gesellschaft (a reasonably cohesive and amicably functioning society or polity). Throughout much of the twentieth century it has been widely contended that in a "modern age," parochial antipathies would dissipate with extended contact between peoples; that, regardless of cultural antecedents or ethnicity, human beings are essentially identical; and that, through exposure of former antagonists to one another, mutual understanding and thus amiable coexistence would be ensured. Yet, empirically, this has not proven to be the case.

Most notably, in Lebanon as in Cyprus, a carefully balanced, internationally sponsored governmental apparatus was established and

---

Publisher's note: The type employed in this book made utilization of diacritical marks unfeasible. Consequently, the German umlaut has been rendered as "ae," "oe," or "ue," respectively, in accordance with traditional practice, while French accents have been omitted, and so have diacritical marks in the case of Turkish, Czech, and other names.

*In view of the particular focus of this study, it will have to refrain from devoting serious attention to such "spillover" effects as the United States embargo on arms to Turkey, the impact on United States military facilities there and in Greece, the resulting disintegration of NATO's southeastern flank, the treatment of the Greek minority in Istanbul and the Turkish minority in Western Thrace after 1974, and other Greek-Turkish disputes, such as those over exploitation of the resources of the Aegean ocean bed and over Greek fortification of Aegean Islands.

was considered at the time of its inception to present a viable solution to the respective ethnic (or "communal") problems of the country. In both cases, international guarantees and sponsorship failed to keep the state concerned from unraveling. Throughout the world, there exist poignant reminders of the failure of modernization to change man's seemingly basic "communal" inclination, i.e., his predilection for his own ethno-cultural environment. It is interesting that, even within "developed" Western Europe, the striving for greater ethnic autonomy is manifested in such diverse environments as Scotland, Catalonia, and the South Tyrol. Thus, the Cyprus case, which is examined here, does not represent an isolated phenomenon, but demonstrates some of the difficulties that have been and may continue to beset contemporary multiethnic states. Cyprus is symptomatic of one of the legacies of the imperial world — the creation of "artificial" states, established without considering the factor of ethnicity.

DEVICES

In general, the problems of multicultural (e.g., multilingual or multi-religious) polities may be addressed through one of the following devices:

1. A unitary centralized state. In most instances, this is virtually synonymous with domination of the polity by the largest — or, at least, the dominant — ethnic group or "nationality." It "solves" the problem by ignoring, or suppressing, the aspirations of the weaker communities, thus giving the state as a whole an artificially "homogeneous" appearance.

2. Regional or provincial autonomy without major population movement. This may not contribute much to conflict resolution if the demographic pattern, i.e., the ethnic geography of a country, is such that no one region or area is linguistically, religiously, or culturally homogeneous. In that case, each autonomous province or canton will replicate the overall problem of domination of one community over another, even if a different nationality is top dog in each of the autonomous areas. Provincial minorities are subject to alien domination no less than countrywide minorities (nor is it much consolation to the vulnerable Croat minority in Bosnia-Hercegovina, for instance, to know that Croats run the neighboring Republic of Croatia). Moreover, the dominant ethnic group in the country as a whole is unlikely to be prepared to allow its kinsmen to be relegated to minority status even within one of the autonomous provinces.

3. Artificially created homogeneity in autonomous provinces. This may be brought about by means of population and property exchanges, voluntary or otherwise, to unscramble an ethnically

heterogeneous map. Of course, this may entail considerable human costs in order to achieve group benefits, i.e., the avoidance of minority status.

4. Nonterritorial, "personal" or "community" autonomy with "functional" self-government. This concept derives from the Ottoman "millet" system, whereby members of the various non-Moslem ethnic-religious "communities," irrespective of territorial or residential considerations, were subject to the civil (usually canon) law of their own communal (usually religious) authorities. This system avoids minority status for any group, however dispersed, but, in a modern state, can be successful only to the degree that governmental functions can be apportioned among ethnic groups in such a manner that none can obstruct or deadlock the basic functions of society. In other words, there may be a dialectical process between autonomy and efficient government.

Variations on all four of these paradigms have been attempted or suggested in Cyprus at various points in time, between 1960 and the present.

ANTECEDENTS OF THE 1974 CRISIS

The 1974 crisis did not arise in a vacuum. Since the formation of the Cypriot state in 1959/1960, there has been ongoing friction between its Greek and Turkish communities, most notably during the confrontation of 1964. (Cyprus, prior to 1974, was approximately 80 percent Greek and 18 percent Turkish, with Armenians and Maronites constituting most of the remainder of the population.(1) Altogether, Cyprus has some 600,000 inhabitants.) On the Greek-Cypriot side, there has been intermittent pressure for _enosis_ or union with Greece itself, especially on the part of members of the ultranationalist EOKA-B organization. The Turkish-Cypriot response to this slogan was _taksim_ or "double enosis," which entailed basically the partition of the island into Greek and Turkish Cypriot zones and the subsequent union of the two areas, respectively, with Greece and Turkey. As will be seen later, taksim de facto entailed major cross-migration of Greeks and Turks within the island, because of its heterogeneous ethnic geography. (See Appendix A.) Increasingly, a major obstacle to both enosis and taksim was presented by Archbishop Makarios, once he became president of the island state, although, as Ethnarch of the Greek Cypriot community, he had once favored enosis. However, he came to savor his power as head of an independent state and found that his personal strength was maximized by the fact that Cyprus was given a "unitary" rather than a "federalist" form of government.

Paradoxically, Makarios' rule, as well as the subsequent Turkish invasion that destroyed his state, theoretically were both based upon the 1959 Zurich and London Agreements, guaranteed by Great Britain, Greece, and Turkey (see Appendix B). These documents constituted the legal basis for the governance of Cyprus, as well as for the Turkish invasion, which, in theory, was carried out by a guarantor of the Cypriot state in defense of the island's constitution.

The Cypriot constitutional system was based loosely on the Ottoman millet concept, employing "personal" rather than "territorial" criteria of minority autonomy – a concept developed further by the Austrian Social-Democrats, Karl Renner and Otto Bauer, as a possible solution for the ethnic maladies of the Habsburg Empire. The basic advantage of the nonterritorial approach is to provide members of ethnic minority groups with protection even where they are interspersed with other ethnic elements, as was the case in Cyprus prior to 1974, when the Turkish minority was spread thinly throughout the island.

The Cypriot constitution, in as far as Archbishop Makarios permitted its provisions to be fulfilled, allowed numerically generous representation for Turkish Cypriots in the civil service and police (30 percent), as well as in the army (40 percent) and the House of Representatives (30 percent). It provided also that the vice-president had to be Turkish and would have the right of veto over legislation passed by the House of Representatives.(2) (Moreover, the Constitution provided, wherever possible, for separate religious, educational, cultural, and legal administrations, an approach typical of personal autonomy systems, or what one author describes as "functional federation," as contrasted to "regional" (i.e., territorial) federation or autonomy).(3) While there may be some validity to Greek arguments, to the effect that this provided a formula for Turkish obstruction (i.e. built-in deadlock), this is the case also with the Turkish argument that obstruction was only a function of the inequitable nature of Makarios' policy. Moreover, the Cypriot Turks would add, a minority of 30 percent in the House of Representatives, while generous for an ethnic group constituting a mere 18 percent of the overall population, nevertheless is a minority and easily (and consistently) outvoted.

However, the demographic situation existing prior to 1974 left no viable alternative for the Turkish population. Their villages were so interspersed with Greek rural areas and with townships of mixed population that no territorial solutions could be found without creating new minorities within whatever autonomous provinces might be established. Since the Greek Cypriots constitute a majority on the island as a whole, they had no interest, prior to 1974, in a new constitutional approach whereby some Greeks would find themselves in a minority within one or two new autonomous regions.

One interesting plan submitted by a Greek scholar (regrettably after 1974) was intended to demonstrate that a territorial approach to the Cyprus problem might have proved viable.(4) This scheme provided for 7 Turkish-Cypriot autonomous zones, each comprising a contiguous (if rather oddly shaped) area of land, amounting altogether to 13 percent of the island's surface (see Fig. 6.2, p. 198), approximately the same proportion of privately owned land held by Turkish Cypriots before

1974. (Officially, 59.6 percent of the land in Cyprus prior to 1974 was Greek-owned, 12.3 percent Turkish-owned, 1.4 percent Armenian, Maronite, or "other" owned; while 26.7 percent comprised state land. Thus, the Turks owned about 16.82 percent of the private land, according to this survey. A British study came up with slightly different statistics, crediting Turkish Cypriots with ownership of 12.9 percent of the island and about 17.5 percent of private land.)(5) This solution, which was suggested by George Karouzis, the head of the Cypriot Land Consolidation Authority, would have required migration of 10.10 percent of the Turkish and only 0.98 percent of the Greek population of Cyprus. On the average, the migrants would have had to move only 3.5 kilometers, and 87.5 percent of Turkish-owned land would have remained under Turkish control.(6) Thus, in exchange for about thirteen percent of its land, the Turkish population would have received comparable Greek and state land under this solution, but, more importantly, could have established territorially contiguous self-governing zones, which would have facilitated greatly de facto autonomy from Greek authority. Unfortunately, this suggestion was offered only after 1974, and by that time the demographic situation in Cyprus had changed so drastically as to render such a settlement unthinkable from the Turkish standpoint. Had such a plan been proposed and implemented before 1974, it might have proven more successful than the system which crumbled completely in 1974.

The fact is that the system provided for in the 1959 Agreements had not been in effect since 1964. In December 1963, Makarios attempted to push through 13 revisions in the Constitution (see Appendix C), which allegedly would have smoothed out the functioning of the state.(7) However, the real effect of these proposals would have been to deprive Turkish Cypriots of some of their basic constitutional guarantees. Even if the latter hampered Makarios' ability to run the state in a manner he deemed appropriate, his revisions were certain to alienate the Turkish community still further. Moreover, the President began to escalate his pressure upon the Turkish minority, establishing a blockade of Turkish enclaves, including interruption of food supplies, and thus jeopardizing, in some instances, the very lives of the island's second largest ethnic community.(8) The Turkish Cypriots reacted by withdrawing from the government and by attempting to run their own affairs, a difficult task, given the ethnic mosaic of Cyprus. De facto, this development initiated the transition toward territorial partition. In 1965, the leaders of the Turkish community proposed bisecting the island along a line from Yialia in the west, through Nicosia, to Famagusta.(9) (See figure 6.3, p. 199.) According to this plan, the unitary state was to be replaced by a loose federal structure, with the Turkish Cypriots controlling a region with roughly twice the area warranted by their proportion of the total population of the island. This proposal followed an abortive attempt by the Ankara government to intervene on behalf of its beleaguered Turkish kinsmen on the island, in accordance with the 1959 Agreements, a military move that was averted by the admonitions of the Johnson Administration.(10) Roughly a decade later, Henry Kissinger was to fail to take similarly timely preventive steps.

In 1968, representatives of the two major Cypriot communities, confronted by a nonviable situation, initiated discussions which were expanded four years later to include the Athens and Ankara governments, as well as U.N. intermediaries, all acting in an essentially advisory capacity.(11) These talks were broken off in April 1974, when the parties reached an impasse. In the meantime, a crisis had developed between Makarios and the Junta that had taken power some years previously in Athens, and which was represented on the island by the small Greek unit stationed there by virtue of the Treaty of Guarantee. Makarios suspected that the Junta and the Greek officers in Cyprus were planning to overthrow him and demanded the withdrawal of the entire unit.(12) At this point, Sampson, representing the rightist EOKA-B sympathetic to the Athens Junta, deposed the Makarios administration in a coup. The removal of the universally recognized Cypriot government, by a group moving openly toward enosis with Greece, provided Turkey with an opportunity to redress long-standing grievances, some of them legitimate. The 1959 Treaty of Guarantee did entitle Ankara to move, particularly in the face of the palpable danger posed to the Turkish-Cypriot minority by the Sampson regime.   Needless to say, Turkey was not concerned with rescuing Archbishop Makarios. Regardless of the merits of the Turkish case during the early stages of the 1974 intervention, Turkey's moves beyond that point became highly questionable. The logic inherent in the situation, as it developed during the decade of 1964 to 1974, seemed to lead inexorably toward some kind of territorial partition, accompanied by a lesser or greater degree of exchange of population in view of the confused ethnic geography of Cyprus. However, the eventual Turkish military occupation of nearly 40 percent of the island far exceeded any measures needed to ensure the safety of the Turkish-Cypriot community. Moreover, Ankara's subsequent policies of permitting Turkish migration from the mainland to Cyprus, as well as the continued Turkish alibis for refraining from engaging in serious negotiations, raised fundamental questions concerning Turkey's ultimate intentions.

POST-INVASION DEVELOPMENTS:
DEMOGRAPHIC AND GEOPOLITICAL ASPECTS

The Turkish invasion encompassed four phases:

1. Initially, the Turks drove a small wedge into Northern Cyprus, from the port of Kyrenia southward to the Turkish sector of Nicosia. On July 22, two days after the beginning of the invasion, the Turkish force agreed to a cease-fire, persuant to UN Security Council Resolution 353.(13) The next day, Sampson was replaced as (Acting) President by the moderate pro-Western statesman, Glavkos Clerides. At this point, the Junta in Athens also fell, and was replaced by the moderately conservative Constantine Karamanlis. Until this juncture, there is little doubt that Turkey was acting in accordance with its legal responsibil-

ities as one of the guarantors of Cyprus and, de facto, of the Turkish-Cypriot community. Moreover, Ankara had achieved major successes in toppling Sampson as well as the Athens Junta, thereby averting the possibility of enosis. Moreover, even Makarios, whose actions had played a significant role in precipitating the July crisis, had been forced to flee the island. He was not to return until December, and his credibility was considerably weakened by the events of July. Thus, Turkey had achieved all that it could wish, short of compelling the Greeks to recognize an autonomous Turkish-Cypriot political entity. Given the events of the previous decade, however, it was to be expected that the Turks should press for full autonomy.

2. Consequently, the Turkish Army violated the cease-fire and continued to widen the wedge it had driven into northern Cyprus.(14) On August 8, serious postinvasion negotiations commenced at Geneva. Whereas earlier contacts had included only the three guarantor states, Greece, Turkey, and Great Britain, the new talks included also Rauf Denktash, representing the Turkish-Cypriot community, and Glavkos Clerides, his counterpart for the Greek-Cypriot side.(15)

Three major plans were presented at the Geneva talks by Clerides, Denktash, and the Turkish Foreign Minister, Turan Gunes, respectively (Appendixes D, E, and F.) The two major "adversaries" Denktash and Clerides, who had confronted one another previously in intercommunal negotiations, actually were old friends dating back to law school days in London.(16)

Clerides had to play with a very weak hand. The presence of the Turkish Army on the island gave the Turkish side tremendous leverage if it wished to impose a victor's peace. At the same time, the specter of Makarios' imminent return had to influence Clerides' thinking. If he signed any agreement without mobilizing for it the wide support of the Greek Cypriot community, Clerides risked giving Makarios (by no means his friend or patron) a pretext for deposing him from the post of Acting President. Clerides presented a plan harking back to the concepts of 1959, based on the continuation of a unitary state but offering a fair degree of autonomy to the Turkish community, with future negotiations to determine the precise division of powers between the President and the two communal administrations to be organized. Turkish villages could be grouped together for administrative purposes.(17) This proposal for functional autonomy perhaps was intended to contain also territorial elements along the lines of the Karouzis Plan, discussed earlier, except that since no map of administrative areas was submitted, it is not clear whether Clerides' approach allowed for population transfers to accomplish the formation of contiguous, ethnically homogeneous zones (as in the Karouzis plan). (To some extent, events were beginning to render these demographic aspects hypothetical. A major factor in the post-intervention negotiations, and particularly after this round of Geneva talks broke down, was the de facto exchange of population that was set in motion, including migration of Turks to the north and Greeks to the south, bringing about the formation of a relatively homogeneous Turkish zone in Northern Cyprus. This question will be discussed later, in greater detail.) However, the seven Turkish zones suggested by Karouzis were so limited in size, oddly shaped, and distant from one another, that, even if preferable to the complete isolation of the numerous tiny Turkish enclaves prior to 1974, they still would not have sufficed to provide meaningful security for the Turkish-Cypriot community.

The Turkish government, on its part, put forth a multizonal proposal, the so-called Gunes Plan, which provided for six Turkish-Cypriot administrative regions, all with coastlines (to guarantee that the 1964 blockades of Turkish villages could not be repeated, since they could be resupplied rapidly by the Turkish Navy). The Gunes Plan demanded 34 percent of the island for the Turkish community, including much choice tourist land and valuable citrus groves.(18) While the precise allocation of administrative functions was negotiable (point 5 of the proposal), it was quite clear that the central authority would have had little power (point 3), understandably, given the previous Turkish experience with a Greek-dominated Cypriot government. There was no reference to the issue of repatriation of refugees, leaving unclear whether this question, too, was negotiable. Presumably, the conceptual framework of the Gunes Plan was meant to follow the general lines of paradigm 3 (see "Devices" section), artificially created ethnic homogeneity in each of several autonomous provinces.

The proposal submitted by Denktash on behalf of the Turkish-Cypriot community, at the same time as the Gunes Plan, also demanded 34 percent of the island for the Turks(19) – actually somewhat less than the Turkish community had requested a decade earlier.(20) Unlike Gunes, however, Denktash called for a bizonal rather than a multizonal structure, with the Turkish zone to extend north of the "Attila line," roughly from Morphou through Nicosia to Famagusta.(21) Presumably, Denktash also took for granted a major population exchange in order to attain a bizonal version of paradigm 3.

The Gunes Plan was not unreasonable, particularly as an opening position from which some (territorial) concessions might be made. However, Turkish behavior at the Geneva Conference raises serious questions regarding whether the Turks were negotiating in good faith, and just how great Turkish territorial appetite had become, now that it had been whetted by Ankara's initial military victories.

While the Gunes Plan hardly was ideal from the Greek perspective, Clerides, perhaps realizing that Makarios' return would undermine his political position on the island (and, hence, his ability to negotiate unfettered), asked for a 36-hour adjournment of the Conference in order to consider the Turkish proposal.(22) (Clerides, Acting President in Makarios' absence,(23) by any standards would have to be considered a flexible, moderate, and pragmatic statesman. He may genuinely have sought an equitable solution to the Cyprus problem. However, he was caught in a vice between Turkish expansionist designs, on the one hand, and the shadow of Makarios, on the other. Even in Makarios' absence, Clerides had to be wary of such dangerous Makarios surrogates as Andreas Azinas and Dr. Vassos Lyssarides. Any concessions that Clerides made would come at the expense of Makarios' authority.

Makarios himself opposed even discussing bi- or multizonal arrangements.(24) Given the violent nature of Cypriot politics, Clerides' flexible and cooperative approach, matched neither by Makarios nor Denktash, could have cost him his life, and eventually did cost him his role as chief negotiator and his position in the Cypriot political arena.)

The Turks refused to grant this brief intermission, perhaps fearing that he might submit a counterproposal that was close enough in substance to the Gunes Plan to deprive Turkey of the option of resuming hostilities. (This concept is valid if one assumes that Turkey was at least marginally concerned with international and, specifically, American reactions. Of course, it may be argued that the American arms embargo, subsequent to the breakdown of the talks, had little, if any, impact on the Cyprus situation. However, it must be pointed out that Turkish self-confidence, after overrunning 40 percent of the island, probably became far more marked than it had been after the initial, less impressive, Turkish gains.) Moreover, after denying Clerides' reasonable request, Ankara delivered a 24-hour ultimatum to the government of Greece to accept the Turkish proposals. Thus the talks collapsed.(25)

3. Within hours the Turkish forces took the military initiative, bombing Nicosia on August 13,(26) and expanded the zone under Turkish control by a factor of several hundred percent. Another cease-fire came into force (actually was declared unilaterally by the Turkish Army) on August 16, by which time the Turkish zone had been enlarged to cover nearly 40 percent of the island.(27)

4. Soon thereafter, the Turks thrust forward in two additional areas, small in size, but strategically significant. They drove a sharp wedge southward, cutting the road from Larnaca, the remaining major Greek-Cypriot port, to the Greek sector of the capital, Nicosia.(28) During the same period, the Turkish army took the remaining portions of Famagusta (part having been seized previously),(29) Cyprus' second largest city and by far its largest port.(30) Thus the Turks, by forcing the termination of the Geneva talks, provided themselves with a pretext for further military operations, extending their lines beyond the parameters of their territorial demands at the conference table.

In retrospect, Greek Cypriots might have been better off immediately and unconditionally accepting the Gunes Plan (if, indeed, it was intended to constitute a serious negotiating position). At least the Turks would have controlled 34 and not 40 percent of the island, while the division of the Turkish sector into 6 separate areas would have severely hampered Turkish attempts to consolidate territorially and form one de facto state. Similarly, it would be harder for a multizonal entity to achieve taksim, union with Turkey, than for a single territorial unit to do so. Since most Greek Cypriots fear, above all, Turkey's sovereignty over the island, or any portion thereof, this consideration should have played a significant role at Geneva in 1974.

On the other hand, from the standpoint of a leader (and merely an Acting President) attempting to consolidate the Greek-Cypriot population after the humiliating and traumatic events of the summer of 1974, as Clerides hoped to do, there were serious inner-political drawbacks to any subdivision into small multizonal entities on an island that, socio-politically, in some ways resembles Sicily. It must be recalled that the Gunes Plan did not merely propose six Turkish zones. The Greek portion of the island, too, was to be split into two zones and, if severed lines of communications are taken into account, the larger of these Greek zones in effect would have consisted of several separated areas. From Clerides' point of view, this would have invited the seizure of local control by various rival political chieftains, not only from EOKA-B on the far right and the protocommunist AKEL on the left, but including such pro-Makarios bosses as Andreas Azinas, the Commissioner of Cooperative Development and a leader of the Cypriot Farmers Union (PEK),(31) and thus a figure with real clout as far as Cypriot peasants are concerned. Moreover, Azinas, who has performed liaison functions with the Soviet bloc on Makarios' behalf,(32) is by no means the only dangerous figure on Cyprus. The leftist EDEK Party under Dr. Vassos Lyssarides (Makarios' physician) controls a private paramilitary force of some significance,(33) while the AKEL leadership, representing the large and powerful Cypriot Communist Party, is extremely well organized.(34) As will be demonstrated subsequently, all of these forces, except for Clerides and the declining EOKA-B, operated in conjunction with Makarios.

The Turkish invasion and subsequent developments brought about demographic and other fundamental changes on the island. Their effect was to make a Turkish-Cypriot autonomous entity much more feasible, both because it had become demographically and economically viable, and because the Turks now controlled key bargaining chips which could be exchanged for Greek recognition of the de facto separation and independence of the Turkish zone from the rest of Cyprus (if not from mainland Turkey).

During the 1974 invasion, all but 20,000 of about 180,000 Greek Cypriots fled or were expelled from the northern, Turkish controlled sector of the island.(35) Meanwhile, most of the Turkish population in the south fled northward to the Turkish zone. However, around 20,000 Turkish refugees (out of a total of 50,000)(36) were unable to reach the north immediately and about one-half of them were given refuge at the British base of Episkopi (held by virtue of Britain's status as a guarantor power). In January 1975, the British Foreign Secretary Callaghan, under strong pressure from Ankara, and to the chagrin of the Greek-Cypriot side, allowed these Turkish refugees to move to the Turkish zone. This deprived the Greeks of a potential hostage population that might have served as a bargaining chip in their quest to compel the Turks to permit Greek refugees to return to their former homes in the North.(37)

The Turks, aiming essentially at the partition of Cyprus into two ethnically homogeneous zones, were eager, of course, to unscramble the heterogeneous ethnic geography of the island, while the Greeks, still clinging to the concept of a basically unitary state with a four to one Greek majority, wanted to return to the status quo ante bellum. Far from agreeing to any repatriation of Greek refugees to the Turkish zone, the Turkish authorities coerced more than half of the small Greek minority remaining there to move south(38) where, by the end of 1974, the refugee population was approaching 180,000.(39)

Subsequently, Denktash and Clerides signed an agreement whereby the remaining 8,000 Turks in the Greek sector were permitted to move to the North, on condition that the Turkish authorities allow the 9,000 Greeks still remaining in the North to stay (and also agree that some 300 Greek refugees in the South could rejoin their families in the North).(40) Thus, the Turkish authorities, who were in need of ethnic Turks to populate their zone (covering almost 40 percent of the area of Cyprus, with Turks constituting a mere 18 percent of the total Cypriot population), were able to bring virtually the entire Turkish community northward into their area of control, without conceding any occupied territory to the Greeks or allowing significant repatriation of Greek refugees to their former homes in the North.   Since the Clerides-Denktash agreement, the migration of Greek Cypriots southward has continued and, by late 1976, there were only about 4,000 Greeks remaining in the North.(41) Moreover, by October 1975, significant Turkish "colonization" of northern Cyprus was under way, with the settlement of up to 15,000 Turkish mainlanders in the region.(42) (Greek sources have claimed that as many as 35,000 new Turkish immigrants arrived in northern Cyprus between 1974 and mid-1976. The Turks claim that they are only returning expatriate Turkish Cypriots to the island. In fact, some 5,000 former Turkish Cypriots, mostly from Great Britain, have returned. However, migration to the Turkish sector appears to exceed considerably this total of 5,000. Apparently included among the Turkish mainlanders converging on northern Cyprus are considerable numbers of Moslem Lazes, a Caucasian, not a Turanian people, who inhabit southern Anatolia, as well as some Gypsies.)(43)

The influx of Anatolian mainlanders, combined with the continued presence of some 25,000 Turkish soldiers (as of the summer of 1977),(44) must be considered in conjunction with the significant wave of Greek emigration from the island.(45) The Greek exodus is due not only to obvious insecurity and fear of further Turkish encroachment, but even more to problems of unemployment in Southern Cyprus, which at one point reached over 25 percent of the working population, and was still hovering around 15 percent in December 1976.(46) Thus, not only was the ethnic geography of the island completely rearranged during this period, but the demographic ratio of Turks to Greeks was beginning to change somewhat, in favor of the former (although they are unlikely to become a majority in Cyprus during the foreseeable future). It should be recalled that massive population exchanges between Greeks and Turks hardly are a novelty in recent history – bearing in mind only the expulsions and forcible transfers in the early 1920s of almost 2 million Greeks from the Ionian coast and Turks from Thrace and Macedonia.(47) This trend, too, has contributed to the Turkish perception that a more or less independent Turkish-Cypriot entity is a viable reality.

It may be assumed that the effect of these demographic factors has been reinforced by Turkey's awareness of the economic potential of the area it seized in 1974. According to the (essentially Greek) Planning Commission in Nicosia, prior to the invasion, this northern sector of Cyprus accounted for 70 percent of the gross output, 65 percent of the tourist accommodation, almost 87 percent of hotel bed space under construction, 83 percent of general cargo handling capacity, 56 percent of mining and quarrying, 48 percent of the agricultural exports, 46 percent of the planned production, and 41 percent of the livestock of the island.(48)

While these statistics may well be exaggerated, there is little doubt that the Turks now control far more of the island's economic potential than they might have been awarded in proportion to their percentage of the total Cypriot population or perhaps even to the percentage of the island's overall area now occupied by the Turkish Army. (The term potential is employed since much of the Cypriot economy has been damaged or, like the tourist industry, almost destroyed. During the fighting, damage, looting, and vandalism led to the destruction of much of the productive capacity of the northern zone of Cyprus, and the Turkish authorities in attempting to take over enterprises requiring refined skills or sophisticated technological knowhow, may encounter difficulties not faced by the previous Greek personnel – now reduced to refugee status. Consequently, considerable time is likely to elapse before the economic potential of the Turkish zone can be utilized fully.)(49) While the Turkish zone may lack the capacity to become a totally self-sufficient economic entity, the Turkish-Cypriot leadership may well feel that its economic basis is sound enough to support a reasonably well-functioning polity, provided there is some linkage to the economy of the Turkish mainland. The functional separation of the Turkish northern sector from the previously unitary Cypriot state has gone well beyond the February 13, 1975 proclamation of an autonomous "Federated Turkish-Cypriot State."(50) Use of the Turkish Lira by the Turkish Cypriots (since the Cypriot Central Bank is located in the Greek Cypriot zone) rather than the Cypriot Pound, and the utilization of the Turkish, rather than the Cypriot, postal system are but two significant indicators of this development. It is not clear, however, whether this is the result of deliberate policy decisions or, as the Turks claim, whether it was a reaction simply to lack of Greek Cypriot cooperation in currency affairs and postal deliveries (although the Greeks have had little choice in these matters, since the Turkish zone has been barricaded off from southern Cyprus).(51)

The cumulative effect of these factors has been to leave the Turks very little incentive to make any concessions. Short of full recognition by Greece and the Greek Cypriots of a nearly independent Turkish Northern Cyprus, comprising almost all of the 40 percent of the island's area now within its boundaries, there is little that the Greek side has to offer in exchange for its demands concerning the return of Greek refugees to the North and the restoration of their former lands and homes to Greek ownership. Considering that the Greek-Cypriot zone now contains roughly 3 refugees from the North to every 5 indigenous inhabitants of the South, a staggering proportion compared to almost any other contemporary refugee problem, the Greek Cypriot effort to deal with the resultant hardships has been little short of heroic. Instead of leaving the refugees to rot under canvas, as a constant reminder and a moving propaganda picture for every visitor to view, the authorities and a majority of Greek-Cypriot families, as well as the refugees themselves, have extended themselves to the utmost to make the expellees productive and to find them more permanent housing. The decline of the unemployment rate from 25 to 15 percent in a relatively short period speaks for itself.(52) Of course, migration from the island has helped also to alleviate the refugee problem.(53)

Nevertheless, during this very complex stage of post-invasion nego-tiations, Clerides and Denktash were able to reach agreement con-cerning the broad principles on which a final settlement would be based. (The first stage of negotiations consisted of the Geneva talks of the summer of 1974, and the third stage of the successful Clerides-Denktash negotiations, in the summer of 1975, concerned the treatment of the remaining ethnic minorities on both sides, following a sterile second stage in Vienna, earlier during 1975.) The general formula devised by the two negotiators provided for the division of Cyprus into two mutually recognized, federated autonomous zones and the reduc-tion of the Turkish-controlled area to less than the nearly 40 percent of Cyprus it constituted at that time.(54) One source claimed subsequently that it had been agreed to limit the Turkish zone to approximately 25 percent of the island,(55) but it is doubtful whether Denktash really would have been prepared, so early in the bargaining, to consent to a territorial concession of such proportions.

Clearly, the concept guiding the negotiators was that recognition by the Greek side of very substantial autonomy for the Turkish zone required meaningful territorial concessions on the part of the Turks. On this basis, Clerides and Denktash continued their talks intermit-tently until April 1976, when Clerides was forced to resign. It was claimed that allegedly without Makarios' authorization or knowledge, he had agreed secretly to allow Denktash to examine and evaluate Greek-Cypriot proposals 10 days before they were due to be submitted officially. (This tactic, known as "prenegotiation," has venerable antecedents and is meant to avert deadlock or breakdown of talks at the official level.) For reasons that remain unclear, Denktash publicly rejected the contents of the Greek-Cypriot plan, on the grounds that he could negotiate only minor border rectifications, 4 days after receiving it, i.e., fully 6 days before he was supposed to see it for the first time. Thus he embarrassed Clerides by revealing the indiscretion entailed in permitting an adversary in negotiations to see proposals prematurely. As a result, a torrent of criticism broke over Clerides' head and he was forced to resign. Since he was President of the Cyprus House of Representatives, he was replaced by the Deputy President, Tassos Papadopoulos.(56) Consequently, Denktash, as Speaker of the Constitu-ent Assembly of the "Federated Turkish-Cypriot State," designated his own Deputy Speaker, Umit Suleyman Onan, to replace him in the talks.(57) The result was that the negotiations were downgraded to the level of lower-ranking officials, decreasing the likelihood of a successful outcome, since such representatives enjoy far less flexibility in bargaining than leaders of great standing and influence.

ADDITIONAL CONSIDERATIONS CONCERNING POLITICAL PARTIES AND LEADERS

It is conceivable that Denktash intended to undermine the talks themselves (the Turkish side, holding all the territory it desired, had no particular reason to press for a compromise), to exacerbate still further the relations between Clerides and Makarios, and, perhaps, to bring about Clerides' removal. Despite the events of April 1976, during the Greek-Cypriot elections of the following fall, Clerides' party, the Democratic Rally, managed to obtain 24.1 percent of the popular vote, despite the superior organization and means of the rival parties and their readiness to resort to intimidation. His sizable popular support did not suffice to gain a single seat in the House for Clerides and his supporters because of the coalition formed against him by the Democratic Front (led by Makarios' former foreign minister and eventual successor, Spiros Kyprianou, who obtained 21 seats), the leftist EDEK (led by Makarios' physician Lyssarides, with 4 seats), and the Communist AKEL (9 seats). Aided by their coalition arrangement and by a plurality constituency electoral system, these pro-Makarios parties swept all the seats except 1, captured by an independent.(58)

The Turks were fully aware of the great reputation and appeal Clerides enjoyed in the West, particularly in the United States, whereas Makarios, in view of his ties with the Soviet Union and his many dubious activities during two decades, was widely mistrusted. Denktash may have hoped that, with Clerides out of the picture, United States pressure on Turkey would be eased further. During the previous fall, the United States embargo on arms to Turkey had been lifted only partially.(59)

With Clerides removed, Makarios had virtually free rein. Unlike the relationships prevailing on the Turkish side, the Greek-Cypriot leadership played a more dominant role in negotiations than the government of Greece. Unlike Turkey, Greece is relatively remote from Cyprus (some 600 miles), and the Greek military presence on the island constitutes little more than a token compared with the Turkish military domination of the northern zone. Whereas Greece itself is governed by a moderate, pro-Western regime under Constantine Karamanlis and his party (New Democracy, which is close in outlook to Mr. Clerides and, like him, flexible on a solution to the Cyprus problem), Cyprus is dominated by parties espousing the Makarios approach, leaning toward the U.S.S.R. and the Third World, and insisting on a hard line vis-a-vis Turkey and the Turkish Cypriots. The opposition parties in Greece, the leftist PASOK of Andreas Papandreou and the two splinters of the Communist Party (the Party of the Exterior and its allies, with Moscow's support, and the more heterodox Party of the Interior) have

Table 6.1. The Greek Elections of 1974 and 1977

PARTY	1974		1977	
	% of Votes	% of Seats	% of Votes	% of Seats
National Rally (Rightist)	---	---	6.8	1.7
New Democracy (Karamanlis)	54.3	73.3	41.8	57.7
Democratic Center (Mavros)	20.5	20.0	11.9	5.0
New Liberals (ex-Dem. Center)	---	---	1.1	0.7
Others	2.2	---	0.9	---
PASOK (Papandreou)	13.6	4.0	25.3	30.7
Left Alliance (C.P. of Interior)			2.7	0.7
Communists (of Exterior, pro-Moscow)	9.4	2.7	9.4	3.7

Note: This tabulation of parties is presented in ideological order, from Right to Left.

Source: Statistics adapted from "Learning to Live with an Opposition," The Economist 265, no. 7004 (November 26, 1977): 54.

The Greek left opposition scored major gains in the 1977 elections at the expense of Karamanlis' New Democracy and George Mavros' Democratic Center party, both in terms of votes and seats. However, Karamanlis still controls a majority of parliamentary seats.

ideological affinity, respectively, with Dr. Lyssarides' EDEK and with AKEL, in the Greek zone of Cyprus. These organizations all are virulently anti-NATO and take a hard-line stance against Turkey and Mr. Denktash.(60)

For these reasons alone, not to mention his personality, the Greek government never felt much sympathy for Archbishop Makarios, who maintained strong links with groups that are anathema to Mr. Karamanlis. Under these circumstances, it is regrettable that Athens' influence in Cyprus negotiations has not been commensurate with that of Ankara, since Mr. Karamanlis could have given strong backing to Mr. Clerides' flexible approach, as well as compensating for the absence of a powerful political organization on Cyprus in support of Mr. Clerides.

Of course, this presupposes a genuine willingness to compromise on the part of Turkish negotiators, an attitude that has not been evident so far. One of the factors contributing to this Turkish stance is believed to have stemmed from the inability of the two major parties in Turkey, Mr. Suleyman Demirel's Justice Party and Mr. Bulent Ecevit's Republican People's Party, to capture an absolute majority of seats in the Turkish Parliament either in the 1973 or 1977 general elections. This has compelled these two major rivals to court the smaller parties that have held the key to the succession of coalition cabinets, led alternately by the R.P.P. and the J.P. (See Appendix G for a list of successive Turkish cabinets in recent years.) A particularly important role in this connection has been played by two parties that, by their very nature and ideology, are inclined strongly toward a very hard line regarding Cyprus. The National Action Party of Colonel Alparslan Turkes, a pan-Turanian organization dedicated to uniting all the Turkic peoples (presumably including Soviet Central Asia), naturally would be disinclined to "abandon" the Cypriot Turks (living on an island "stolen" from Turkey just under a century ago).(61) The National Salvation Party of Mr. Necmettin Erbakan, a pan-Islamic party of dubious legality under Turkey's strongly secularist constitution,(62) clearly would not tolerate relegating a Turkish-Moslem population on Cyprus to the status of a helpless minority engulfed in a Greed Orthodox "ocean."

Ecevit, the "hero of Cyprus," discovered only two months after his victorious invasion of the island in 1974 that he could not offend the N.S.P. and continue to govern, since his ruling coalition started to fall apart at that stage over a number of issues, including Cyprus.(63) Mr. Demirel is even more vulnerable on the Cyprus issue since, if he were to make really significant concessions, he would be subject to a propaganda campaign by Mr. Ecevit, accusing the J.P. of surrendering the fruits of a great victory won under R.P.P. leadership (at the expense of Turkish blood).(64)

Of course, it is by no means clear to what extent Ecevit and Demirel themselves really are inclined to grant meaningful concessions to resolve the Cyprus problem. (If anything, it seems that Mr. Demirel, who is more vulnerable on this issue, may be slightly less intransigent than Mr. Ecevit, who could, perhaps, draw upon some of the credit gained in 1974 as a result of his successful incursion into the island.) In

Table 6.2. The Turkish Elections of 1973 and 1977

PARTY	1973		1977	
	% of Votes	% of Seats	% of Votes	% of Seats
N.A.P. (Turkes)	3.4	0.7	6.4	3.6
N.S.P. (Erbakan)	11.9	10.7	8.6	5.3
D.P. (J.P. splinter)	12.0	10.0	1.8	0.2
J.P. (Demirel)	30.0	33.1	36.9	42.0
T.U.P.	1.1	0.2	0.4	---
Independents	2.8	1.3	2.5	0.9
R.R.P. (R.P.P. splinter)	5.3	2.9	1.9	0.7
R.P.P. (Ecevit)	33.5	41.1	41.4	47.3
T.L.P. (Protocommunist)	---	---	0.1	---

Note: This tabulation of parties is presented in ideological order, from Right to Left.

Source: Adapted from statistics in Keesing's Contemporary Archives 23 (October 7, 1977): 28597.

The two major parties could dispense with the support of the N.A.P. or the N.S.P. only at the price of forming a "Big Two" coalition of the R.P.P. and the J.P., which would be comparable to a British Labor-Conservative coalition and must be regarded, therefore, as politically implausible.

any case, the Turkish domestic political situation provides an excellent pretext for the two main leaders not to take risks concerning Cyprus, since they can plead that concessions on this sensitive issue would produce dangerous instability at home. Thus the absence of a political concensus on foreign and security affairs is tactically advantageous to the main Turkish figures, since each of them can claim to be personally moderate while pursuing intransigent national policies under the guise of being compelled to do so for the sake of the country's unity. Weakness at home can translate into strength at the bargaining table, when properly manipulated.

Whatever may be the real motivations of Mr. Demirel and Mr. Ecevit, however, it is a fact that on at least three occasions since the invasion, in September 1974,(65) May 1975, and June 1977,(66) the smaller parties have been able to enforce a change in government by withdrawing from a coalition and, in the first and the last of these instances, Cyprus proved to be a significant issue in causing the downfall of the Cabinet. It must be recalled also that the Turkish Army, which established and sustains the "Federated Turkish-Cypriot State," remains the most important pillar of the mainland Turkish state and can be offended only at grave political risk. Unlike the Greek side, therefore, it is Ankara and not (Northern) Nicosia that makes the final decisions concerning Cyprus.

Nevertheless, political divisions within the Turkish-Cypriot community do play a role of some significance. Existing differences derive mainly from the clan rivalries between the Denktash and Kucuk families, even if this antipathy has taken on ideological coloring. The son of Rauf Denktash, the leader of the ruling National Unity Party, publishes the organ reflecting the views of the present regime, Cyprus Times (or Zaman). The major opposition newspaper, Halkin Sesi, is published by the son of Dr. Fazil Kucuk, former vice-president of Cyprus, who is regarded as the elder statesman of Turkish-Cypriot politics. The Kucuk family's newspaper generally represents the views of the center-left opposition parties (the Popular Party, the Communal Liberation Party, and the Republican Turkish Party), which control 10 out of the 40 seats in the Turkish-Cypriot Legislative Assembly. (The clan rivalries among Turkish Cypriots, no less than the highly personal nature of Greek-Cypriot politics (see pp. 179-181, 184-187) once again illustrate the resemblances between Cyprus and Sicily.) Halkin Sesi tends to adopt a more conciliatory approach toward the Greek Cypriots than Denktash's Zaman,(67) and accuses Denktash of resorting to intimidation (by organized gangs).(68) It voices criticism also of members of the Turkish armed forces(69) (who are reported to have mistreated their ethnic kinsmen, as well as Greek Cypriots). Mainland Turks, including the armed forces, on their part are reported to be less than enamored of Turkish Cypriots, who are viewed as lacking the proverbially fierce pride and fighting spirit of the Turkish nation.

One source cites a prevalent attitude in Turkey which believes that "Cyprus is not a great prize."(70) Whether the Turkish Cypriot opposition elements would maintain their current views if they were in power themselves is a moot point. At the moment, Denktash is solidly ensconced and the Turkish Army, which backs him, continues its highly visible presence in Cyprus. Of course, if the political situation in Ankara were to change, with one party capturing an absolute majority of seats in Parliament, it is conceivable that Turkey might decide to make some concessions amounting to a sufficiently significant adjustment in the Cypriot status quo to permit a mutually recognized, reasonably final solution.

PROSPECTS

Since Clerides' resignation, limited progress has been recorded on the negotiating front. On February 12, 1977, following a summit meeting between Makarios and Denktash under the auspices of UN Secretary-General Kurt Waldheim, four fundamental principles were agreed upon as the basis for future negotiations:(71)

1. We are seeking an independent, nonaligned, bicommunal, federal Republic.
   (While details would have to be worked out, the implication is that each of the two ethnic communities essentially would continue to govern itself, but a central state framework would be reconstituted and the Greeks would abandon enosis and the Turks give up taksim. (An incentive for the Turks to agree to the reconstitution of a Cypriot state — with much weakened powers, of course — is that, as long as their zone of the island remains an entity without international recognition, all international aid — save that of Turkey, which faces major economic burdens of its own — to Cyprus will continue to flow to the recognized government of the island — i.e., Kyprianou, which is less than likely to distribute funds to the Turkish sector.)(72))

2. The territory under the administration of each community should be discussed in the light of economic viability or productivity and land ownership.
   (The implication is that the autonomy enjoyed by the two communities would be based on territorial, rather than functional, division, but that the size of the Turkish zone would be reduced in the light of some of the criteria mentioned.)

3. Questions of principles, like freedom of movement, freedom of settlement, the right of property, and other specific matters, are open for discussion, taking into consideration the fundamental basis of a bicommunal federal system and certain practical difficulties which may arise for the Turkish Cypriot community.

(This paragraph is beset with pitfalls, as far as future negotiations are concerned. Needless to say, there is no freedom of movement, freedom of settlement, right of property, etc., since the free and unrestricted application of these principles would break up precisely what the Turks have achieved — i.e., a territorially contiguous, ethnically homogeneous zone, that can be defended with relative ease.)

4. The powers and functions of the central federal government will be such as to safeguard the unity of the country, having regard to the bicommunal character of the State.
   (Thus the main function of the central authority would appear to be the safeguarding of the state rather than its actual administration. This implies that both sides understand clearly that the federal government would handle external affairs (i.e., foreign relations and defense — an empty function, since relations with the two countries that really matter to Cyprus will be decided by them, in Athens and Ankara, respectively), and little else.)

While these principles have been agreed upon, essential differences remain concerning actual implementation, i.e., the specifics of an agreement.

Quantitatively, with regard to the size of the Turkish zone, the parties would not appear to be worlds apart. The Turks are speaking now in terms of 32.8 percent of the area of Cyprus,(73) although they continue to refrain from producing a map specifying just where the boundaries are to be drawn (despite repeated promises to this effect over several years). The Greek Cypriots did submit a map in 1977, according to which the Turkish zone would contain only 20 percent of the island.(74) (See Fig. 6.6) However, Makarios at the time let it be known that his side, in fact, might be willing to agree that the Turks should have "more than 25 percent," although "somewhat less than 30 percent."(75) (According to another report, the Ethnarch specified 25 to 27 percent.)(76) Thus, the gap between the Turkish demand for 32.8 percent and the Greek willingness to concede somewhat less than 30 percent is hardly earthshaking.

However, Makarios, at the same time, also insisted upon the return of 60 to 70,000 Greek Cypriots to their former homes in the North, a condition that is most unlikely to prove acceptable to the Turkish side, since it would threaten to disrupt the homogeneity of the Turkish zone.(77) Late in 1977, a breakthrough appeared imminent, when Demirel offered to allow up to 10,000 Greek Cypriots to return to the area of Varosha,(78) a former Greek portion of Famagusta that was seized by the Turkish Army at the very end of its drive (causing particular bitterness among Greek Cypriots). However, when the Demirel government fell, Ecevit, back in office, proved unwilling or unable to confirm the offer. This may have been due to the fact that, when last in power (July 1976), he had taken a particularly hard line on this issue and had announced that Varosha, at that point virtually uninhabited, would be settled by Turks.(79) Thus Ecevit may have felt that to backtrack and permit Greek Cypriots to return to the area would stand in flat contradiction to his former declaration and, therefore, would make him appear vacillating and rather foolish. Moreover, his current cabinet rests on a parliamentary minority plus some defectors from the coalition that supported the previous Demirel government. This leaves Ecevit in an uncomfortable and exposed position. However, he has come up with a new concept whereby, in the context of an overall settlement, Famagusta, together with its suburb of Varosha, would become the Cypriot capital, having special federal status and permitting both Greeks and Turks to live there, but ensuring that Varosha would not be incorporated into the Greek zone.(80) This trizonal approach (with one Turkish, one Greek, and one mixed area) may be attractive at first sight, not merely as a solution for the Varosha problem, but also as a bridge for the quantitative gap between the 32.8 percent the Turks are demanding and the 27 to 30 percent Makarios appears to have been willing to concede.

However, the question has to be posed whether this proposal would not simply replicate, in the microcosm of Famagusta-Varosha, the Cyprus problem as a whole – as it existed between 1959 and 1974. Once again, there would be an area, albeit much smaller (but also very significant, as the third or federal zone), inhabited by both communities, with each attempting to fill the political vacuum created by the constitutional "neutralization" of the urban area, i.e., to gain domination there. It seems doubtful whether such artificial "solutions" can deal satisfactorily with the regions that are most hotly contested, e.g., Varosha or the Morphou citrus groves (which are on the opposite, western end of the island). Both of these areas now are in Turkish hands, but were designated specifically as part of the Greek-Cypriot zone on the map submitted by the Greeks in 1977.

It appears that an acceptable settlement, if indeed the circumstances on Cyprus, in Ankara, and in Athens would be propitious for an agreement, must be based on a Turkish concession of territory in return for Greek-Cypriot recognition of a Turkish-Cypriot zone that will retain both ethnic homogeneity and a high degree of autonomy. The more significant the Turkish territorial concessions, the less likely the Turks are to accept back any Greek refugees into a reduced Turkish zone. Having unscrambled the ethnic geography of Cyprus, no leader on the Turkish side is likely to jeopardize his community's security by returning to the preinvasion demographic kaleidoscope.

Thus, the problem probably will boil down to two issues:

1. Will the Greek Cypriots be willing to abandon the demand for the return of Greek refugees to the areas that will remain in the Turkish zone?

The answer to this question probably will be positive, although, perhaps, not explicitly so. The refugees have been integrated quite well into the economy of the South, as demonstrated by the declining unemployment rate and the recovery of the GNP.(81) The number of

Greek Cypriots prepared to live as a minority under Turkish rule must be quite insignificant.

2. Will the Turks be prepared to concede enough territory to make it worthwhile for the other side to agree to recognize the virtually complete autonomy of the Turkish zone?

Given the current de facto independence of that zone, plus Turkish military predominance, it is unlikely that the Turks will be willing to give up much more than they offered already. This is likely to be the case particularly so long as the present political stalemate continues in Ankara, with no party capable of winning a clear electoral mandate. The only real incentive for greater Turkish flexibility is economic, leaving aside the complex issue of weapons supply. However, throughout most of the world and not least in the Eastern Mediterranean, considerations of national pride (and security) usually triumph over "rational" economic considerations.

APPENDIX A

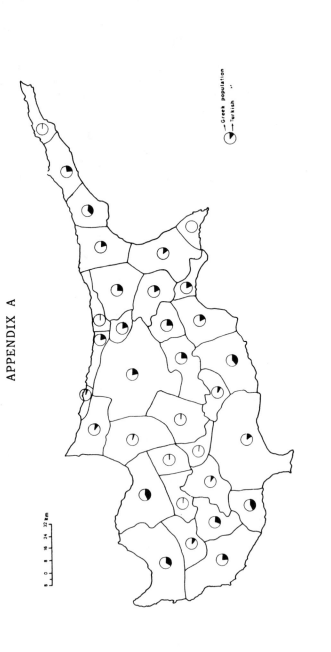

Fig. 6.1.: Heterogeneous pattern of Turkish-Cypriot settlements prior to 1974 (population distribution based on town and country planning regions).

Source: Map contained in George Karouzis, Proposals for a Solution to the Cyprus Problem, p. 43. For more detailed breakdown, please refer to the folded map in the rear of this study.

APPENDIX B

1959
Treaty of Guarantee*

The Republic of Cyprus of the one part, and Greece, Turkey and the United Kingdom of Great Britain and Northern Ireland of the other part,

I.   Considering that the recognition and maintenance of the independence, territorial integrity and security of the Republic of Cyprus, as established and regulated by the Basic Articles of its Constitution, are in their common interest,

II. Desiring to co-operate to ensure respect for the state of affairs created by that Constitution.

Have agreed as follows:

ARTICLE I

The Republic of Cyprus undertakes to ensure the maintenance of its independence, territorial integrity and security, as well as respect for its Constitution.

It undertakes not to participate, in whole or in part, in any political or economic union with any State whatsoever. It accordingly declares prohibited any activity likely to promote, directly or indirectly, either union with any other State or partition of the Island.

ARTICLE II

Greece, Turkey and the United Kingdom, taking note of the undertakings of the Republic of Cyprus set out in Article I of the present Treaty, recognise and guarantee the independence, territorial integrity and security of the Republic of Cyprus, and also the state of affairs established by the Basic Articles of its Constitution.

Greece, Turkey and the United Kingdom likewise undertake to prohibit, so far as concerns them, any activity aimed at promoting, directly or indirectly, either union of Cyprus with any other State or partition of the Island.

---

*Published in Necati M. Ertekun. Intercommunal Talks and the Cyprus Problem, which contains the entire series of agreements, pp. 45-60.

APPENDIX B (Cont.)

ARTICLE III

The Republic of Cyprus, Greece and Turkey undertake to respect the integrity of the areas retained under United Kingdom sovereignty at the time of the establishment of the Republic of Cyprus, and guarantee the use and employment by the United Kingdom of the rights to be secured to it by the Republic of Cyprus in accordance with the Treaty concerning the Establishment of the Republic of Cyprus signed at Nicosia on to-day's date.

ARTICLE IV

In the event of a breach of the provisions of the present Treaty, Greece, Turkey and the United Kingdom undertake to consult together with respect to the representations or measures to ensure observance of those provisions.

In so far as common or concerted action may not prove possible, each of the three guaranteeing Powers reserves the right to take action with the sole aim of re-establishing the state of affairs created by the present Treaty.

ARTICLE V

The present Treaty shall enter into force on the date of signature. The original texts of the present Treaty shall be deposited at Nicosia.

The High Contracting Parties shall proceed as soon as possible to the registration of the present Treaty with the Secretariat of the United Nations, in accordance with Article 102 of the Charter of the United Nations.

APPENDIX C

1. President Makarios' 13 Points*

1. The right of veto of the President and the Vice-President of the Republic to be abandoned.

2. The Vice-President of the Republic to deputize for the President of the Republic in case of his temporary absence or incapacity to perform his duties.

3. The Greek President of the House of Representatives and the Turkish Vice-President to be elected by the House as a whole and not, as at present, the President by the Greek Members of the House and the Vice-President by the Turkish Members of the House.

4. The Vice-President of the House of Representatives to deputize for the President of the House in case of his temporary absence or incapacity to perform his duties.

5. The constitutional provisions regarding separate majorities for enactment of certain laws by the House of Representatives to be abolished.

6. United Municipalities to be established.

7. The administration of Justice to be unified.

8. The division of the Security Forces into Police and Gendarmerie to be abolished.

9. The numerical strength of the Security Forces and of the Defense Forces to be determined by a Law.

10. The proportion of the participation of Greek and Turkish Cypriots in the composition of the Public Service and the Forces of the Republic to be modified in proportion to the ratio of the population of Greek and Turkish-Cypriots.

11. The number of the Members of the Public Service Commission to be reduced from ten to five.

12. All decisions of the Public Service Commission to be taken by simple majority.

13. The Greek Communal Chamber to be abolished.

---

*Published in Nicos Kranidiotis, The Cyprus Problem, p. 53.

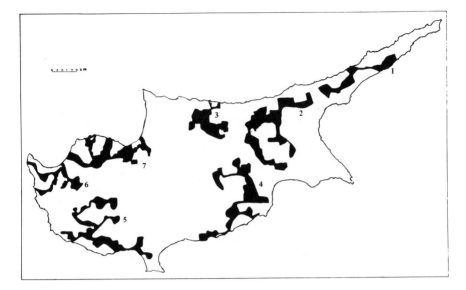

Fig. 6. 2.   The Karouzis Plan.

Source: Map contained in George Karouzis,   <u>Proposals for a Solution to the</u>
<u>Cyprus Problem</u>,   pp. 122-123.

Turkish Cypriot Regions	Privately owned Property (donums)	State Property (εi(donums)	Total Area (donums)
1. Galinoporni - Galatia	68,529	32,416	100,945
2. Chatos - Ay.Andronikos extending to Pergamos and Kouklia	181,524	102,321	283,845
3. Nicosia - Kyrenia	113,565	475	114,040
4. Louroudjina - Kophinou	154,770	62,486	217,256
5. Evdhimou - Mandria - Ay. Ioannis	180,860	22,297	203,157
6. Khrysokhou	57,806	25,822	83,628
7. Lefka - Yialia - Gaziveran	84,024	88,722	172,746
TOTAL	841,078[59]	334,539	1,175,617

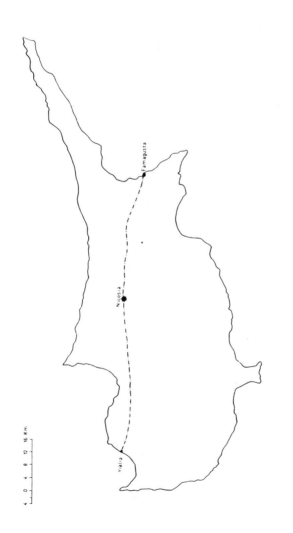

Fig. 6.3. 1965 Turkish-Cypriot proposal to Dr. Galo Plaza for division of the island.

Source: Map contained in George Karouzis, Proposals for a Solution to the Cyprus Problem, p. 86.

APPENDIX D

Clerides' 1974 Proposal at Geneva*

The representative of the Greek Cypriots, Glavkos Clerides, proposed the following:

1. The constitutional order of Cyprus shall retain its bicommunal character based on the co-existence of the Greek and Turkish communities within the framework of a sovereign, independent and integral Republic.

2. This constitutional order shall, through an appropriate revision and the active cooperation and free consent of the two communities, ensure an enhanced feeling of security for both.

3. The co-existence of the two communities shall be achieved in the context of institutional arrangements regarding an agreed allocation of powers and functions between the Central Government, Communal Administrations exercising their powers on all other matters within areas to be established as in paragraph (5) herein below provided.

4. The structure of the Central Government shall continue to be based on the presidential regime.

5. The Greek and Turkish communal administrations shall exercise their powers and functions in areas consisting respectively of the purely Greek and Turkish villages and municipalities. For the purpose of communal administration such villages and municipalities may be grouped together by the respective communal authorities. For the same purpose mixed villages shall come under the communal authorities of the community to which the majority of their inhabitants belong.

6. Legislative authority over the respective Communal Administrations shall be exercised by the Greek and Turkish members of the House of Representatives constituted in separate Councils for this purpose.

---

*Published in Nicos Kranidiotis, The Cyprus Problem, pp. 34-35.

APPENDIX E

The Denktash Plan, 1974

The Turkish-Cypriot proposals tabled in Geneva by Rauf Denktash were:

1. The Republic of Cyprus shall be an independent binational state.

2. The Republic shall be composed of two federated states with full control and autonomy within their respective geographical boundaries.

3. In determining the competence to be left to the Federal Government, the binational nature of the state shall be taken into account and the federal competence shall be exercised accordingly.

4. The area of the Turkish-Cypriot Federated State shall cover 34% of the territory of the Republic falling north of a general line starting from the Limnitis-Lefka area in the west and running towards the east, passing through the Turkish controlled part of Nicosia, including the Turkish part of Famagusta, and ending at the port of Famagusta.

5. Pending an agreement on the final constitutional structure of the Republic, the two autonomous administrations shall take over the full administrative authority within their respective areas as defined above and shall take steps to normalize and stabilize life in the Republic and refrain from acts of violence, harassment and discrimination against each other.

---

*Published in Nicos Kranidiotis, The Cyprus Problem, p. 36.

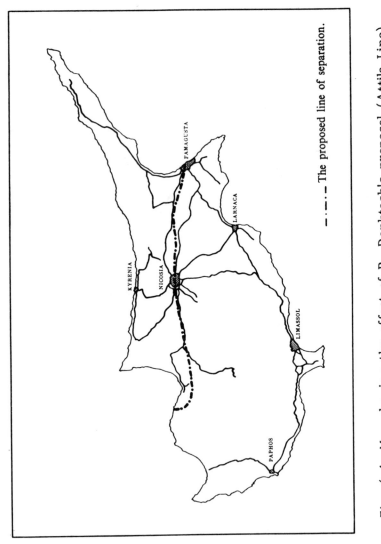

Fig. 6.4 Map showing the effect of R. Denktash's proposal (Attila Line).

Source: Map contained in Kranidiotis, The Cyprus Problem, p. 58.

—·—·— The proposed line of separation.

202

APPENDIX F

The Gunes Proposal at Geneva, 1974*

The proposals of the Turkish Foreign Minister, Turan Gunes, were the following:

1. The Republic of Cyprus is a bicommunal and independent state.
2. The Republic will be constituted by one Turkish-Cypriot autonomous zone, comprising six districts, and by one Greek-Cypriot autonomous zone, comprising two districts:
a) Greek-Cypriot autonomous zone:
  i) Main Greek-Cypriot district.
  ii) Greek Cypriot district of Karpassia.
b) Turkish-Cypriot autonomous zone:
  i)   Main Turkish-Cypriot district, the boundaries of which follow from west to east a line including Panagra – Myrtou – Asomatos – Skylloura – Yerolakkos – Sector of Nicosia controlled by Turks – Moka – Angastina – Yanagra – Maratha – Styllos – "Fresh Water Lake" – Turkish part of Famagusta, and to the northwest by a line excluding Galounia, including Komi Kebir, Ayios Efstathios and excluding Gastria.
  ii) Turkish district of the region of Lefka.
  iii) Turkish district of the region of Polis.
  iv) Turkish district of the region of Paphos.
  v)   Turkish district of the region of Larnaca.
  vi) Turkish district of the region of Karpassia.

The area of the Turkish-Cypriot autonomous zone will be equivalent to nearly 34% of the Republic's territory.

The area and the boundaries of each of the districts other than the main district of the Turkish-Cypriot autonomous zone will be fixed by the provisions which will be added to the present Declaration.

The main district of the Turkish-Cypriot autonomous zone will be evacuated by units of the Greek armed forces and of the so-called Greek-Cypriot National Guard as well as by Greek irregulars within a time.

---

*Published in Nicos Kranidiotis, The Cyprus Problem, pp. 36-37.

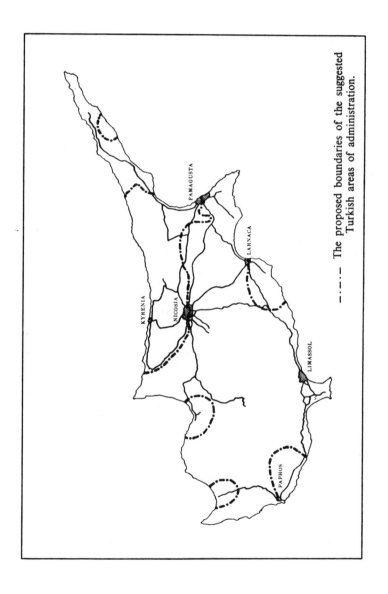

----- The proposed boundaries of the suggested Turkish areas of administration.

Fig. 6.5. Map showing the effect of proposal of the Turkish Foreign Minister T. Gunes.

Source: Map contained in Kranidiotis, The Cyprus Problem, p. 59.

APPENDIX G:
CHANGES IN THE TURKISH GOVERNMENT, 1974 to 1978

July 1974

Turkey ruled by a coalition of Bulent Ecevit's Republican People's Party and the National Salvation Party of Necmettin Erbakan.

September 1974

This coalition breaks up over a number of issues.

March 31, 1975

Following months of chaotic attempts to form a government, a minority Nationalist Front coalition is formed under the leadership of Suleyman Demirel's Justice Party, including the National Salvation Party, the National Action Party led by Colonel Alparslan Turkes, and the Republican Reliance Party under Turhan Feyzioglu.

June 5, 1977

Premature elections held in Turkey. Once again, no party gains a majority. After Ecevit fails to form a coalition acceptable to the National Assembly, Demirel forms a coalition with the NAP and the NSP.

January 4, 1978

Demirel's coalition government dissolved after New Year's Eve no confidence vote in National Assembly. Ecevit forms a government with the help of eleven deputies who had deserted the Justice Party.

The following sources were used in compiling this appendix:

Keesing's Contemporary Archives:

June 10-16, 1974 (Vol. 20), pp. 26562-26563,
January 1-5, 1975 (Vol. 21), pp. 26885-26887,
April 28-May 4, 1975 (Vol. 21), pp. 27093-27094,
October 7, 1977 (Vol. 23), pp. 28597-28599;

The Washington Post

John Lawton, "Leave Greece, Turkey Alone, Ankara's Leader Urges U.S.," January 5, 1978, p. 23.

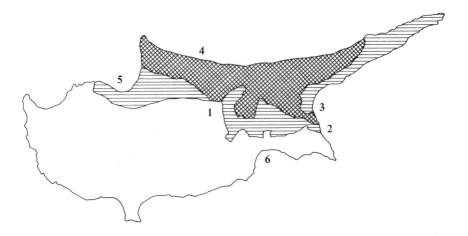

Fig. 6.6. Map depicting Greek-Cypriot territorial proposals of March 31, 1977.

Key:

     -- area now held by Turkish Cypriots to be returned to Greek control.

     -- area to remain under Turkish Cypriot Administration.

(1) Nicosia; (2) Varosha; (3) Famagusta; (4) Kyrenia; (5) Lefka-Morphou; (6) Larnaka.

Source: Map adapted from Cyprus Intercommunal Talks - New Series, First Round - Vienna, March 31-April 7, 1977, issued by Public Information Office, Nicosia, 1977. pp. 12-13.

NOTES

(1) U.S. Senate, Crisis on Cyprus: 1974, p. 9.

(2) Necati M. Erketun, Intercommunal Talks and the Cyprus Problem. (Nicosia, 1977), pp. 45-60.

(3) George Karouzis, Proposals for a Solution to the Cyprus Problem, p. 96.

(4) Ibid., pp. 122-137.

(5) Ibid., pp. 60-62.

(6) Ibid., pp. 136-138.

(7) Kyriacos C. Markides, The Rise and Fall of the Cyprus Republic, p. 28.

(8) Ertekun, Intercommunal Talks, pp. 12-14.

(9) Polyvios G. Polyviou, Cyprus - The Tragedy and the Challenge, p. 109. Also see Karouzis, Proposals, p. 86.

(10) Polyviou, Cyprus, pp. 46-47.

(11) U.S. Senate, Crisis on Cyprus: 1974, p. 13.

(12) Markides, Rise and Fall, p. 174.

(13) U.S. Senate, Crisis on Cyprus 1976: Crucial Year for Peace, p. 37. See also Keesing's Contemporary Archives 20 (August 12-18, 1974): 26663.

(14) U.S. Senate, Crisis on Cyprus: 1974, p. 15.

(15) Nicos Kranidiotis, The Cyprus Problem, p. 34.

(16) Keesing's Contemporary Archives 20 (August 12-18, 1974): 26666.

(17) Kranidiotis, Cyprus Problem, pp. 34-35.

(18) "Drink Me," The Economist 265, no. 7002 (November 12, 1977) 56. See also U.S. Senate, Crisis on Cyprus: 1975, p. 25.

(19) Kranidiotis, Cyprus Problem, p. 36.

(20) Karouzis, Proposals, p. 85.

(21) Kranidiotis, Cyprus Problem, p. 36.

(22) Ibid.

(23) "The Man Clerides has to Deal With," The Economist 232, no. 6831: (July 27, 1974) 22-23.

(24) Eric Baker and Michael Harbottle, Cyprus 1975, pp. 8-9.

(25) Henry Giniger, "Cyprus Fighting Resumes as Peace Talks Collapse, U.N. Called into Session," New York Times, August 14, 1974, p. 1.

(26) Ibid.

(27) Henry Giniger, "Cyprus Fighting Goes on South of Turkish Sector," New York Times, August 19, 1974, p. 1.

(28) U.S. Senate, Crisis on Cyprus 1976, p. 38.

(29) Please refer to Fig. 6.6

(30) Eugene K. Keefe et al., Area Handbook for Cyprus, p. 20.

(31) "Soviet Tactician in Cyprus," Foreign Report (of The Economist), no. 1515 (December 7, 1977): 6.

(32) F.B.I.S., "Azinas to Visit Cuba," Nicosia Alithia in Greek (March 1, 1976): 1.

(33) "Cyprus after Makarios," Foreign Report (of The Economist), no. 1499 (August 10, 1977): 2.

(34) Stanley R. Sloan, "The Communist Party of Cyprus," in Report on Western European Communist Parties, pp. 199-207.

(35) Kranidiotis, Cyprus Problem, p. 60.

(36) Ibid.

(37) "Where's the Cyprus Pay-off?" The Economist 254, no. 6857 (January 25, 1975): 15-16.

(38) "De Facto Partition of Cyprus," Times (London), September 8, 1975, reprinted in Crisis on Cyprus 1976, pp. 100-101.

(39) U.S. Department of State, Background Notes - Cyprus, p. 6.,

(40) Steven P. Roberts, "Freedoms Few in Cyprus Area," New York Times, September 23, 1975, reprinted in Crisis on Cyprus 1976, pp. 78-79.

(41) U.S. Department of State, Background Notes - Cyprus, p. 6.

(42) Christopher Hitchens, "How Cyprus Was Betrayed," The New Statesman, October 24, 1975, reprinted in Crisis on Cyprus 1976, p. 93.

(43) John Hooper, "Unwanted Dumped in Cyprus," Manchester Guardian Weekly, October 19, 1975, reprinted in Crisis on Cyprus 1976, p. 91.

(44) Foreign Report, "Cyprus after Makarios," August 10, 1977, p. 1.

(45) Discussion with Cypriot Ambassador to the United States, Mr. Nicos Dimitriou.

(46) U.S. Department of State, Background Notes - Cyprus, p. 6.

(47) G. Westermann, Atlas zur Weltgeschichte (Part III; Neuzeit), p. 153, map V.

(48) These statistics are taken from a map prepared by the Department of Lands and Surveys, Cyprus, May 1975, with statistical data provided by the Planning Bureau of the Planning Commission in Nicosia.

(49) John Fielding, "U.N. Report on Cyprus Looting Suppressed," Boston Globe, May 7, 1976; see also Crisis on Cyprus: 1975, pp. 24-26 and Crisis on Cyprus 1976, pp. 7-13.

(50) Kranidiotis, Cyprus Problem, p. 42.

(51) Based on conversations with Bulent Shemi, a Turkish-Cypriot graduate student at The Fletcher School of Law and Diplomacy.

(52) See p. 182.

(53) See p. 182.

(54) "Slow Death," The Economist 256, no. 6895 (September 13, 1975): 61.

(55) Crisis on Cyprus 1976, p. 45.

(56) Keesing's Contemporary Archives 22 (July 30, 1976): 27866.

(57) Ibid.

(58) Ibid. (October 8, 1976): 22: 27980.

(59) Crisis on Cyprus 1976, pp. 47-48.

(60) Ibid., also Keesing's Contemporary Archives 24 (January 28, 1978): 28781-28782; also Sloan, "Communism in Greece," pp. 247-265 and "The Communist Party of Cyprus," in Report on Western European Communist Parties.

(61) "The Turkes Factor," The Economist 265, no. 7007 (December 17, 1977): 52; see also Keesing's Contemporary Archives 21 (April 28-May 4, 1975): 27093.

(62) "Stirring It Up," The Economist 261, no. 6952 (November 27, 1976) pp. 62-65. It is noteworthy that Erbakan was ordered to disband an earlier party he had headed (the National Order Party) in a 1971 Constitutional Court decision to the effect that the party's theocratic nature violated the secular tenets of the Turkish Constitution. Richard F. Nyrop, Area Handbook for the Republic of Turkey, p. 231.

(63) Keesing's Contemporary Archives 21 (January 1-5, 1975): 26885.

(64) "Two Men, One Island," The Economist 257, no. 6900 (October 18, 1975): 12-13; also see "When Excuses Run Out," The Economist 265, no. 6992 (October 11, 1977): p. 62.

(65) Keesing's Contemporary Archives 21 (January 1-5, 1975): 26885.

(66) Keesing's Contemporary Archives 23 (October 7, 1977): 28599.

(67) Discussion with Bulent Shemi.

(68) F.B.I.S., Fazil Kucuk, "Dangerous Games," Nicosia Halkin Sesi in Turkish (June 1, 1976): 1.

(69) F.B.I.S., "Turkish-Cypriot Students Score Denktash Administration," Nicosia Halkin Sesi in Turkish (June 1, 1976): 1; also "Denktash Scores Turkish-Cypriot Opposition Parties," Nicosia Zaman in Turkish, (June 4, 1976): 1.

(70) Baker and Harbottle, Cyprus 1975, p. 31.

(71) Cyprus Intercommunal Talks - New Series, First Round - Vienna, March 31-April 7, 1977, issued by Public Information Office, Nicosia, 1977, p. 3.

(72) Discussion with Bulent Shemi.

(73) "Home Soon?" The Economist 262, no. 6967 (February 5, 1977): 59.

(74) Cyprus Intercommunal Talks, pp. 12-13.

(75) "The Old Fox Winks," The Economist 262, no. 6965 (January 22, 1977): 15.

(76) "Back on Speaking Terms," The Economist 266, no. 7011 (January 14, 1978): 40-41.

(77) "Shifting Ice," The Economist 261, no. 6950 (November 13, 1976): 64.

(78) "Trying to Square the Triangle," The Economist 265, no. 7007 (December 17, 1977): 55.

(79) "Ecevit's Return," Foreign Report no. 1518 (January 11, 1978): 3-5.

(80) Ibid.

(81) U.S. Department of State, Background Notes - Cyprus, p. 7.

BIBLIOGRAPHY

Books and Monographs:

Attalides, Michael A., ed. Cyprus Review. Nicosia: The Jus Cypri Association, 1975.

Baker, Eric and Harbottle, Michael. Cyprus 1975. London: A report for the Friends Peace and International Relations Committee, 1975.

Cyprus Geographical Association, International Symposium on Political Geography - Proceedings. Nicosia: February 17-19, 1976.

Cyprus Intercommunal Talks, New Series, First Round - Vienna, March 31-April 7, 1977. Nicosia: Issued by Public Information Office, 1977.

The Cyprus Problem. Nicosia: Issued by Public Information Office, 1977.

Denktash, Rauf R., The Cyprus Problem. Nicosia: Turkish Cypriot Administration, Public Information Office, 1974.

Ertekun, Necati M. Intercommunal Talks and the Cyprus Problem. Nicosia ("Turkish Federated State of Cyprus"): 1977.

Karouzis, George. Proposals for a Solution to the Cyprus Problem. Nicosia: Cosmos Press, 1976.

Keefe, Eugene K., et al. Area Handbook for Cyprus. Washington, D.C.: Foreign Area Studies Handbook, The American University, 1971.

Kranidiotis, Nicos. The Cyprus Problem. Athens: C. Michalas S.A. Press, 1975.

Markides, Kyriacos C. The Rise and Fall of the Cyprus Republic. New Haven and London: Yale University Press, 1977.

Nyrop, Richard F. Area Handbook for the Republic of Turkey. Washington, D.C.: Foreign Area Studies Handbook, The American University, 1973.

Polyviou, Polyvios G. Cyprus - The Tragedy and the Challenge. Washington, D.C.: American Hellenic Institute, 1975.

United States Department of State, Background Notes - Cyprus. Washington, D.C.: December 1976.

United States Senate, Subcommittee to Investigate Problems Connected with Refugees and Escapees of the Committee on the Judiciary, Report on Cyprus: Crisis on Cyprus: 1974. Washington, D.C.: U.S. Government Printing Office, 1974.

_____. Crisis on Cyprus: 1975.

_____. Crisis on Cyprus 1976: Crucial Year for Peace.

_____. Report on Western European Communist Parties. (Survey) submitted by Senator Edward W. Brooke to the Committee on Appropriations. Washington, D.C.: U.S. Government Printing Office, 1977.

Xydis, Stephen. Cyprus - Reluctant Republic. The Hague: Mouton and Co., 1973.

Interviews and Discussions:

Celik, Vedat, Foreign Minister of the "Federated Turkish-Cypriot State," fall 1977.

Dimitriou, Nicos, Cypriot Ambassador to the United States, February 16, 1978.

Shemi, Bulent, Turkish-Cypriot graduate student at The Fletcher School of Law and Diplomacy, several discussions, fall 1977.

Magazine and Newspaper Articles

Boston Globe. Fielding, John. "U.N. Report on Cyprus Looting Suppressed." May 7, 1976.

The Economist. "Back on Speaking Terms." January 14, 1978, 266, no. 7011: 40-41.

_____. "Drink Me." November 12, 1977, 265, no. 7002: 56.

_____. "Home Soon?" February 5, 1977, 262, no. 6967: 59.

_____. "Learning to Live with an Opposition," November 26, 1977, 265, no. 7004: 54.

_____. "The Man Clerides Has to Deal With," July 27, 1974, 232, no. 6831: 22-23.

_____. "The Old Fox Winks," January 22, 1977, 262, no. 6965: 15.

_____. "Shifting Ice," November 13, 1976, 261, no. 6950: 64.

_____. "Slow Death," September 13, 1975, 256, no. 6895: 61.

_____. "Stirring It Up," November 27, 1976, 261, no. 6952: 62-65.

_____. "Trying to Square the Triangle," December 17, 1977, 265, no. 7007: 55.

_____. "The Turkes Factor," December 17, 1977, 265, no. 7007: 52.

_____. "Two Men, One Island," October 18, 1975, 257, no. 6900: 12-13.

_____. "When Excuses Run Out," October 11, 1977, 265, no. 6992: 62.

_____. "Where's the Cyprus Pay-Off?" January 25, 1975, 254, no. 6857: 15-16.

Foreign Report (of The Economist). "Cyprus after Makarios," August 10, 1977, no. 1499, pp. 1-3.

_____. "Ecevit's Return," January 11, 1978, no. 1518, pp. 3-5.

_____. "Ecevit's Troubleshooter for Cyprus," February 8, 1978, no. 1522, pp. 6-7.

_____. "Soviet Tactician in Cyprus," December 7, 1977, no. 1515, pp. 5-6.

Foreign Broadcast Information Service: (Nicosia) Alithia. "Azinas to Visit Cuba," (in Greek) March 1, 1976, in F.B.I.S. (Cyprus) March 3, 1976, p. 6.

_____. Cyprus Public Information Office Press Release. "Review of the Question of the Colonization of Cyprus," (in English) May 17, 1976, in F.B.I.S. (Cyprus) May 21, 1976, pp. 1-6.

_____. Fazil Kucuk, "Dangerous Games," (Nicosia) Halkin Sesi (in Turkish) June 1, 1976, p. 1. in F.B.I.S. (Cyprus) June 3, 1976, p. 7.

_____. Halkin Sesi, "Turkish-Cypriot Students Score Denktash Administration," (in Turkish) June 1, 1976, p. 1. in F.B.I.S. (Cyprus) June 3, 1976, p. 7.

_____. (Nicosia) Zaman "Denktash Scores Turkish Cypriot Opposition Parties," (in Turkish) June 4, 1976, p. 1. in F.B.I.S. (Cyprus) June 4, 1976, p. 1.

Keesing's Contemporary Archives:
June 10-16, 1974, vol. 20, pp. 26562-26563.
July 1-7, 1974, vol. 20, p. 26603.
August 12-18, 1974, vol. 20, pp. 26661-26666.
September 9-15, 1974, vol. 20, pp. 26709-26710.
January 1-5, 1975, vol. 21, pp. 26885-26887.
March 24-30, 1975, vol. 21, pp. 27033-27035.
April 28-May 4, 1975, vol. 21, pp. 27093-27094.
July 7-13, 1975, vol. 21, pp. 27219-27220.
November 17-23, 1975, vol. 21, p. 27450.
December 15-21, 1975, vol. 21, p. 27489.
July 30, 1976, vol. 22, p. 27866.
April 8, 1977, vol. 23, p. 28290.
October 7, 1977, vol. 23, pp. 28597-28599.
January 20, 1978, vol. 24, p. 28781.

Manchester Guardian. Harbottle, Michael. "Cypriot Date with Destiny." May 30, 1976, p. 7.

Manchester Guardian Weekly. Hooper, John. "Unwanted Dumped in Cyprus." October 19, 1975, as reprinted in Crisis on Cyprus 1976, p. 91.

New York Times.
Giniger, Henry. "Cyprus Fighting Goes on South of Turkish Sector." August 19, 1974, p. 1.
Giniger. "Cyprus Fighting Resumes as Peace Talks Collapse, U.N. Called into Session." August 14, 1974, p. 1.
Roberts, Steven P. "Freedoms Few in Cyprus Area." September 23, 1975, as reprinted in Crisis on Cyprus 1976, pp. 78-79.

The New Statesman. Hitchens, Christopher. "How Cyprus Was Betrayed." October 24, 1975, as reprinted in Crisis on Cyprus 1976, pp. 92-96.

Times (London). "De Facto Partition of Cyprus." September 8, 1975 as reprinted in Crisis on Cyprus 1976, pp. 100-101.

Washington Post. Lawton, John. "Leave Greece, Turkey Alone, Ankara's Leader Urges U.S." January 5, 1978, p. 23.

Cartography:

Westermann. Atlas zur Weltgeschicte (Part III: Neuzeit). Berlin: G. Westermann Verlag, 1963) p. 153, map V.

All other maps taken from above books and monographs as cited (except Fig. 6.6 which is an original drawing).

7 Koreans in Japan: Ethnic Problems in a Developed Asian State*
Grant F. Rhode

While riding on the night ferry between Shimonoseki in southwest Japan and Pusan on the southern Korean coast, I was struck by the feeling I had been on the run before. But it wasn't the same run. The deja vu illusion had its roots in a night ferry run from Liverpool to Dublin that I had made a few years ago. Temperamentally, the Koreans on board returning to their homeland were very like the Irish who had been on their way to the Emerald Isle. Whiskey flowed and stories of the homeland were told, not of Kilarney and Cork, but of Andong and Daegu. There is something apt in calling the Koreans the Irish of Asia in terms of similarity of temperament, in terms of treatment of their nation by greater powers nearby, and in terms of their treatment abroad.

This paper is a discussion of the situation and treatment of Koreans residing in Korea's near neighbor, Japan. The data consist of a combination of statistical and anecdotal material. The data have been interwoven and arranged under the headings of history, politics, economy, education, psychology, security issues, legal issues, statistics, geography, and language and religion. This account certainly does not say everything that can be said or needs to be said about the Koreans in Japan, but it tries to say something about each of the most important aspects of the problem. The headings are not mutually exclusive in any

*I wish to thank Professors Cole, Henderson, and Ra'anan of The Fletcher School of Law and Diplomacy for their guidance in preparing this study. Funds for fieldwork were graciously provided by the John Anson Kittredge Educational Fund and by the International Security Studies Committee of The Fletcher School. Of the many Japanese and Koreans who assisted me I wish to give special thanks to Akihiko Tanaka for his help in translating Japanese materials and his continued interest in my study of Japanese society.

sense.   Legal issues bear on politics; education bears on economy; language bears on psychology; and vice-versa. The headings are heuristic devices for organizing the presentation, but it is the interrelation of these various facets and the institutions that represent them which makes up the more important whole. This holistic approach discloses the disciplinary bias brought to bear on the subject, that of social anthropology.

A discussion section follows the main body of the paper. In the discussion some comparisons are made, theoretical formulations tried out, and normative thoughts allowed expression.

The research for the paper is based on a combination of library materials and a period of field research conducted during the summer of 1977.

HISTORY

During the Tokugawa period Koreans visiting or living in Japan were treated with respect. Japanese had high regard for their classical learning from the Chinese traditions. Koreans were brought into Japan as scholars and as teachers of the feudal lords, the daimyo, and their children.(1) After Commodore Perry steamed into Tokyo Bay in 1853 with his Black Ships, Japan was not long in developing its own ideas of conquest. Korea sat dangerously perched between Japan and the Asian mainland, a corridor for Japanese troops during both the Sino-Japanese War of 1895 and the Russo-Japanese War of 1905. In 1910 Japan annexed Korea, both to gain a foothold on the mainland and to gain a breadbasket to feed her increasing population.

Before the Annexation there were few Koreans in Japan. Fukuzawa, the founder of Keio University, brought a few Koreans to study in Japan. He was enamored of Europe's industrialized ways, and did not feel that the Koreans were as fit for modernization as were the Japanese.

After the Annexation in 1910 the number of Koreans emigrating to Japan slowly began to increase. Some went for the employment opportunities in Japanese cities. Some went to avoid land taxes newly imposed by the Japanese on Korean lands. These taxes continued to go up as Japanese produced more rice in Korea for their own domestic purposes.

At the time of Annexation there were fewer than 3,000 Koreans in Japan. By the end of World War II there were close to 2.5 million. The table below indicates the rate of growth of the Korean community in Japan:(2)

The great majority of the immigrating Koreans came from the southern end of the Korean peninsula, from the area around Pusan and Che Ju Island. They tended to be very poor upon arrival, and worked primarily in the industrial or mining areas. Literacy rates were low and living conditions were poor. Japanese prejudice was strong.

Table 7.1.

Year	Koreans in Japan
1904	229
1911	2,527
1916	5,638
1920	30,175
1925	133,710
1930	298,091
1935	625,678
1939	961,591
1940	1,190,444
1941	1,469,230
1942	1,625,054
1943	1,882,456
1944	1,936,843
1945	2,365,263

Following the Great Kanto Earthquake of 1923, thousands of Koreans were killed by Japanese for alleged mass looting, poisoning wells, setting fires, and planning to attack the Japanese. There seems to be little evidence to support the strong Japanese overreaction to the Koreans during the aftermath of the earthquake. The following account indicates the kind of story circulated at the time of the 1923 earthquake that built up Japanese feeling against the Koreans:(3)

The alarm that reached Omori and Osaki, both only a few miles west of Tokyo, on the afternoon of the second day was to the effect that riotous Koreans were coming in force, freely committing looting, incendiarism, well-poisoning, and other atrocities on the way, and that the inhabitants were trying desperately to check their progress. Alarm bells were wildly rung in all the adjacent villages and women and children pale with terror fled to safe retreats.

The Korean scare in the downtown quarter of Tokyo at Honjo and other places originated from the isolated malpractices perpetuated in the hour of confusion following the shock and fire by a number of disorderly Koreans. About fifty criminal acts by Koreans were reported in Tokyo and properly dealt with. One case that occurred early in the morning of the third day near the only remaining water tap in the Kikugawa-cho, Honjo, is significant. A suspicious-looking Korean in Japanese dress was noticed loitering nearby. He was seized and examined by the refugees when a paper wrapper containing about an ounce of whitish powder was discovered about his person. He insisted it was common salt. He was forced to swallow it and soon died in agony. The powder was arsenic.

Although the period of the 1920s was difficult for the Koreans, problems were further complicated in the 1930s. Many Koreans were forcibly brought into Japan to stoke Japanese industry after the Manchurian Incident in 1931. More and more young Japanese men were becoming soldiers, and had to be replaced in factory jobs by imported Koreans. This accounts for the extremely rapid increase of the Korean population in Japan during the 1930s, which continued right up until the end of the war in 1945.

Immediately following the end of the war several hundred thousand Koreans in Japan repatriated to Korea, uncontrolled by the American occupying forces. The Supreme Command of the Allied Powers (SCAP) took control of the repatriation procedures, and had things well in hand by early 1946. Wagner presents the statistics regarding repatriation.(4) (See Table 7.2 below.)

It seems clear that all of the repatriation of an uncontrolled nature was voluntary. Data does not seem to be available on the aspirations of those who returned to Korea during the controlled repatriation. Virtually all of the immediate postwar repatriation was to the southern part of Korea, the original homeland of most of the Koreans in Japan. South Korea was at that time occupied by the United States, while North Korea was occupied by the Soviet Union.

Socialist and communist movements in Japan before the war had had an impact on some of the Koreans in Japan who were strongly represented in the urban proletariat. It appears that a certain portion of those Koreans who remained in Japan after the war did so because of a fear of returning to a United States backed South Korea.

During the late 1950s, Pyongyang, through its political arm among the Koreans in Japan, Chosoren, pressured the Kishi government to allow Koreans to repatriate to North Korea.(5) Signatures were obtained supporting the movement in a door to door petition. The South Korean government attacked the Kishi government for developing a "deportation" plan for Koreans. The Kishi government responded by invoking the doctrine of freedom of domicile recognized by both the Universal Declaration of Human Rights and the Japanese Constitution. Negotiations were carried on through the North Korean Red Cross in Geneva. By the mid-1960s approximately 88,000 Koreans had been repatriated to North Korea according to these agreements.

In the early 1960s approximately 60 percent of the Korean population in Japan owed their political allegiance to North Korea.(6) In 1965 Japan normalized relations with South Korea. Negotiations for this treaty had been impaired by the repatriation of Koreans to North Korea, but the treaty itself signifies a turning point in Japan's policies toward the Koreans in Japan, a turning point that favors South Korea. Nationals of South Korea were given permanent residency status. A shift took place among the population such that a majority of the Korean population in Japan for the first time since the Second World War owed their political allegiance to South Korea.

Table 7.2. Volume of Korean Repatriation, 1945-1949

| | Repatriation | | Koreans |
	Controlled	Uncontrolled[a]	in Japan
Status as of March 1945			2,400,000[a]
Mar-15 Aug 45		400,000	
1st Period 15 Aug - 30 Nov 45	275,000[b]	550,000	
2nd Period 1 Dec 45 - 30 Apr 46	469,511	50,000	
1 May 46 - 30 Dec 46	54,634	[c]	
3rd Period 1 Jan 47 - 30 Oct 47	7,551	[c]	
1 Nov 47 - 31 Aug 48	5,006	[c]	
4th Period 1 Sep 48 - 31 Dec 49	6,590	[c]	
Total	818,292	1,000,000	
Status as of November 1948			611,758[d]

[a] Estimated. Both SCAP and USAMGIK underestimated the number of Koreans in Japan at the end of the war, and failed to take into consideration the extent of the uncontrolled population movement. Official count did not begin until 1 October 1945, although SCAP estimated that 150,000 had crossed, controlled and uncontrolled, prior to that time. SCAP and Japanese Government repatriation figure was 945,420 as of 30 April 1950. USAMGIK final figure was 1,115,550 as of 31 August 1948. Republic of Korea revised figure as of 31 December 1949 was 1,414,258.
[b] Estimated from official sources.
[c] Negligible uncontrolled movement during this period.
[d] Does not correspond exactly to total derived by subtraction because of estimated nature of status as of March 1945 and of uncontrolled movement.

Source: Controlled movement – USAMGIK, South Korean Interim Government Activities
SCAP, Summation of Non-Military Activities in Japan
Republic of Korea, Statistical Summation
Status as of March 1945, League of Koreans Residing in Japan cited in USAMGIK, Repatriation, Seoul, Korea, 1946, p. 14.
Status as of November 1948, Japanese Government, Attorney General's Office, Civil Affairs Bureau, cited in Nippon Times, March 9, 1949, p. 4.

POLITICS

Korean nationalism and factionalism have characterized the political involvements of the Korean minority in Japan. The long and complicated history of Korean associations and organizations in Japan reflects the social forces at work in relation to this immigrant minority.(7)

In 1909 the Taehan Hunghak-hoe (Greater Korean Promotion of Education Association) published articles in Tokyo denouncing the contemplated annexation of Korea. Several Koreans at Meiji University were arrested after the Hagu-hoe (Student Fraternal Organization) published anti-Japanese material from 1914 to 1916. Some support for Korean independence could be found among Japanese intellectuals through organizations such as the Shinjinkai (New Man's Society). They backed the student demands of the Hagu-hoe for Korean independence at the time of the March First Movement in 1919. Korean nationalist leaders in Seoul proclaimed a declaration of independence that was in fact much more moderate in tone than the one the Korean students in Japan advocated. At this time many Japanese as well as Koreans spoke against the Japanese policy of assimilation. Japanese policy remained essentially the same although some surface concessions were made in terms of public statements and educational programs. Many Korean students were embittered by the failure of the March First Movement.

In the 1920s and 1930s a number of leftist organizations appealed to the growing Korean minority. In 1924 the Chosen Musansha Shakai Renmei (Korean Proletarian Social League) worked for Korean rights in cooperation with the Zenkoku Suiheisha (National Levelling Society) which worked with the Burakumin for human rights. Four associations together formed the Korean Communist Organization in Japan. Two of them were legal — the Zainihon Chosen Rodo Sodomei called Rodo (Federation of Labor of Koreans in Japan) established in 1925, and the Zainihon Chosen Seinen Domei (Korean Youth League in Japan). The other two were illegal — the Chosen Kyosanto Nihon Sokyoku (Korean Communist Party, General Bureau) and the Korai Kyosan Seinenkai Nihonbu (Korean Communist Youth Society). These communist organizations had close ties with organized labor in Japan and represented many Korean workers, the bulk of whom were engaged in manual jobs.

On the other side of the fence from these organizations were those that were founded by the government largely for the purpose of controlling the Korean minority. These included the Soaiki (Mutual Love Society), founded in Osaka in 1923, which later became the Kyowa Jigyo (Concordia Enterprise) in 1926 subject to the Home Ministry. In 1939 the police established the Chuo Kyowakai (Central Concordia Association) whose intention was to turn the Koreans into "soldiers for industry" for the war effort.

Korean organizations in Japan following the Second World War reflected the division of the Korean peninsula into North and South. The communist association oriented toward the north was the Zainichi Chosenjin Renmei called Choren (League of Koreans in Japan), established in 1945. In 1950 its name was changed to the Zainichi

Chosen Toitsu Minshu Sensen called Minsen (Korea's United Democratic Front in Japan). In 1955 the name was again changed to the Zainichi Chosenjin Sorengokai called Chosoren (General Federation of Korean Residents in Japan). Chosoren has given support to a number of left-wing organizations of importance to Koreans in Japan, including the Association of Korean Businessmen in Japan, the Korean Cultural Art Group, the Korean Problems Research Center, the Japanese-Korean Society, the Japanese-Korean Trade Society, and the Cooperation for the Repatriation of Korean Nationals in Japan. Chung states that in 1964 Chosoren controlled the allegiance of 60 percent of the Koreans in Japan. Before 1961, the year in which President Park of South Korea began to woo the Korean community in Japan, the percentage with allegiance to North Korea was probably much higher.

The association oriented toward South Korea is the Zainichi Daikan Minkoku Kyoryu Mindan called Mindan (Community of Korean Residents in Japan). From its founding in 1946 until 1960, Mindan tended to be identified with prosperous Koreans in Japan. Unlike Kim Il-sung uses of Chosoren, Syngman Rhee did not choose to use Mindan to support or influence the Korean minority in Japan. South Korea adopted a point of view much more supportive of the Koreans in Japan following the military coup of Park Chung-hee in 1961. In 1961 64 Korean business-men living in Japan visited Korea at Park's invitation. They pledged support of South Korea's economic programs and General Park promised that he would do everything possible to advance the interests of Koreans in Japan. In 1965 South Korea established diplomatic relations with Japan and in the same year made an agreement concerning the legal status of Koreans residing in Japan which made it possible for 500,000 out of 600,000 Koreans to apply for permanent residency in Japan.   By 1971 over 350,000 had applied and they were expected to receive rights of permanent residency which would make them eligible for National Health Insurance benefits and compulsory education privi-leges.   Through the establishment of these agreements and programs since the early 1960s, South Korea's image has considerably improved among the Koreans in Japan.

In 1957 a neutralist group, the Chosen Churitsuka Undo Iinkai (Korean Committee for the Neutralization of Korea), was established. The group attracted considerable publicity, but little power. Chosoren and Mindan have been able to rely on strong institutional backing from North Korea and South Korea respectively, and it has been difficult for effective new organizations to enter into competition with them.

More recently a new faction has been organized that associates itself with the movement for the democratization of South Korea. This group, Han Chong(8) was founded by Kim Dae Jong and continues to operate in Japan in spite of the fact that its founder is now in prison in South Korea. The numbers of this group are considered confined to a few outspoken intellectuals by government officials, but Korean ac-tivists indicate the group has considerably more grassroots support.

Despite the appearance of small spin-off factions such as Chosen Churitsuka Undo Iinkai and Han Chong, the main division of the Koreans in Japan is between those oriented toward North and South Korea, respectively. A Japanese government official responsible for monitoring the activities of Koreans in Japan estimates that 350,000 of the approximately 650,000 Koreans have registered as permanent residents under the provisions of the normalization treaty of Japan with South Korea in 1965.(9) The other 300,000 Koreans remain registered as aliens and must periodically renew their visas, having no permanent residency status. These statistics seem to indicate that since 1965 there has been a shift of allegiance of the majority of the Koreans in Japan from North Korea to South Korea. In part this may be true. But it appears that the Koreans with allegiance to North Korea are considerably more highly politicized. Of the 350,000 permanent Korean residents ostensibly having ties to South Korea, only 200,000 are members of Mindan, leaving 150,000 relative apoliticals. On the other hand, 280,000 to 290,000 of the nonpermanent residents are members of Chosoren, leaving only 10,000 to 20,000 apoliticals. It should be noted that there is considerable advantage and sometimes overt pressure for a Korean to become a permanent resident. Besides the advantage of relative security of residence, there is also economic incentive to become a permanent resident because only permanent residents are granted permission to establish businesses.(10) A permanent resident may apply for a South Korean passport through Mindan. They may also obtain reentry permits to come back to Japan if they leave Japan with one of these passports. Nonpermanent residents cannot secure these reentry permits.

ECONOMY

The overwhelming majority of Koreans in Japan are members of Japan's lowest economic stratum. There are three reasons for this. First, the Koreans who were brought from Korea before the war were primarily laborers who were put into manual jobs from the time of their arrival in Japan. Second, few Koreans take or are able to take Japanese citizenship through naturalization, and hence many jobs and businesses are closed to them through legal restrictions. Third, there is a heavy wall of prejudice confronting Koreans who wish to enter the job market.

Many Koreans attempt to become involved in small businesses of their own since it is difficult for them to find employers. The streets of Korean areas in Osaka and Kyoto show evidence of many small business efforts. Scrap metal junkyards and carts with cardboard and rags for recycling abound. In the downstairs portions of homes there are cottage industries, often for making sandals or shoes, making traveling bags, and processing rubber goods.

In one such cottage operation, run by an illegal Korean immigrant, four women and two men manufacture 600 to 800 pairs of sandals each day.(11) The retail price of a pair of the sandals is approximately 980 yen. Profit to the manufacturer is 10 yen per pair or approximately $25.00 per day. It is not a high profit margin for an entrepreneur giving up part of his home and having a family to support. Many small industries such as this exist. They are precarious, dependent as they are on such a small profit margin. Small fluctuations in the market destroy these businesses quickly, but new ones soon pop up in their place. Sato reports that in 1969, 150,000 of 600,000 Koreans were reported to hold jobs; 33.8 percent (50,700) were engaged in small enterprises and 45.5 percent (68,260) were engaged in hard or simple labor.(12)

Lee presents a more complete overview of the recent kinds and frequency of employment engaged in by Koreans in Japan.(13) (See Table 7.3 below.)

There are examples of important and successful Korean businesses in Japan. Many of the pachinko (pinball) parlors are Korean owned. The large Lotte Chewing Gum Company is also Korean owned. While they do exist, these successful businesses are the exception and not the rule.

Many Koreans live in slum areas of the large cities, sometimes close to the areas occupied by Burakumin, Japan's outcasts. One such area exists in central Kyoto. Housing is small and ramshackle. The housing problem has not been an easy one for Koreans to tackle. Only recently have Koreans been granted occupancy in apartments built by public housing corporations. In the midst of this Kyoto ghetto a new high rise apartment complex has been built by a private housing corporation.(14) In spite of the fact that the building has gone up in a predominantly Korean area, the private corporation does not allow Koreans to rent apartments in the new building.

The means by which Japanese attain entry into the most prestigious jobs, those with the famous large corporations, is through education. Those who receive degrees from the finest universities have a good chance to obtain these jobs. Koreans have had virtually no chance to move into this privileged area of employment in spite of the fact that a number of Koreans have achieved good university educations.

The case of Park Chong Suk highlights this phenomenon. A Korean born in Japan, Mr. Park applied for work with Hitachi Industries in 1970. As a part of his application, he completed successfully the stiff company examination procedure. But when he could not produce a certificate of family registration, a document not possessed by second-generation Koreans residing in Japan, he was discharged by Hitachi with the statement: "Ordinarily we do not employ foreigners."(15)

Mr. Park refused to accept his dismissal for being Korean without a fight. He filed suit against Hitachi for infringement of his personal rights. Hitachi changed its position at the trial from "ordinarily we do not employ foreigners" to an accusation that Mr. Park had lied on his application by saying that Japan was his native land and permanent place of residence. Park Chong Suk consistently maintained that he was dismissed strictly on the grounds of discrimination, and that this was an abuse of the right of dismissal according to the Labor Standards Law.

In January 1975, Abrams reported:(16)

Last June, nearly four years after the case was brought to court, the decision came down: Hitachi had to rehire Park, give him retroactive salary from the time he was dismissed, and pay a substantial compensation fee. Last, but hardly least, Hitachi officials apologized to the Korean youth.

Table 7.3.

The 1974 Statistics of the Gainfully Employed Koreans in Japan

Classification	Total Number of Koreans 638,806	
	Male 336,787	Female 302,019
Engineer	615	16
Teaching Profession	756	283
Doctor and Medical Worker	544	323
Clergy	204	70
Writer and Author	108	8
Correspondent	162	21
Scientist	320	81
Artist and Entertainer	457	246
Other Professional	568	99
Managerial Worker	4,595	202
Office Worker	16,796	3,973
Trader (Import and Export)	181	4
Scrap Iron and Ragpicking Business	7,112	382
Other Sales Work (retail and wholesale)	19,041	4,058
Agriculture and Forestry including Farmer	2,737	962
Fishery and Fisher	243	130
Miner and Stone Cutter	463	21
Transportation and Communication	804	22
Builder and Construction Worker	10,681	134
Other Technical Workers and Manufacturer	31,051	3,858
Simple Manual Laborer	15,177	1,744
Chef	1,422	116
Barber and Beautician	470	576
Receptionist in the Leisure Industry	697	98
Restaurant, Cabaret, and other Service Entertainment Business	2,069	956
Driver	12,794	67
Housewife	–	724
Student	2,735	1,792
Unemployed	155,929	218,711
Unclassified	492	209
Unreported	47,564	62,133

Park is now back on the job, but he and his supporters tend to minimize the victory; they stress instead that Park's case involved only him, and that hundreds of thousands of Korean compatriots still must contend with discriminatory practices when seeking employment and trying to better their lives.

On August 19, 1977, a case similar to that of Park Chong Suk was announced in the press.(17) Zendetsu, the All Japan Telecommunication Workers' Union, demanded that NTT (Nippon Telegraph and Telephone Public Corporation) employ Korean residents in Japan. The case under consideration involved a Korean student in Nishinomiya City, Hyogo Prefecture, whom NTT refused to hire on the grounds that he did not have Japanese nationality. An NTT spokesman said the public nature of the corporation made the hiring of foreign nationals problematical with possible leaking of communications secrets. Due to union pressure, the corporation agreed to study the case and announced it would reach a conclusion within a month.

EDUCATION

The key to upward mobility in Japanese society is education. The most desired jobs, those as executives with large corporations or as administrators in the elite bureaucratic positions of Japanese government, are available only to those with education at the finest universities.   To gain a position in one of these universities, it is necessary to have gone to a good school. Some people say that the key to success begins with getting into the right kindergarten.

For Koreans it is difficult to gain a good education in Japan and more difficult still to gain a job in one of the top corporations. The areas in which Koreans live are generally depressed and the schools in these areas are not the best ones. The vicious cycle of poverty is hard at work in the Korean community in Japan; living in a slum area gives few opportunities to a Korean child growing up there. Schools are bad. Housing is cramped, noisy, and rundown, giving little place for study. Education suffers. Menial and uncertain employment follows.   There is no place possible to go outside the slum so one's children are born there and encounter the same problems. For the Koreans, the cycle is exacerbated by extreme prejudice against Koreans and by the tenuous legal position that Koreans hold in Japanese society.

The Nakagawa kindergarten in Osaka's Ikuno ward has been much sought after by Korean parents as a place to send their children.(18) The school's policy concerning Korean children has been openly discriminatory.   The tuition fee for Japanese children at the school in the early 1970s was 16,000 yen. Korean parents were forced to pay 30,000 to 50,000 yen, or, if they had a successful go-between argue their case, it might be reduced to 25,000 yen. Koreans were excluded from the kindergarten's recommendation system. There was a 15 percent limit on Korean enrollment in the school. The attitude of the kindergarten was that they had done nothing wrong since other schools were more expensive or didn't admit Koreans at all.

The position of the principal of the Nakagawa kindergarten was: "If too many Korean children come, the school's level and quality will decline. Japanese will stop coming and we'll have to go out of business. This kindergarten was built by Japanese for Japanese, so that we have no choice but to charge twice for Koreans. Further, Korean households that can afford the extra expense would be of middle class or above, which is the level we wish to keep our institute at, with Korean enrollment no higher than 15 percent. This way we can maintain our business smoothly. If possible, though, we'd like to reduce the percentage of Korean enrollment."

Incensed by this attitude, Korean parents in Ikuno ward organized under the direction of activists from the Korean Christian Center. A committee was formed to negotiate with kindergarten officials and was successful in securing guarantees that Koreans would be charged no more than Japanese for attending the school, that Koreans would be included in the recommendation system, and that the 15 percent limit on Korean enrollment would be ended. The parents won a battle in gaining these concessions, but they realize it is only one battle in a large war.

The majority of Korean children attend Japanese schools. However, both <u>Chosoren</u> and <u>Mindan</u> operate schools for Koreans only in a number of Japanese cities. Of the 140,000 or so Korean school age children in Japan, approximately 30,000 attend schools run by <u>Chosoren</u>, and 3,000 attend schools run by <u>Mindan</u>.(19) The Korean schools emphasize Korean pride and their curriculum includes Korean culture and history.

Hondayama(20) is the site of a projected new Korean high school in a hilly wooded area on the southeast outskirts of Kyoto. The present Korean high school in north Kyoto is in a dilapidated building. Funds are available for the construction of a new high school building, but local Japanese opposition has already caused the proposed site of the new high school to be changed twice. When Hondayama was chosen, local residents protested against the Koreans coming into the neighborhood. The Kyoto municipal government informed the locals that such outright discrimination was not permitted. Immediately, the anti-Koreans slogans were changed to those for environmental protection. Every fence and post in the area was plastered in kanji with a sign like "Don't Construct Here...Preserve Nature and the Environment." The shift was a thin disguise for true sentiment. The city government has told the Koreans that it must work out its plans in negotiation with the local residents. Hondayama is the third site on which Koreans have tried to build the high school. There is considerable determination not to be moved again, but to stay and build. The problem is complicated by the fact that the money to build the school is from <u>Mindan</u>, and as a result there are <u>Chosoren</u> opponents to its construction.

Discrimination against Koreans in education continues beyond the kindergarten and high school levels into the colleges and universities. In January 1974, a Korean woman named Kim was refused permission to take the entrance examination for Otemae Women's College.(21) Lobbying by twelve organizations, including the Foreign Resident's Rights Protection Committee, the Burakumin Liberation League, and Japanese teacher's organizations, eventually secured a statement from the college that it would admit non-Japanese, and furthermore would introduce lectures and seminars on Korean and minority issues.

The tone for successor attitudes toward Korean education in Japan was set during the Occupation period by an event now referred to as the Hanshin Korean School's Incident.(22) After World War II, Korea was liberated from Japanese control for the first time since the Annexation in 1910. Many Korean educational institutions sprang up in Japan as Koreans tried to reassert their historical, cultural, and linguistic identity. The American occupation command considered such ethnic education to be a threat to internal security, as did the Japanese Ministry of Education, who ordered all Korean schools closed in 1948. On April 24, 1948, Koreans held sit-in demonstrations demanding educational self-determination. The Japanese prefectual Governor revoked the order closing the Korean schools, but the Occupation authorities declared a state of emergency, and invalidated the Governor's revocation. Many of the demonstrators received stiff sentences for their participation, including sentencing of up to ten years of hard labor by a military court. Since that time the overwhelming majority of Korean children have had to enroll in Japanese public schools. Only about 20 percent of Korean children are now in Korean schools.

It should be noted that the North Korean government through Chosoren has applied large quantities of money for the support of Korean schools. In 1960 Chosoren operated 280 Korean schools in Japan and between 1945 and 1960 had received 1.2 billion yen for educational purposes from Pyongyang. Mindan had received only about 100 million yen from the South Korean government up until 1960.(23) By 1965 North Korea had supplied Chosoren with 4.2 billion yen ($11.2 million)(24) for support of schools in Japan ranging from kindergartens through a university in Tokyo.

Governor Minobe of Tokyo decided to allow a Korean language university to open in Tokyo.(25) The decision was resented by the government on the grounds that it was likely to inculcate political subversion.

PSYCHOLOGY

I am a Korean

Although I'm a Korean
Until now I've used a Japanese name.
Why that's nothing short of telling a lie!
When my mother said to us sisters –
"Since you are Koreans, you are to use
    your Korean names,"

We opposed her. After all,
When even now everyone says
"You Koreans, go back, go back to Korea"
Wouldn't they hound us even more
If once we changed our names?

But, you know, it was actually a relief
To use my own country's name.
From now on I'll tell everybody –
"I'm a Korean," and even if they don't
Call me Kyung Ja, they'll see it
Written on my nametag and know anyway,
Since I've begun to use that name,
My friends call me "Hwan San" or "Kyon Chan"
It makes me so happy!
But, of course, there are still those who try to
Make fools of us, shouting "Korean, Korean!"
It annoys me, I admit, for though I pretend
Not to hear, it's hard to take.
Yet I'm Korean,
And no matter what they say to me,
I won't be discouraged.

Hwang Kyung Ja

This poem,(26) by an eight-year-old Korean girl resident in Japan, well illustrates the central psychological problem facing the Koreans in Japan, that of sense of identity and dignity.

In order for a Korean to naturalize and become a Japanese citizen, he or she must give up his or her Korean name and adopt a Japanese name. The impact of this regulation is that one is required through the giving up of the outward symbol of one's name to give up one's Korean background and national heritage. The unwillingness of Koreans to make this denial is one reason for the extremely low rate of naturalization amongst Koreans in Japan.

As a despised minority, there are internal pressures for Korean individuals to accept society's judgement and to despise themselves for being Korean. Yet at the same time there is a pull to look to one's roots for identification. Suzuki believes that language use is a good guide to the strength of one's ethnic identity. His research has shown that children of Chosoren parents tend to speak Korean more and be proud of speaking Korean than do the children of Mindan parents.(27)

In a recent study of Koreans from Che Ju Island now living in Tokyo, Kim has found that for first generation Koreans, the primary locus of identity is in Che Ju Island, where the adults spent their childhood.(28) This is true even for those who have spent more than thirty years in Japan. They have not internalized Japanese values even though they well understand them. However, their children, the second generation Koreans in Japan, are unable to find any locus for their identity, and are ambivalent about committing themselves to Korean identity alone. Many try to pass into Japanese society, which is possible because there are no overt physical differences between Japanese and Koreans. The attempt to pass usually results in an identity crisis.

Chai gives an account of a young Korean driven to suicide through self-immolation on account of a denial of his Korean past:(29)

"My parents had themselves naturalized in order to avoid obstacles to my education and career future. But for myself, where can I feel at home?" This was the dilemma of a young naturalized Korean, Yamamura Masaaki, whose alienation led him to take his own life by self-immolation. His tragic suicide gave witness to the futility of seeking freedom through naturalization.

The other side of the psychological problem of identity felt by Koreans is the problem of the Japanese attitude in relations with the resident Koreans — an attitude of discrimination. Statistics from the poll survey of the Japanese National Character held every five years included the question "Please select any of the peoples on this list you think are superior (yushu)." The results for the 1958 poll are as follows:(30)

Rank	Nationality	Percent
1	Japanese	57
2	Germans	52
3	Americans	47
4	Englishmen	31
5	Russians	20
6	Frenchmen	17
7	Chinese	9
8	Jews	8
9	Indians	7
10	Koreans	1
11	Arabs	1
12	Micronesians	0

The Koreans as a nationality stand very near the bottom of the list in terms of Japanese perceptions of non-Japanese. The Japanese stereotype of Koreans is that they are wild, deeply emotional, dirty, lazy, and alcoholic. Their homes and their bodies are considered to have a bad smell. Such stereotypes hold even among some Japanese that have little contact with Koreans.

There have been government programs with the goal of changing majority attitudes. UNESCO sponsored a program in Kawasaki aimed at teaching Japanese students Korean culture, history, and geography and made possible exchange of letters with Korean children.(31) The aim of the program was to lessen discriminatory attitudes. What did the results of this program show? "The percentage of those who said they could be friends with Koreans rose from 20 to 70 after the program; those who said the Koreans were 'dirty' and could not be accepted dropped from 60 to 10; 20 percent held a middle view before and after the program." Even though the program seems to have been a solid success, the government does not seem likely to encourage many such programs. One problem with it, as far as Chosoren was concerned, was that it was geared toward South Korea.

SECURITY ISSUES

The Japanese government considers the Korean minority in Japan as having the potential to threaten the internal security of Japan. Members of the National Police have been assigned within the Self-Defence Agency to monitor the activities of the Korean residents. Chosoren is listed with the Police Investigation Office as a potentially subversive organization, and as such is probably the most closely watched Korean organization in Japan,(32) although it is not the only one under scrutiny. Police concerned with the Koreans study Korean and keep track of all aspects of Korean life in Japan – political, economic, legal, and criminal.

Proportionate to their numbers, Koreans have a high crime rate, running about six times that of Japan as a whole. The marginal nature of the economic activities that many of the Koreans are consigned to often brings them close to the limits of the law.

DeVos and Wagatsuma present the table below which allows comparison of Korean delinquency rates with that of majority Japanese and outcaste Japanese, Burakumin, in Kobe, Japan's largest exporting port.(33)

Table 7.4. Estimated Rate of Delinquency in
Minority Group Youth in Kobe

	Number of Cases	Total Population	Rate per 1,000
Those residing in majority areas	493	1,098,546	4.49
Those residing in ghettos	71	47,023	15.10
Korean registrants	63	22,365	28.17
Other non-Japanese	6	10,468	5.73

Sentences for Korean prisoners sometimes seem overly severe. Shin Kyon Whan(34) was sentenced to eight years in prison for an armed robbery attempt shortly after he graduated from high school, despite the fact that he was a minor. The Japanese youth involved received maximum sentences of three years. Shin was paroled as a model prisoner after five years. Upon his release he was taken into custody and given a deportation order. According to Japanese law, non-Japanese sentenced to seven or more years in prison are subject to deportation.

Shin was born in Japan and held permanent residency status under the provision of the Japan-Korea treaty of 1965. He knows no home other than Japan. Nevertheless, he was sent to the deportation camp at Omori which now holds approximately 500 individuals awaiting deportation.

In the Japan-Korea Normalization Treaty the article concerning the legal status of Koreans in Japan states that "In the case of deportation proceedings against families holding permanent residence permits, attention shall be paid to the family's composition and other such factors, and special consideration applied from a humanitarian point of view." Shin's family was clearly destitute, his father suffering a disabling illness and his mother working as a day laborer. The treaty article was being ignored. Activist demonstrations and petitions on behalf of Shin eventually secured his release from the Omori camp in February 1974.

It is possible that in some instances the Japanese authorities perceive a greater threat to internal security from the Korean minority than actually exists. The social and economic conditions under which Koreans live exaggerate their proclivity to take part in criminal activities.

In addition to incidental crime, Koreans are also disproportionately heavily represented in organized crime amongst the yakuza, the gangster element in Japanese cities, including over half the membership in the famous Yamaguchi group. Gangsters are said to be involved in the illicit smuggling of Koreans into Japan by boat on the north coast.

A recent case highlighted the Korean involvement in gangsterism. Kinkiro,(35) a known Korean gangster, was sought for the murder of a Japanese gangster in Yokohama. Kinkiro sought refuge in a spa, holding several Japanese hostage. He then gave interviews to a number of Japanese officials and academics. He eloquently argued that although he spoke only Japanese and had taken a Japanese name, he could not obtain legal employment and was forced into a life of crime. The academics were impressed by his ability to articulate, and by how widely read he was. His own hostages were taken by his personal charm and insisted that he treated them well. Kinkiro was apprehended and his pleading proved of no avail. He is still in prison.

Crime, both incidental and organized, and potential subversion by Chosoren, are not the only threats to Japan's internal security faced by the Japanese authorities. Pro-South Korea factions also occasionally have disruptive influence.

On August 12, 1977, a three-day conference began in Tokyo at Ikenohata Bunka Center in Taito ward, sponsored by South Korea dissidents.(36) The goal of the conference was to form a democratic people's league to oppose the Park administration in the Republic of Korea. Approximately 100 were to attend the meeting, among them prominent South Koreans and high ranking government officials from 10 countries in North America and Europe. The dissidents announced a message advocating "restoration of democracy and the expulsion of Park." The message was supported by Yun Po Sun, former South Korean president, and Hanmintang, the South Korean National Congress for the Restoration of Democracy and Promotion of Unification.   The dissidents called for immediate and unconditional release of all political prisoners in the Republic of Korea, and abrogation of laws which suppress human rights.

During the Tokyo meeting, the Federation of Overseas South Koreans for Democracy and National Unification was formed. Lim Chung Young, former Republic of Korea ambassador to the United Nations, was elected as chairman of the federation. Tokyo was chosen as the site of the federation's international secretariat. On August 14, 1977, writer Makoto Oda announced the formation of an international liaison committee for the democratization of the Republic of Korea at a separate symposium in Tokyo's Gakushi Kaikan Hall. Shin Aochi, a critic, was named chairman of the committee, and Oda was named secretary general.

On August 13, approximately 300 pro-Park South Korean residents in Japan supported by Mindan invaded the Ikenohata Bunka Center where the dissident meeting was being held. In the violent demonstration which followed, more than 10 people were injured. Later in the week the Seoul government lodged a note of protest with the Japanese government over the arrest of these individuals.

There is historical precedent for the operation of Korean political activity in Japan under the protection of the Japanese government. Korean dissidents to the Japanese annexation of Korea in 1910 had more freedom of expression in Tokyo than they did in Seoul, and they exercised that freedom.

If Japan harbors violent pro-Park elements, it also harbors violent anti-Park elements. The house of Mun Se Kwang(37) in Osaka's Ikuno ward is pointed out to passersby as a reminder of a notorious incident. During the 1974 mid-August National Day ceremonies in Seoul, a series of shots rang out while Park Chung-hee presided over the celebration of Korea's liberation from Japan in 1945. The shots were fired by 22-year-old Mun Se Kwang, a Korean youth born and raised in Japan. He had entered Korea by obtaining a false passport under a Japanese name. Mun failed in his attempt to assassinate Park, but succeeded instead in killing Park's wife. The incident brought relations between South Korea and Japan to their lowest point since World War II. The Seoul government demanded a crackdown by the Japanese government on Koreans in Japan with political sympathies to Pyongyang.

The South Korean government began to watch Korean residents from Japan visiting or studying in Korea more closely. On November 22, 1975, the Korean Central Intelligence Agency announced that it had arrested 21 North Korean spies who were involved in a "campus spy ring" in Pusan and Seoul.(38) Of the 21, 13 were Zainichi Kankokujin, resident-in-Japan Koreans. All of the defendants were found guilty and given stiff sentences, including the death penalty for 4. According to observers at the time many of the defendants seem to have been declared guilty based on little evidence other than self-confession. Some of the defendants seemed to show marks of torture. In many ways the "November 22nd Spy Case" showed striking parallels to the "People's Revolutionary Party Spy Case" uncovered by the KCIA in May 1974. Eight of the "ringleaders" of this group were put to death in 1975, not long after an Amnesty International mission(39) to Seoul concluded that the defendants had been tortured. Rightly or wrongly the Zainichi Kankokujin have had to bear the brunt of these KCIA investigations.

Korean-Japanese relations were seriously affected in 1973 by the kidnapping of South Korean opposition leader Kim Dae Jung from the Grand Palace Hotel in Tokyo.(40) On August 8, 1973, Kim disappeared, having been drugged, blindfolded, and carted off by five Korean-speaking men. Five days later he was deposited in Seoul near his home. An organization called the National Salvation Society claimed responsibility for the kidnapping, but evidence of the number of men involved (at least 20), money (an estimated $500,000), and equipment (cars, boats, and houses) indicated that more than a private organization was involved. Kim attributed the sparing of his life to pressure brought to bear on the Seoul government by Japan and the United States immediately following the kidnapping.

Kim was placed under house arrest until October 26, 1973. He announced upon his release that he was giving up political activities for the time being. Speculation at the time linked his release with the attempt to avoid an internal crisis over the death of a prominent Seoul law professor, Choi Chong-Kil. The South Korean government announced that Choi had committed suicide while being interrogated by the KCIA on charges of spying for North Korea.

On November 18, Kim applied for the exit clearance permit necessary in obtaining a passport in order to travel to the United States to take up a fellowship at Harvard University that had been pending. Japanese Foreign Minister Ohira said that Japan had been assured that Kim Dae Jong would be allowed to travel abroad. The Korean response was that he would be treated "just like any other Korean." Edwin Reischauer, Harvard professor and former ambassador to Japan, traveled to Korea to lobby for Kim's exit permit. The permit was never granted.

Instead, Kim was put on trial for violation of election laws. As the opposition candidate to President Park Chung-hee, Kim won an official 46 percent of the votes in the 1971 election. When Park declared martial law in October 1972 and altered the constitution so that elections were limited to the easily controlled National Conference for Unification, Kim was in Japan. From that time until the kidnapping, Kim denounced Park's moves in Japan and in the United States as dictatorial, unconstitutional, and unjustified. His trial and subsequent sentence seems to have been more a reaction to these statements abroad than to the charges of election law violations. Kim remains in jail.

The case of Kim Dae Jong indicates the importance of Koreans in Japan for Japanese-Korean relations. At the time of Kim's kidnapping, a breach was established between the governments of Tokyo and Seoul. Japan felt that there was evidence that her sovereignty had been breached by KCIA operations in Japan. On August 24, following the kidnapping, Japan postponed a meeting of Japanese and South Korean cabinet members as a register of public displeasure over the abduction until the Koreans helped to settle the affair to the satisfaction of the Japanese. The focus of the talks was $200 million in Japanese economic aid to Korea. The pressure did not succeed in allowing Kim to return to Japan to help the Japanese in the investigation. The Japanese did not wish a complete break with Korea over the Kim Dae Jong affair, so they alternatively toughened and weakened their stand. Kim's release from house arrest provided a face-saving compromise for both sides, but the Japanese continued to make embarassing revelations, such as the fact that the car in which Kim was kidnapped belonged to the Korean vice consul in Yokohama.

Before his kidnapping, Kim had organized a group of Koreans in Japan to oppose the Park government and its arm in Japan, Mindan. This activity attracted a small group of vocal supporters who continue to operate without the presence of their leader and organizer.

Japan continues to be an arena of political debate for Koreans over developments on the Korean peninsula. These debates from time to time erupt into violence that affect internal Japanese security. At other times, as in the case of the Mun Se Kwang assassination attempt and in the case of the Kim Dae Jong kidnapping, the debates erupt into breaches of Japan's relations with Korea. These debates continue to have repercussions long after their initial impact. A mock trial of Kim was held in Tokyo, in September 1977, to parody the system of justice in South Korea.

These debates of South Korean political factions are only part of the security concerns of the Japanese government regarding the Korean minority in Japan. The North Korean organization Chosoren continues to be labeled a potentially subversive organization and is kept under close observation by national police trained especially for monitoring such activities. The high crime rate of Koreans in Japan, in both incidental crime and organized gangsterism, is a security problem also under constant surveillance. The existence of the deportation camp for Koreans at Omura provides a safety valve for eliminating undesired Koreans.

The Korean minority in Japan is one of considerably political volatility. Its activities are characterized by high crime and low level violence. Considerations of policy toward the minority by Japan has influence on and is influenced by Japan's relations with both Koreas. Occasional incidents of a dramatic nature subsequently affect the climate of relations between Japan and the Koreas.

LEGAL ISSUES

The legal position of the Koreans in Japan is complex. Relatively few Koreans are taking Japanese citizenship through naturalization. In fact, the rate of naturalization of Koreans is lower than the rate of growth of the Korean community in Japan. An accounting of the naturalization rate appears in the following section on statistics. Because few Koreans have become or are becoming citizens of Japan, they are consigned to an ambiguous status. Many Koreans have been born in Japan, but if their parents have not naturalized, they are considered Korean – not Japanese. The great majority of Koreans are considered aliens or residents, but not citizens. Citizens' rights or privileges are not extended to the Koreans in the same way they are to Japanese.

Some of the more important regulations affecting the Koreans in Japan have been the National General Mobilization Act of 1938, the Alien Registration Law of 1947, Law 126 of 1952, and the Agreement on the Legal Status and the Treatment of the Nationals of the Republic of Korea Residing in Japan of 1965.(41)

Through the National General Mobilization Act enacted by the Japanese Diet in 1938, Koreans were legally brought by force into Japan. Koreans in Korea as well as in Japan were considered Japanese nationals at that time, as they had been since the Annexation of Korea in 1910. Immediately following World War II, the SCAP decreed on November 20, 1946 that Koreans in Japan were to be treated as Japanese nationals. The Koreans did not like this idea and wished to be given status equal to the Allied nationals in Japan. On May 27, 1947, the Alien Registration Law was enacted requiring Koreans to register as "Chosen" (North Korea) or "Kankoku" (Republic of Korea) nationals, following the split on the peninsula. In June 1948, the SCAP accorded Koreans a special status, semi-independent from Japanese nationality. Later, in June 1950, a SCAP memorandum declared the status of the Koreans in Japan to be undetermined until an agreement was reached between Japan and the Republic of Korea.

In October 1951, negotiations between Japan and the Republic of Korea resulted in Japan refusing to grant special legal status to the Korean minority. Eleven countries signed the Peace Treaty with Japan which came into force on April 28, 1952. The text of this treaty mentions nothing about the Koreans in Japan, but on the same day that the Treaty came into force, Law 126 was enacted in Japan. This law gave permission for continued residence in Japan by Koreans until the issue was settled. Koreans continued to be registered as nationals of Chosen or Kankoku. It should be remembered that events immediately following World War II were affected by the massive repatriation to Korea, and that events in the early 1950s were affected by the Korean War.

For a period in the late 1950s, relations between Japan and South Korea soured when Japan gave permission for a major repatriation to North Korea. Koreans registered as either Chosen or Kankoku were treated more or less equally right up through the early 1960s. The status of the Koreans after World War II had been reduced from that of Japanese nationals to that of aliens, undesired aliens at that. The Koreans never succeeded in gaining the status of Allied nationals in Japan as they had hoped. As aliens, Koreans had to register and reregister and do without many of the rights given to Japanese nationals in matters of education, employment, housing, and health care.

In January 1965, Japanese Minister of Justice Ishii Mitsujiro testified in the Diet that of the Koreans in Japan, 347,407 were registered as Chosen (North Koreans) and 230,072 were registered as Kankoku (South Korean). Figures released by the Republic of Korea at the time indicated a somewhat different assessment, for they showed Mindan membership at 230,000, Chosoren membership at 170,000, and neutrals at 175,000.

On June 22, 1965, the important Agreement on the Legal Status and Treatment of the Nationals of the Republic of Korea in Japan was put into effect as a part of the treaty and normalization agreement between Japan and the Republic of Korea. This Agreement applied to all those Koreans in Japan who wished to be Kankoku, nationals of the Republic of Korea. Those who wished to remain Chosen, nationals of North Korea, continued to hold the same limited legal status as before.

The views of the Republic of Korea were generally well reflected in the 1965 Agreement. Koreans in Japan wishing to associate with South Korea were allowed to apply for the right of permanent residency in Japan, eliminating the need for constant reregistration. Their living situation became more secure. They were to be given "due consideration" in matters of education, protection of livelihood, and health insurance. They were to be allowed remission of funds and property should they choose to return to Korea to reside. The full text of the 1965 Agreement between Japan and the Republic of Korea concerning ROK nationals in Japan appears at the end of this section (fig. 7.1).

The complex history of the status of Koreans in Japan has run the gamut from nationals, to aliens, Chosen, Kankoku, Allied nationals, residents, permanent residents, and to naturalized citizens. Many Koreans feel the route via naturalization is not a viable one, because taking Japanese citizenship means taking up Japanese nationality to the point of giving up Korean nationality and adopting a Japanese name. There seems to be evidence that in any event naturalization results in aryun Nihonjin, second class Japanese citizenship.(42) Even if one passes the severe requirements to naturalize, kika seraru, one becomes identifiable as a new Japanese, Shin Nihonjin. In a sense, the Korean fight for permanent residency rights was a fight for citizenship rights without the necessity of giving up one's Korean nationality.

Many Koreans had been very displeased by the 1947 Alien Registration Law which specified that those Koreans who had come to Japan before World War II, even those who had been brought forcibly under the provision of the National General Mobilization Act of 1938, were to be treated like tourists, kankosha, exactly like other foreigners who came to Japan of their own free will. Through a strange quirk, it appears that in the immediate postwar period Koreans did not have the right to vote unless they registered as aliens. Subsequently they lost all voting rights, and became full-fledged foreigners following the San Francisco Peace Treaty of 1952.

The trend since the 1965 Agreement seems to be that gradually the Koreans, at least those Koreans falling under the terms of this Agreement (roughly half the Koreans in Japan), are gaining a more solid legal position in Japanese society. Government decisions such as those involving Park's employment with Hitachi or the Koreans' desire to build a school in Kyoto at Hondayama have supported the Koreans' point of view. The more difficult aspect of the problem, popular prejudice against Koreans, remains strong, although there is some evidence that this too is decreasing, perhaps with the change in generation.

Koreans take Japanese citizenship for a number of reasons. The first and perhaps most important reason is relationship by kin, either through marriage or adoption. Evidence indicates that the greatest single group of Koreans to be naturalized are Korean women who marry Japanese men.(43) If there is no kinship relationship involved, reasons for naturalizing include the attempt to provide better educational activities for one's children, preparation for employment, or to ease the way for going into legitimate business.

Necessary preconditions for being accepted for naturalization according to the law are a minimum of five years continued residence in Japan; good behavior (avoidance of illegal activities); and ability to live (economic stability and ability to pay taxes without being a burden on the state).

The procedure involved in processing an application for naturalization involves going to the Registration Division of the appropriate Bureau of the Ministry of Justice in a prefectural capital, or to the appropriate office of a subbureau of the Department of Justice if one lives in a smaller city or town.(44) Nine documents must be completed and submitted for naturalization procedures: a naturalization application, a photograph taken within six months of the date of application; a statement of motivation; a personal history including addresses, education, and professional status arranged chronologically; a certificate of nationality; a certificate of registration as a foreigner; an oath of loyalty to obey Japanese law; an account of assets, income, and proof of ability to live unsupported; and tax records. Help may be obtained in preparing the documents for submission, but the documents must be signed by anyone 15 years of age or older to demonstrate that the application is voluntary. For children under 15 not all the documents are necessary, but those that are must be signed by either the child's father, mother, both parents, or guardian.

Applications may be rejected for a number of reasons including violation of traffic regulations, problems of individual status such as multiple marriage, or inability to meet the legal requirements already mentioned of financial ability and a clear criminal record. It appears that 80 to 90 percent of rejections are the results of applicants having committed too many traffic violations.(45)

Most applications take one to one and a half years to process, perhaps an indication of Japanese restraint in processing applications, in spite of the official position of neither encouraging nor discouraging attempts to naturalize.

Naturalized Koreans tend to emphasize the legal problems and inferior status of Koreans who choose not to naturalize or who are not accepted in the naturalization process. In Osaka the Seiwa Club of Naturalized Koreans has been formed who attempt to contact newly naturalized Koreans through the list of those naturalized published by the Department of Justice. There appears to be some confusion over the nationalities of those naturalizing, since some Korean and Chinese names are identical, and those naturalizing are not listed by nationality. On the other hand, those Koreans who choose not to naturalize emphasize problems faced by the Koreans who naturalize, such as loss of Korean identity, the giving up of Korean national education, and the inability to avoid second-class citizenship.

The opposing points of view were graphically put forward by two men interviewed in 1975.(46) Kim Rong-hai, a teacher of national education in a Korean primary school in Japan, discussed the identity problems of those Koreans who chose to naturalize. He saw naturalization as a road to abandoning family and nation, a road that could only be blocked by teaching Korean children in Korean history, culture, and language. Shirai Minoru, executive director of the Seiwa Club of Naturalized Koreans, took the view that there was an inevitable historical process at work in which those Koreans who chose to remain in Japan must eventually naturalize. He pointed out that since there was no racial distinction between Koreans and Japanese, and since there were considerable economic benefits to naturalization, it was the best course to take for those Koreans wishing to remain permanently in Japan.

It is possible that the reasons and emotions expressed by these two men have had differential impact on the Korean community in Japan at different points in time.

According to Table 7.5 in the following section, the number of Koreans in Japan taking Japanese citizenship through naturalization slowly increased between 1952 and 1965. After normalization with South Korea in 1965, with the Agreement between Japan and South Korea concerning the possibility of Koreans in Japan obtaining a new permanent residency status, the rate of naturalization steadily decreased up until 1970. This may have been because Koreans preferred to try for permanent residency rather than naturalization, or because the Japanese government preferred to award permanent residency rather than naturalization status to Koreans. The number of Koreans naturalizing after 1970 began to rise again with a significant jump in 1973, related by some to the Kim Dae Jong kidnapping in Tokyo which took place during that year.(47) It appears that the naturalization rate bears some relationship to the state of Japanese-Korean state relations.

The matter of naturalization is somewhat obscured because of the lack of precise data available on those naturalizing. The Korean embassy reports that it does not receive statistics on naturalization of Koreans in Japan since there is no intergovernmental agreement that specifies that this should take place. According to law, members of a Korean family are required to report any member of their family who takes Japanese citizenship, but this law is little heeded in practice.(48)

[TRANSLATION[1]—TRADUCTION[2]]

No. 8474. AGREEMENT[3] ON THE LEGAL STATUS AND THE TREATMENT OF THE NATIONALS OF THE REPUBLIC OF KOREA RESIDING IN JAPAN BETWEEN JAPAN AND THE REPUBLIC OF KOREA. SIGNED AT TOKYO, ON 22 JUNE 1965

Japan and the Republic of Korea,

Considering that nationals of the Republic of Korea residing in Japan for many years have come to have special relations with Japanese society; and

Recognizing that enabling these nationals of the Republic of Korea to lead a stabilized life under the social order of Japan will contribute to the promotion of friendly relations between the two countries and their peoples;

Have agreed as follows :

Article I

1. The Government of Japan shall give permission for permanent residence in Japan to a national of the Republic of Korea falling under either of the following categories, if he applies for such permission within five years from the date of the entry into force of the present Agreement in accordance with the procedure to be established by the Government of Japan for the implementation of the present Agreement :

(*a*) A person residing in Japan since August 15, 1945, or a date prior thereto, continuously until the time of his application; or

(*b*) A person born in Japan on or after August 16, 1945 and before the period of five years from the date of the entry into force of the present Agree-

---

[1] Translation by the Government of Japan. The Secretariat also received an English translation of this agreement from the Government of the Republic of Korea which on certain points differs from that provided by the Government of Japan. At the request of the Government of the Republic of Korea, these differences have been shown by printing in italics the pertinent word of phrase in the translation of the Government of Japan and providing in square brackets the corresponding expression in the translation by the Government of the Republic of Korea.

[2] Traduction du Gouvernement japonais. Le Gouvernement de la République de Corée a également communiqué au Secrétariat une traduction anglaise de cet accord qui diffère en certains points de celle transmise par le Gouvernement japonais. À la demande du Gouvernement de la République de Corée, on a indiqué en italique dans la traduction transmise par le Gouvernement japonais chaque mot ou groupe de mots donnant lieu à divergence et introduit à la suite entre crochets l'expression correspondante dans la traduction fournie par le Gouvernement de la République de Corée.

[3] Came into force on 17 January 1966, the thirtieth day following the exchange of the instruments of ratification, which took place at Seoul on 18 December 1965, in accordance with article VI.

Figure 7.1.

(continued)

Figure 7.1.   (continued)

ment expires, as a lineal descendant of a person falling under (a) above, and residing in Japan continuously until the time of his application.

2.   The Government of Japan shall give permission for permanent residence in Japan to a national of the Republic of Korea who is born in Japan after the lapse of five years from the date of the entry into force of the present Agreement as a child of a person who is given permission for permanent residence in Japan in accordance with the provisions of paragraph 1 above, if such child applies for such permission within sixty days from the date of birth in accordance with the procedure to be established by the Government of Japan for the implementation of the present Agreement.

3.   Notwithstanding the provisions of paragraph 1 above, the application period for permission for permanent residence shall be sixty days from the date of birth in the case of a person who falls under paragraph 1 (b) above and is born after the lapse of four years and ten months from the date of the entry into force of the present Agreement.

4.   No fee shall be levied for the above-mentioned applications and permissions.

Article II

1.   With respect to the residence in Japan of the nationals of the Republic of Korea born in Japan as lineal descendants of the persons who are given permission for permanent residence in Japan in accordance with the provisions of Article I, the Government of Japan agrees, if requested by the Government of the Republic of Korea, to holding consultations *until twenty-five years will have elapsed* [by the lapse of twenty-five years] from the date of the entry into force of the present Agreement.

2.   In the consultations under the preceding paragraph, the spirit and purposes which form the basis of the present Agreement shall be respected.

Article III

A national of the Republic of Korea who is given permission for permanent residence in Japan in accordance with the provisions of Article I shall not be deported from Japan unless he comes to fall under any of the following categories by his *act* [acts] committed on or after the date of the entry into force of the present Agreement :

(a) A person who, for crimes concerning insurrection or crimes concerning foreign aggression, is sentenced in Japan to imprisonment or to a heavier punishment (except a person who is granted the suspension of execution of such sentence or who is sentenced for reasons of responding to an agitation or following the lead of another in an insurrection);

No. 8474

Figure 7.1.   (continued)

(*b*) A person who, for crimes concerning foreign relations, is sentenced in Japan to imprisonment or to a heavier punishment, or a person who, for his criminal acts committed against the head of a foreign state, a diplomatic envoy or his official premises, is sentenced to imprisonment or to a heavier punishment and thereby prejudice vital interests of Japan in its foreign relations;

(*c*) A person who, by violating the laws and regulations in Japan concerning control of narcotics with profitmaking intents, is sentenced to penal servitude or imprisonment for life or for not less than three years (except a person who is granted the suspension of execution of such sentence), or a person who, by violating the laws and regulations in Japan concerning control of narcotics, is sentenced to penalties not less than three times (twice in the case of a person who was sentenced to penalties not less than three times by his acts committed prior to the date of the entry into force of the present Agreement); or

(*d*) A person who, by violating the laws and regulations in Japan, is sentenced to penal servitude or to imprisonment for life or for more than seven years.

Article IV

The Government of Japan shall pay due consideration to the following matters :

(*a*) Matters concerning education, livelihood protection and national health insurance in Japan for the nationals of the Republic of Korea who are given permission for permanent residence in Japan in accordance with the provisions of Article I; and

(*b*) Matters concerning taking property with them and remitting funds to the Republic of Korea in the event that nationals of the Republic of Korea, who are given permission for permanent residence in Japan in accordance with the provisions of Article I (including persons who are qualified to apply for permission for permanent residence in accordance with the provisions of the said Article), renounce their intention of residing permanently in Japan and return to the Republic of Korea.

Article V

It is confirmed that, with regard to all matters, including entry into and exit from Japan and residence in Japan, the nationals of the Republic of Korea who are given permission for permanent residence in Japan in accordance with the provisions of Article I shall be subject, unless specifically provided for in the

Figure 7.1.   (continued)

present Agreement, to the laws and regulations in Japan applicable equally to all aliens.

Article VI

The present Agreement shall be ratified.   The instruments of ratification shall be exchanged at Seoul as soon as possible.   The present Agreement shall enter into force on the thirtieth day after the exchange of the instruments of ratification.

IN WITNESS WHEREOF the undersigned, being duly authorized thereto by their respective Governments, have signed the present Agreement.

DONE in duplicate at Tokyo, in the Japanese and Korean languages, both being equally authentic, this twenty-second day of June of the year one thousand nine hundred and sixty-five.

> For Japan :
>> Etsusaburo SHIINA
>> Shinichi TAKASUGI

> For the Republic of Korea :
>> TONG WON LEE
>> DONG JO KIM

AGREED MINUTES TO THE AGREEMENT ON THE LEGAL STATUS AND THE TREATMENT OF THE NATIONALS OF THE REPUB-LIC OF KOREA RESIDING IN JAPAN BETWEEN JAPAN AND THE REPUBLIC OF KOREA

The representatives of the Governments of Japan and the Republic of Korea have reached the following understandings concerning the Agreement on the Legal Status and the Treatment of the Nationals of the Republic of Korea Residing in Japan between Japan and the Republic of Korea signed today :

Re *Article I* :

1. For the purpose of certifying that a person who applies for permission for permanent residence in accordance with the provisions of paragraph 1 or 2 of the Article has the nationality of the Republic of Korea

(i) Such person shall produce his passport or a certificate in lieu thereof, or shall submit a written statement that he has the nationality of the Republic of Korea; and

No. 8474

Figure 7.1.   (continued)

(ii) The competent authorities of the Government of the Republic of Korea will reply in writing in case the competent authorities of the Government of Japan make inquiries in writing.

2. For the purposes of paragraph 1 (*b*) of the Article, " a person falling under (*a*) " *will* [shall] include a national of the Republic of Korea residing in Japan since August 15, 1945 or a date prior thereto, continuously until the time of his death.

Re *Article III* :

1. For the purposes of (*b*) of the Article, " his official premises " are the buildings or parts of buildings and the land ancillary thereto, irrespective of ownership, used as embassy or legation (including the residence of the diplomatic envoy).

2. The Government of Japan *will* [shall], when it intends to deport a person falling under (*c*) or (*d*) of the Article, take into consideration the composition of his family and other circumstances from a humanitarian standpoint.

3. The Government of the Republic of Korea *will, in accordance with* [shall, at the request of] the request of the Government of Japan, co-operate in accepting a person who is to be deported from Japan under the provisions of the Article.

4. It is the policy of the Government of Japan that, when deportation procedures are taken with respect to a person qualified to apply for permission for permanent residence in accordance with the provisions of Article I of the Agreement, it will, taking into account that should he be given permission for permanent residence he shall not be deported from Japan unless he falls under either of (*a*) through (*d*) of Article III, withhold the enforcement of his deportation :

(i) in case he has already applied for permission for permanent residence, until decision is given on his application; or

(ii) in case he has not applied for permission for permanent residence, until whether or not he intends to apply is confirmed, and in case he applies, until decision is given on his application.

Re *Article IV* :

1. In accordance with the laws and regulations, the Government of Japan *will* [shall], when nationals of the Republic of Korea who are given permission for permanent residence in Japan in accordance with the provisions of Article I of the Agreement wish to enter a public primary or secondary school of Japan, take such measures as it deems necessary so that such entrace may be permitted, and *will* [shall], when they finish a secondary school of Japan, recognize their qualification for applying for higher schools of Japan.

Figure 7.1.   (continued)

2. The Government of Japan *will* [shall] have for the time being the present livelihood protection for the nationals of the Republic of Korea who are given permission for permanent residence in accordance with the provisions of Article I of the Agreement continued.

3. The Government of Japan *will* [shall] take such measures as it deems necessary in order to insure under the National Health Insurance the nationals of the Republic of Korea who are given permission for permanent residence in Japan in accordance with the provisions of Article I of the Agreement.

4. When the nationals of the Republic of Korea who are given permission for permanent residence in Japan in accordance with the provisions of Article I of the Agreement (including persons who are qualified to apply for permission for permanent residence) renounce their intention of residing permanently in Japan and return to the Republic of Korea, the Government of Japan *will* [shall] permit in principle that they may take all their property with them or remit all their funds.

For this purpose :

(i) with respect to their taking their property with them, the Government of Japan *will* [shall], within the scope of the laws and regulations, permit their taking with them their personal effects, household goods and professional tools and equipments, and pay due consideration as much as possible in authorizing their exportation; and

(ii) with respect to their taking with them or remitting their funds, the Government of Japan *will* [shall], within the scope of the laws and regulations, permit their taking with them or remitting their funds not exceeding ten thousand United States dollars per family at the time of their returning home, and their taking with them or remitting the exceeding amount as the case may be.

Tokyo, June 22, 1965

E. S.

T. W. L.

RECORD OF DISCUSSIONS

In the course of the negotiations for conclusion of the Agreement on the Legal Status and the Treatment of Korean Nationals residing in Japan, the following statements were made respectively by the Japanese and Korean sides :

Figure 7.1.   (continued)

Japanese Representative :

(*a*) In the application of the provisions of paragraph 1 (*a*) of Article I of the Agreement, it is the policy of the Government of Japan to regard the period between the departure from Japan for military service or for compulsory labour recruitment and the arrival in Japan under the repatriation programme as the period of continued residence in Japan.

(*b*) The following will be included among those which a person applying for permission for permanent residence in accordance with the provisions of Article I of the Agreement is to submit or produce :

(i) Application for permission for permanent residence

(ii) Photograph

(iii) Statement on family relations and residence record in Japan

(iv) Certificate of alien registration.

(*c*) The term " such measures as it deems necessary " referred to in paragraph 1 of the part of the Agreed Minutes to the Agreement regarding Article IV of the Agreement means guidance, advice and recommendation given by the Ministry of Education in accordance with the laws and regulations presently in force.

(*d*) The term " such measures as it deems necessary " in paragraph 3 of the part of the Agreed Minutes to the Agreement regarding Article IV of the Agreement includes amendment of the ordinance of the Ministry of Welfare. However, since a preparatory period of considerable length will be necessary for taking such measures, the Government of Japan will ensure that those Korean nationals will be insured under the National Health Insurance as from the first day of the fiscal year following the fiscal year to which the first day after the lapse of one year from the date of the entry into force of the Agreement belongs.

(*e*) The Republic of Korea is designated in the notification under the Cabinet Order concerning the Acquisition of Properties by Aliens as a country to which the said Order shall not apply, and the Government of Japan has no intention to delete it upon the entry into force of the Agreement.

(*f*) It is the policy of the Government of Japan that, when a national of the Republic of Korea who is given permission for permanent residence in Japan in accordance with the provisions of Article I of the Agreement intends to leave Japan and applies for re-enty permission, it will, within the scope of the laws and regulations, handle such application as favourably as possible.

Korean Representative :

(*a*) It is the policy of the Government of the Republic of Korea that, after the entry into force of the Agreement, it will co-operate with the Government of

Figure 7.1.   (continued)

Japan in accepting nationals of the Republic of Korea to be deported from Japan under the laws and regulations of Japan concerning immigration control.

(b) The Government of the Republic of Korea, while recognizing that a preparatory period of considerable length will be necessary for taking " such measures as it deems necessary " referred to in paragraph 3 of the part of the Agreed Minutes to the Agreement regarding Article IV of the Agreement, expects that such measures will be taken as soon as possible.

(c) The Government of the Republic of Korea is prepared to consider with the Government of Japan measures for co-operating with the latter to the extent possible at the latter's request in order to stabilize the life of the nationals of the Republic of Korea residing in Japan and relieve the poor among them.

M. Y.
K. H. L.

STATISTICS ON POPULATION GROWTH
AND RATE OF NATURALIZATION

The Department of Justice of Japan publishes annually the number of Koreans officially registered in Japan. The table below summarizes the growth of the number of Koreans in Japan during the decade 1965 to 1974 based on these statistics:(49)

Table 7.5. Increase of Koreans in Japan
1965-1974

Year	Number of Koreans in Japan
1965	583,837
1966	585,278
1967	591,345
1968	598,076
1969	607,316
1970	614,202
1971	622,690
1972	629,809
1973	636,346
1974	639,652
TOTAL INCREASE	55,815

These statistics include only those Koreans officially registered in Japan as Koreans. It is acknowledged by all people concerned with the issue that there are many Koreans residing illegally in Japan, but there is no accurate means of determining the number of these illegal aliens since they attempt to remain anonymous. Estimates range from 10,000 to 300,000. Thus we may conclude that at the present time there are more than 650,000 Koreans in Japan, but the total number is somewhat less than 1 million.

Table 7.5 indicates that the average rate of growth of the Korean community in Japan during the past decade has been less than 1 percent per year, averaging about .91 percent annually.

The Koreans are distributed throughout the heavily urbanized and industrialized areas of Japan. Osaka has consistently been home for the largest number of Koreans in Japan. The greatest concentration of Koreans in Osaka is in the Ikuno ward, often the first stop upon arrival in Japan before dispersal to other areas. In 1974 the official statistics showed 179,315 Koreans in Osaka, more than twice as many as the 73,473 in Tokyo, the second largest concentration in the country. Following Osaka (179,315) and Tokyo (73,473) in numbers, are Hyogo Prefecture including the port city of Kobe (67,375); Aichi Prefecture including industrial Nagoya (54,163); Kyoto (44,236); Kanagawa Prefecture including Yokohama (28,952); and Fukuoka in Kyushu (25,475). These are the 7 cities in Japan with populations over 1,000,000.

The table below summarizes the number of Koreans in these cities as well as those of Yamaguchi and Hiroshima for 1964 through 1966.(50)

Table 7.6. Number of Koreans in Japan
(registered)

District, City or Prefecture	1964	1965	1966
Osaka	154,868	158,596	159,446
Tokyo	65,516	66,678	67,503
Hyogo (Kobe)	57,923	58,786	59,223
Aichi (Nagoya)	45,147	46,267	46,876
Kyoto	38,967	39,487	39,706
Kanagawa (Yokohama)	24,890	25,592	25,822
Fukuoka	25,978	25,518	25,486
Yamaguchi	16,862	16,166	15,942
Hiroshima	14,237	14,406	14,445
Other areas	113,157	132,041	130,889
Total	578,545	583,537	535,278
Total number of foreigners in Japan	659,789	665,989	668,318

Table 7.6 shows that for the years under consideration, 1964 through 1966, there was a tendency for Koreans to migrate into the larger urban centers. Each of the seven largest cities except for Fukuoka showed steady increases in their Korean populations, relatively large increases compared to the overall growth rate of the Koreans in Japan. Conversely, the category Other areas (the less densely populated regions), showed considerable reduction in Korean population.

For comparative purposes with another minority group in Japan, it may be useful to note below the geographical concentrations for the Chinese for 1964 through 1966 in the same way that we have done for the Koreans.(51)

The lack of rights that Koreans have in Japan can be attributed to a certain extent to their not having the legal status that other Japanese have. The legal questions involved are complicated and have already been discussed in the preceding section. Here we will observe that a certain small number of Koreans are becoming naturalized citizens of Japan. Each year several thousand aliens apply for Japanese citizenship. Table 7.8 summarizes action taken on these applications.(52)

The statistics, supplied annually by the Japanese Department of Justice, are incomplete from 1965 onward. Up until that time there is a steady rise in the number of new applications for citizenship each year. We might have expected that rising trend to continue, but surprisingly the later statistics are not available. It might be noted that the number of applications accepted for citizenship after 1965 declined and did not reach the 1965 level again until 1972.

Table 7.7 Chinese and Foreigners in Japan

District, City, or Prefecture	1964	1965	1966
Tokyo	15,652	15,867	15,804
Hyogo (Kobe)	9,184	9,140	9,172
Osaka	6,608	6,628	6,622
Kanagawa (Yokohama)	6,194	6,316	6,283
Fukuoka	1,282	1,275	1,299
Kyoto	1,112	1,112	1,120
Nagasaki	867	851	842
Aichi (Nagoya)	798	825	843
Kumamoto (Kyushu)	493	496	482
Others	6,984	6,908	6,920
Total Chinese in Japan	49,174	49,418	49,387
Total foreigners in Japan	659,789	665,989	668,318

The exact number of Koreans in these annual Justice Department statistics for aliens taking Japanese citizenship is not specified. The Justice Department indicates that the number of Koreans in the total is around 90 percent. The table below summarizes the number of Koreans taking citizenship each year, based on estimates between 80 and 90 percent.(53)

These statistics, admittedly estimates, show that the number of Koreans naturalizing each year is somewhat lower than the number of additional Koreans immigrating into or born into Japan each year. For instance, in Table 7.5, we noted that the increase of registered Koreans in Japan in the decade 1964 through 1974 was 55,815. During the same years the number of Koreans naturalizing in Japan according to the estimates in Table 7.9 was 49,373. Thus we can see that the rate of increase for Koreans in Japan is higher than the rate of naturalization. If this pattern continues to prevail we cannot expect the problem of the Koreans in Japan to be solved, or partially solved, through the melting pot phenomenon that has been at work in the United States.

If we add the 49,373 naturalized Koreans to the 55,815 increase in Koreans between 1965 and 1974, we can determine that the annual real growth rate of Koreans in Japan for the decade was not the .91 percent cited earlier, but 1.72 percent, the difference accounted for by the disappearance of Koreans through naturalization.

Somewhat different statistics from those appearing in Table 7.8 have been compiled from the daily bulletins of the Bureau of Civil Affairs in the Ministry of Justice. Table 7.10 summarizes applications accepted for Japanese citizenship by a number of nationalities between 1952 and 1966.(54)

Lee (Table 7.11) has presented a recent account of the place of birth of Koreans in Japan.(55)

Table 7.8 Applications for Citizenship by Aliens in Japan

Year	Pending Applications	New Applications	Total	Accepted	Rejected	Deferred
1949				1		
1950				4		
1951				21		
1952		1,095		209	219	586
1953	628	2,737		1,428	568	1,369
1954	1,394	4,347		2,806	1,223	1,712
1955	1,712	5,585	7,297	2,744	2,332	2,218
1956	2,218	5,756	7,974	2,834	2,385	2,755
1957	2,755	5,993	8,748	2,632	2,909	3,207
1958	3,207	5,990	9,197	2,794	2,896	3,507
1959	3,507	7,482	10,989	3,196	3,020	4,773
1960	4,773	8,130	12,903	3,857	2,955	6,091
1961	6,091	7,671	13,762	3,240	2,933	7,589
1962	7,589	8,297	15,886	3,614	3,433	8,839
1963	8,839	8,271	17,110	4,100	2,519	10,491
1964	10,491	8,759	19,250	6,572	1,217	11,461
1965				6,687	1,186	
1966				5,409	1,620	
1967				4,786		
1968				3,501		
1969				2,153		
1970				5,379		
1971				3,386		
1972				6,825		
1973						

Table 7.9. Number of Koreans Naturalized
1952 through 1974

Year	Estimate Number of Koreans Naturalized
1952	232
1953	1,326
1954	2,435
1955	2,434
1956	2,290
1957	3,310
1958	2,246
1959	2,737
1960	3,763
1961	2,710
1962	3,222
1963	3,558
1964	4,632
1965	5,617
1966	4,543
1967	4,020
1968	2,941
1969	1,808
1970	4,518
1971	2,844
1972	5,733
1973	11,448
1974	5,901
Total	83,268

GEOGRAPHY

Table 7.6 summarized the numbers of Koreans in the prefectures of greatest Korean concentration. Koreans reside in every prefecture of Japan, from Hokkaido in the extreme north to Okinawa in the extreme south. Table 7.12 below gives the number of Koreans living in each prefecture in 1974. Reference may be made to the accompanying prefectural map (fig. 7.2) in order to gain a clearer understanding of the distribution of the Korean population throughout Japan.

It has already been noted that there is a trend toward increasing concentration of the Korean population in the largest urban centers. Within the largest cities there are areas where Koreans tend to concentrate. Sometimes Koreans live in close proximity to Burakumin, as they do along the west side of the river in south central Kyoto. In Tokyo the greatest concentration of Koreans is in the northern Arakawa ward, characterized by a Korean market. In Osaka, as has been mentioned, the greatest concentration of Koreans in all Japan is in the Ikuno ward.

Table 7.10. Naturalization by Natity, 1952-1966

Year	Koreans	Stateless	Brazilians	Americans	Canadians	Peruvians	Filipinos	Argentinians	Indonesians	French Indians	Indians	Others	Total
1952	232	42	6	1	1	0	0	0	0	0	0	0	282
1953	1,326	56	34	10	1	2	0	0	0	0	0	2	1,431
1954	2,435	112	45	6	2	2	1	0	0	1	1	3	2,608
1955	2,434	127	72	11	3	4	5	0	1	2	0	2	2,661
1956	2,290	152	17	3	3	10	4	0	1	1	0	5	2,547
1957	2,312	174	45	29	6	2	2	0	0	2	0	10	2,582
1958	2,246	224	60	46	9	0	0	0	3	0	0	6	2,594
1959	2,737	251	38	31	5	1	3	1	0	0	5	4	3,076
1960	3,763	284	32	32	13	7	8	1	0	1	5	10	4,156
1961	2,410	222	32	35	4	5	3	1	1	1	0	1	3,013
1962	3,222	259	28	73	8	3	7	1	1	0	0	12	3,614
1963	3,558	458	19	48	1	3	2	0	0	1	1	9	4,100
1964	4,632	674	39	58	10	5	6	4	5	1	2	9	5,445
1965	3,438	550	25	38	10	0	1	4	5	2	1	14	4,088
1966	3,816	766	54	48	5	1	16	3	6	1	0	19	4,735
Totals	41,151	4,351	593	483	81	43	58	15	23	13	15	106	46,932

Table 7.11. The Place of Birth of Koreans in Japan

Total Number of Koreans in Japan, 1974	638,806
Born in Japan	483,185
Born in Korea	154,054
Born in China	96
Born in Sakhalin (U.S.S.R.)	262
Born elsewhere	50
Unknown	1,159

LANGUAGE AND RELIGION

Language and religion play an important part in the life of most ethnic groups. The Koreans in Japan are no exception. Korean and Japanese are related but not mutually intelligible languages. They have evolved different sorts of writing systems, both originally dependent on Chinese characters. A sophisticated syllabary was developed for Korean in the fourteenth century and it is still in use. A classical scholarly education in Korea also requires learning Chinese characters. Japanese is written with a combination of Chinese characters, Kanji, and two separate and uniquely Japanese alphabets, hirangana and katakana.

The first generation of Koreans arriving in Japan suffered a severe language handicap in Japan. Figures from 1922 showed that 54 percent of the Koreans in Osaka were illiterate in both Japanese and Korean, only 15 percent were able to understand Japanese, and 31 percent understood the language slightly.(56) Later prewar figures showed a similar low level ability in Japanese. Second and third generation Koreans tend to speak Japanese better than Korean. For these generations the importance of language as an emblem of ethnic identity has become crucial. Those that wish to emphasize Korean heritage stress pride in speaking Korean. This is especially true for those in Chosoren schools, but pride in speaking Korean is not limited only to these children. On the other hand, there are those Koreans who strive to speak Japanese perfectly in order to pass for Japanese in Japanese society. For these people the Korean language is no longer important.

The religion of the Koreans is a difficult problem to discuss. Suzuki feels that beneath South Korean Christianity and North Korean Communism there is an underlying Korean Confucianism.(57) This Confucian mode of thinking shows up most in family life, especially in the guise of respect for one's elders which is still a marked trait in North Korea as well as South Korea. As a communist country North Korea encourages no form of religion except Marxist dogma, and this attitude permeates through Chosoren to a large number of the Koreans in Japan. Many of the Mindan supporters are Christian. But a number of Korean Christians in Japan are also critics of the Park regime. The Korean Christian Center in Osaka is one of the prominent activist groups working to alleviate problems of the Korean minority in Japan.

Table 7.12.   Population of Koreans Residing in Each
Prefecture of Japan, 1974*

Hokkaido	7,117	Kyoto	44,236
Aomori	1,869	Osaka	179,315
Iwate	1,497	Hyogo (Kobe)	67,375
Miyagi	3,601	Nara	5,653
Akita	1,083	Wakayama	4,935
Yamagata	672	Tottori	1,471
Fukushima	2,141	Shimane	1,327
Ibaraki	3,877	Okayama	8,181
Tochigi	2,116	Hiroshima	16,039
Gunma	2,790	Yamaguchi (Shimonoseki)	14,816
Saitama	9,684	Tokushima	278
Chiba	9,615	Kagawa	974
Tokyo	73,473	Ehime	2,040
Kanagawa (Yokohama)	28,952	Kochi	909
Niigata	2,537	Fukuoka	25,475
Toyama	1,909	Saga	1,332
Ishikawa	3,374	Nagasaki	2,534
Fukui	4,781	Kumamoto	1,629
Yamanashi	1,679	Oita	2,983
Nagano	4,862	Miyazaki	1,040
Gifu	10,924	Kagoshima	500
Shizuoka	8,368	Okinawa	198
Aichi (Nagoya)	54,163		
Mie	7,938		
Shiga	6,887		

*Names in parentheses indicate the major city in the Prefecture.

Source: Toyo Keizai Nippo, January 17, 1975.

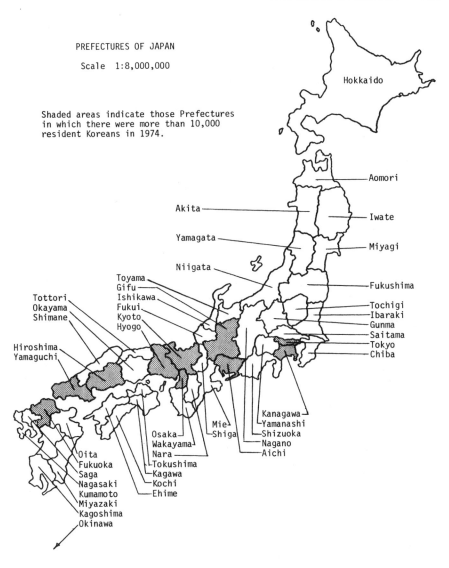

Fig. 7.2.   Prefectures of Japan.

Source: Adapted from the Atlas of Japan: Physical, Economic, and Social, International Society for Educational Information, Tokyo, 1970, p. 69.

THE PLACE AND PROSPECTS OF KOREANS IN
JAPANESE SOCIETY

Many of the characteristics of the Korean minority in Japan are not unlike those of oppressed minorities in other countries. Compared with majority Japanese, Koreans in Japan suffer from political powerlessness, economic depression and low status occupations, educational inferiority, lack of self-esteem, discrimination, government suspicion, legal inequality, and language handicap. This formidable list of obstacles has been demonstrated by both statistical evidence and by individual cases such as those of Park Chong Suk (Hitachi), Hondayama (Kyoto Korean High School), Yamamura Masaaki (self-immolation), Shin Kyon Whan (deportation), Kinkiro (gangster), and a number of others. The patterns and case examples have rough parallels in many instances of majority/minority ethnic interrelations throughout the world, but there are a number of kinds that are unique to the case of the Koreans in Japan.

Except for a few hundred individuals, the Koreans all came to Japan after the Japanese annexation of Korea in 1910. In the 1930s they were forcibly brought to Japan to work in manual jobs under adverse conditions. Under these terms the minority was created by Japanese choice, not Korean choice. After the defeat of Japan in war, 80 percent of the Korean minority returned to Korea, but a 20 percent residue remained for a variety of reasons. Because Japan lost Korea during the war, Koreans lost Japanese nationality at the end of the Occupation period. Hence they lost certain minimum rights of citizenship, an ironic twist of history in which the oppressed became legally more oppressed because the oppressor lost her power. The division of Korea into North and South after the war also had its effect by fragmenting the loyalties of those Koreans who remained in Japan. The accidents of history have shaped the legal and political particulars of the position of the Koreans in Japan in unique ways, although the dominate/subordinate relationship pattern is clearly similar to that of majority/minority relations elsewhere.

It is not only the historical circumstances that give particular color to the case of the Koreans in Japan. Attitudes of the Japanese and the way they are reflected in politics, economics, and law are in a number of ways quite different from those of Western industrial and post-industrial societies.

Nakane(58) and other Japanese social scientists have pointed out the strongly hierarchical nature of Japanese society. The Japanese associate very strongly with their school or firm, having a higher degree of loyalty to those inside their organization than Westerners tend to have, and having few ties outside the organization they work or study in. Within the organization there is a well-defined set of obligations to those above and below one's own position. There is a strong tendency for Japanese to classify in a hierarchical way. I have argued that this tendency to classify hierarchically affects both Japanese relations with minority groups living in Japan and Japanese relations with other countries.(59) Minority groups tend to be either inferior to Japanese, such as the Koreans, Burakumin, or Ainu, or superior to Japanese, such as Americans and Europeans living in Japan. The case of the Chinese is somewhat ambiguous, perhaps because the Japanese feel indebted to the Chinese for a good part of their cultural heritage on the one hand, while on the other hand Japan has clearly outshadowed China in her prodigious effort to modernize. The feeling of the superiority of Westerners is probably also fading as Japan increases her technological capability and economic power.

Besides the deeply embedded hierarchical concept in the Japanese social psyche, there is also a conception of purity and defilement that may play a part in Japanese relations with ethnic minorities or with other nations.(60) In this conception, peoples or states may be viewed as impure, and hence inferior. This attitude is most clearly marked in majority Japanese interaction with the Burakumin. The Burakumin are considered unclean, more in a ritual than actual sense, and are consigned to the lowest rung of Japanese society. This kind of outcaste status may also acrue to others, such as the Koreans, through demonstration of political weakness or technological inferiority. In other words, this tendency to view peoples as pure or defiled intensifies their positions on the hierarchical ladder.

In a penetrating essay on the problems of cultural identity of majority Japanese,(61) Wagatsuma documents the Japanese need to establish a unique and powerful Japanese identity. In spite of the historical facts of Chinese cultural influence and Western industrial diffusion, the powerful Japanese synthetic imagination speaks through Japanese anthropologist Yoshio Masuda: "The Japanese, as a homogeneous ethnic group, have maintained a homogeneous culture since the pre-historic age. . . ."(62) Not all Japanese intellectuals are as sure of Japanese identity as Masuda was at the point of time he wrote his statement. Yukio Mishima, the famous novelist, gave dramatic highlight to the spiritual crisis involved in choosing between traditional and modern values by committing hara-kiri in assertion of bushido, the traditional way of the samurai warrior. He was unwilling or unable to adopt an altered value system more in tune with modern Japan. One is reminded of Yamamura Masaaki's spiritual crisis that led to self-immolation. Wagatsuma concludes that "a strong collective feeling remains that the Japanese must cultivate something uniquely theirs."(63)

It is clear that the Japanese are not as monolithic or as homogeneous in sentiment or in fact as is often taken for granted by foreigners, or as the Japanese often present themselves. Symbols taken at first glance as being particularly Japanese may not necessarily be Japanese at all. During the past summer Saduharu Oh was given plaudits by all levels of Japanese society from the man in the street to the emperor. He had established Japanese preeminence in sport by breaking the American Hank Aaron's all-time home run record in baseball. Once Oh hit his 757th home run, breaking Aaron's record by one, he became a national hero, even a national treasure. To be sure, he had to share the top notch hitting honors with his Tokyo Giants teammate Harimoto, who ranks only slightly behind Oh in poster-selling competition. The irony is that neither of these national heroes, symbols of Japanese international supremacy in baseball, is Japanese. Harimoto is Korean.   Oh's father is Chinese, and Oh's passport is from the Republic of China.   His name is in fact the familiar Chinese surname Wang and Oh is the Japanese pronunciation. Thus sport is an area where other ethnics can compete on a more or less equal basis with Japanese.

In spite of these gaps in Japanese homogeneity, Japan is closer to being a nation-state than any other modern democratic state. Ninety-nine percent of the people in Japan are racially, linguistically, and culturally Japanese. Of this figure two to three percent are Burakumin, Japanese who effectively operate outside the pale of mainstream Japanese society in an economically and politically subordinate position. The very fact that Japan is as homogeneous as it is makes it relatively difficult for Japanese to cope with people from minority groups. Contact with members of other ethnic groups is relatively rare, especially since Burakumin, the largest minority, tend to live in quite separate and discrete areas from majority Japanese. The concept of cultural pluralism that has been developing in other industrial democracies is slower in coming to Japan, partially on account of the small size of the minority groups and their relative isolation. The political leadership of the minority groups (Koreans, Burakumin, and Ainu), on the other hand, are quite conscious of the activities and gains of prestige and power of ethnics in the United States and Europe. Advocates of Buraku power and Ainu power exist. Korean community organizers train in American cities. This training has proved of some use, as is witnessed by the successes in such cases as the eventual Hitachi hiring of Park Chong Suk and the staying of the deportation order for Shin Kyon Whan.

There is evidence that the attitudes ostracizing despised minorities in Japan are weakening. Hierarchy and purity in recent years appear to be losing their full force as categorizing tools. To a certain extent the change is one of generation. On the whole, younger Japanese seem to be accepting Koreans and Burakumin in a way that their parents did not, and this points to a trend of increasing acceptance of cultural pluralism. It is possible that the West is having a certain influence as a model of social development in the same way that it served as a model for technological development. As long as Japan maintains its present pacifistic and nonmilitaristic mood, we might expect increased acceptance of minority groups in Japan. If the mood of Japan changes to a militaristic phase, it is possible that increased nationalistic feelings might make it more difficult for the minorities.

Marxist class analysis sheds relatively little practical light on the situation of the Koreans in Japan. It is true and has been amply demonstrated that as an aggregate the Koreans fit into the lower class of Japanese society in political and economic terms. But it is unlikely that the Japanese lower class will be able to launch a class revolution before it is absorbed into the rapidly expanding middle class. Japan is becoming a welfare state as are the other modern democratic states. Social programs and welfare schemes have increased, and Koreans are increasingly eligible for benefits. The problems of the Koreans are very real, but it does not follow that the solution for them, in Japan, is class warfare. The position of the Koreans in Japan can be substantially altered for the better through appropriate government action coupled with more slow-moving changes in Japanese and Korean attitudes. The key to Korean success in Japan lies as much with development of ethnic consciousness as with development of class consciousness.

There have been a number of indicators that the Japanese government has been more willing to accommodate Koreans than they have been in the past. They grant permanent residency status to those who choose it and meet the requirements; court decisions award jobs to Koreans where they had formerly been refused employment, and Koreans are granted the right to reside in public housing. An advocate of cultural pluralism could point out a number of other steps that might be carried out to enhance the position of the Koreans in Japanese society, especially as far as law is concerned. Requirements for naturalization might be simplified for those that wish to take this route. Perhaps the requirement of adopting a Japanese name should be dropped. Evidence shows that the melting pot idea does not work in practice. The government should be more willing to publish the statistics related to naturalization applications. If naturalization is still not possible or desirable for the majority of the Koreans, some method of political enfranchisement should be devised so that there is legitimate political representation for Korean interests. The government should take a stand that Koreans be given equal opportunity for education and jobs through development of affirmative action programs.

It is in the best interest of both Koreans and Japanese to have a better off and more accepted Korean minority in Japan. From the Korean perspective a greater degree of welfare and increased sense of legitimacy would be achieved. From the Japanese perspective the disruptive effects of a politically volatile minority could be avoided.

NOTES

(1) Conversation with Professor Hatada Takashi of the Tokyo Metropolitan University.

(2) Kim Chan Jon, ed., Chosenjin Kyosei Renko (Koreans Forcibly Abducted) (Tokyo: Shin Jinbutsu Orai Sha, 1975), p. 140. Ministry of the Interior Security Affairs Bureau Statistics.

(3) The Japan Yearbook, 1924-35, p. 241.

(4) Edward W. Wagner, The Korean Minority in Japan (New York: Institute of Pacific Relations, 1951), p. 96.

(5) Koh Byong Chul, The Foreign Policy of North Korea (New York: Praeger, 1969), p. 192.

(6) Chung Kiwon, "Japanese-North Korean Relations Today," 1964, p. 789.

(7) Richard H. Mitchell, The Korean Minority in Japan (Berkeley and Los Angeles: The University of California Press, 1967).

(8) Conversation with Rev. Chai of the Korean Christian Center in Osaka.

(9) Conversation with a member of the National Police in the Japanese Self-Defense Agency.

(10) Conversation with Professor Suzuki Jiro of the Tokyo Metropolitan University.

(11) Based on observations made in August 1977, in Osaka.

(12) Kim Su Il, "The Korean Ethnic Minority in Japan," unpublished paper, 1977, p. 6.

(13) Changsoo Lee, "Ethnic Discrimination and Conflict: The Case of the Korean Minority in Japan," in Case Studies on Human Rights and Fundamental Freedoms: A World Survey (The Hague: Nijhoff, 1976), vol. 4, p. 270.

(14) Based on observations made in September 1977, in Kyoto.

(15) This account of Park Chong Suk vs. Hitachi is based on the International Documentation report, "Racial Oppression in Japan," September 1974, p. 25.

(16) Arnold Abrams, "The Shantytowns of Japan," The Asia Magazine, January 12, 1975, p. 5.

(17) Asahi Evening News, August 19, 1977.

(18) Chai Choong Shik, "The Struggles of Koreans in Japan," unpublished paper, 1974, p. 5.

(19) Conversation with Bae Jong-Do, Secretary to the Research-Action Institute for Koreans in Japan (RAIK).

(20) Based on observations made in September 1977, in Kyoto.

(21) Chai, "Struggles of Koreans," p. 6.

(22) Ibid., pp. 3-4.

(23) Mitchell, The Korean Minority, p. 128.

(24) Koh, Foreign Policy, p. 195.

(25) J.A.A. Stockwin, Japan: Divided Politics in a Growth Economy (New York: Norton, 1975), p. 230.

(26) Christian Conference on Asia. Identity and Justice: Report of an Ad Hoc Meeting on Race and Minority Issues in Asia, Hong Kong, 1977, p. 9.

(27) Conversation with Professor Suzuki Jiro.

(28) Kim, "Korean Ethnic Minority," pp. 8-10.

(29) Chai, "Struggles of Koreans," p. 7.

(30) Akihiko Tanaka, "A Transformation of the Japanese People's Image of the United States – A Case of Correlation between the Cognitive and the Affective Image," unpublished paper, 1977, p. 17, based on the source Tokei Sun Kankyujo, Kokumin Chosa Iinkai, ed., Dai ni Nihonjin no Kokuminsei (Tokyo, 1970), pp. 396-397.

(31) Mitchell, The Korean Minority, p. 161.

(32) Conversation with a member of the National Police.

(33) George DeVos and Hiroshi Wagatsuma, Japan's Invisible Race (Berkeley and Los Angeles: University of California Press, 1966), p. 266.

(34) Chai, "Struggles of Koreans," p. 3.

(35) Conversation with Professor Hatada.

(36) Asahi Evening News, August 12-15, 1977.

(37) Abrams, "Shantytowns," p. 5.

(38) November 22nd Rescue Society, "The November 22nd Spy Case," Osaka, 1976.

(39) Amnesty International, Report of an Amnesty International Mission to the Republic of Korea, 27 March-9 April 1975. London: Amnesty International Publications, 1977.

(40) This account of the Kim Dae Jong Kidnapping is taken largely from newspaper coverage from the New York Times, Christian Science Monitor, and Washington Post.

(41) Kim Kwan Bong, The Korea-Japan Treaty Crisis and the Instability of the Korean Political System (New York: Praeger, 1971), pp. 65-68.

(42) IDOC, "Racial Oppression," pp. 16-17.

(43) Toyo Keizai Nippo (Orient Economic Times), September 10, 1976.

(44) Kan-po (Government Daily Register), June 7, 1967.

(45) Toyo Keizai Nippo (Orient Economic Times), January 17, 1975.

(46) Ibid.

(47) Toyo Keizai Nippo, September 10, 1976.

(48) Toyo Keizai Nippo, January 17, 1975.

(49) Ibid.

(50) Kan-po, June 7, 1967.

(51) Ibid.

(52) Toyo Keizai Nippo, January 17, 1975.

(53) Toyo Keizai Nippo, September 10, 1976.

(54) Kan-po, June 7, 1967.

(55) Lee, "Ethnic Discrimination," p. 268.

(56) Mitchell, The Korean Minority, p. 30.

(57) Conversation with Professor Suzuki Jiro.

(58) Chie Nakane, Japanese Society (Berkeley: University of California Press, 1970).

(59) Grant F. Rhode, "Anomalies in a Homogeneous Society: Burakumin, Koreans, and Ainu," December 1976, and "The Place of Purification, Defilement, and Hierarchy in the Japanese Ethos, and the Implications of the Values for Japan's Minority Groups," April 1977, unpublished papers.

(60) Ibid.

(61) Hiroshi Wagatsuma, "Problems of Cultural Identity in Modern Japan," in George DeVos and Lola Romanucci-Ross, eds., Ethnic Identity: Cultural Continuities and Change (Palo Alto, California: Mayfield Publishing Company, 1975.)

(62) Ibid., p. 329.

(63) Ibid., p. 331.

Index

About the
Contributors

URI RA'ANAN is Professor of International Politics and Chairman of the International Security Studies Program, the Fletcher School of Law and Diplomacy. He is author or co-author of many books on recent and contemporary history and on international conflict. Before resuming academic life in 1964, he spent a number of years in international diplomacy and political journalism.

JOHN P. ROCHE is Henry R. Luce Professor of Civilization and Foreign Affairs, the Fletcher School of Law and Diplomacy. Former Special Consultant to President Lyndon Johnson, he is now also a syndicated columnist and author of many works on constitutional, social, and political aspects of recent and contemporary history.

URSULA MEHRLAENDER is Project Director at the Friedrich-Ebert Institute, Bonn, and an internationally recognized authority with many publications on migrant labor.

HENRY M. DRUCKER is Professor of Politics, University of Edinburgh, author of The Scottish Government Yearbook and other publications on Scotland and its politics.

JEAN ELLEN KANE is a graduate of Mount Holyoke College and at present is a doctoral candidate at the Fletcher School of Law and Diplomacy, Tufts University. Part of her education was attained in Belgium.

GAVRIEL D. RA'ANAN, legislative assistant on foreign affairs and defense to Senator R. Boschwitz, is author of a book on NATO's Southeastern Flank, Yugoslavia After Tito: Scenarios and Implications (Westview Press, 1978). As a consultant at the Rand Corporation, he authored a monograph on The Evolution of the Soviet Use of Surrogates in Military Relations with the Third World. At the Fletcher School, he is completing his Ph.D. dissertation on Soviet Decision-Making.

GRANT F. RHODE is visiting lecturer in the comparative anthropology of China and Japan at Tufts University. His graduate training in anthropology was undertaken at the Institute of Social Anthropology, Oxford University. At present he is a doctoral candidate in Asian Diplomatic History and Foreign Policies at the Fletcher School of Law and Diplomacy. He is co-author of <u>Treaties of the People's Republic of China, 1949-1978: An Annotated Compilation,</u> and author of articles on Chinese foreign policy and on Japanese values and ethnic minority relations.